The
PROMISE *of* PARTY
in a
POLARIZED AGE

The
PROMISE *of* PARTY
in a
POLARIZED AGE

Russell Muirhead

Harvard University Press

Cambridge, Massachusetts & London, England

2014

Library of Congress Cataloging-in-Publication Data

Muirhead, Russell, 1965–
    The promise of party in a polarized age / Russell Muirhead.
      pages cm
    Includes bibliographical references and index.
    ISBN 978-0-674-04683-2 (hardcover : alk. paper)
1. Political parties—United States. 2. Two party systems—
United States. 3. Republican Party (U.S. : 1854–) 4. Democratic
Party (U.S.) 5. Political culture—United States. 6. Divided
government—United States. I. Title.
    JK2265.M85 2014
    324.273—dc23   2014003559

For Toni

CONTENTS

PREFACE

As a partisan myself, I know a bit of what party spirit feels like. I have been moved—by anger, by conviction, by hope, by affection, and sometimes by hate—to hold signs, to sit through caucuses, to make calls, to write checks, and to vote. On those election nights when my party was defeated, I have crawled early into bed full of woe. And I will never forget the nights when my party has won, celebrating with friends into the sunless hours of morning.

Perhaps this experience gives me a sympathy for those who find it in them to take a stand and carry this stand to the political world. From a combination of habit, affection, and conviction, such people stand with a party. These may be "passive partisans" who think about politics only now and then. Or they may think about it a lot and try to talk their friends into voting this way or that. They are also the ones who make elections happen—they vote, stuff envelopes, knock on doors, drive people to the polls, make phone calls, contribute money, design strategy, and run for office. They are the ones who cheer in joy and who mourn in sorrow on election night—and either way, steel themselves for another fight. If they are prejudiced, narrow, and blind in some respects (and they can be), they are also idealistic, inspired, and knowing. Partisanship does not entirely deserve its bad name.

It is hard to imagine life without political friends—those with whom I can take a certain measure of agreement for granted.

But it is also stimulating and provocative to be with political opponents. They remind me of the mystery of political disagreement: Why would someone so decent and so thoughtful *disagree* with what seems, to me, so obvious, so true? Are they blinded by selfish interests? Are they heartless? Or . . . am I . . . not entirely right after all? What is it about the political world that can give rise to such disagreement? Party spirit is the starting point for a basic curiosity about political things.

But party spirit is less an intellectual than an active thing: partisans take a stand. They stand *with* others and stand *for* something. As a partisan, I have sometimes allied with groups I otherwise disagree with, for the sake of standing *for* the larger goals of the party. This is never solely a matter of sober calculation, as if any algorithm could be up to the job. It is always, in part, a matter of the heart. That is why I prefer the eighteenth-century phrase "party spirit" to the social-scientific "partisanship." Partisanship is not a dispassionate "identification," nor is it simply what happens to you while you are not looking (as a child); it is spirited, or prideful. It originates in the desire for recognition, is sustained by the way being disagreed with is experienced as an insult, and is not without a noble willingness to fight (in a sense) for the sake of the common good. Reason can—and should—inform, guide, and chasten party spirit, but it is rarely only the consequence of a conclusion based in reason, the way we might conclude that the square root of two is irrational when we study geometry.

In principle, the common good should be a matter of agreement—it is, after all, common. Since Plato, political philosophy has been devoted largely to articulating a rational basis for agreement about the common good. In this sense, the purpose of political philosophy is to eradicate partisanship: in principle, the idea of justice itself may require believing that reason can displace contestation. The aspiration to base politics on reason informs the social-scientific ideal of a politics of problem solving by informed experts who do not let disagreements on small questions of technique get in the way of mutually advantageous accommodations. It is also aligned with the common understanding that partisanship is an affliction of political elites, a self-serving game that distracts us from the common good.

But the hope that we could take the politics out of politics blinds us to the way every effort to denude politics of disagreement must silence some interests, some understandings, some groups, some persons. What makes politics magnetic is that the common good is ever a matter of dispute. To serve the common good implicates us in a contest. What that contest is for, how it should be fought, and how it might be the basis of a political community are urgent questions of politics and political philosophy.

Yet amid the resurgence of partisan passions in the 2000s—following the impeachment of President William Clinton in 1998 and President George W. Bush's contested victory in 2000—it struck me that we lacked a vocabulary by which to understand and value partisanship. Other than the language that justifies one's own partisan commitments and the language that piously condemns all partisanship, we lacked a way to locate the important place of party spirit in our politics.

To make sense of partisanship, political theory needs to give an account of what can be said in its favor—one that goes beyond the partisan's own, one-sided account. In my first efforts to do this, a 2006 essay in *Perspectives in Politics,* I focused on defending the place of partisanship in democratic politics. Since then I have come to see that while partisanship needs a defense, it also invites profound pathologies that can corrupt democratic politics.

Part of this corruption comes in the form of money, of course: parties funded by the few are unlikely to connect citizens' trust and affection with the institutions of government. But the more severe threat comes from the spirit of party itself. In particular, the danger arises when party spirit pervades life and extends to all of government, the press, scholarship, and friendship.

Working out the limits of party spirit requires more than a defense of partisanship on one hand, and more than a general condemnation of party on the other. It requires a more nuanced consideration of public institutions, one that makes room for partisanship in some places while containing it in others. That is what I have tried to do in this book.

Partisanship is appropriate for citizens and legislators, for instance—but is a far more potent threat in other institutions that house the executive or judicial functions of government. Partisanship is not the sort of force that can easily be contained. Rather than expect that partisanship can be overcome, or transcended, or simply turned off in those places where its presence would be corrupting, it is better—more true to the real possibilities for democratic politics—to differentiate between more elevated and more base expressions of party spirit.

High partisanship is oriented to convictions, principles, and conceptions of the common interest. Low partisanship is about strategy, power, and ultimately, victory. The two are intimately connected, but they have different roles. Low partisanship has its place in campaigns, elections, and legislatures. But even there it can corrode cooperation and trust. High partisanship by contrast does not necessarily corrupt. The task for institutions like the executive or the judiciary is not to insulate them from all partisanship, as if political decisions could be made according to a handy nonpartisan algorithm. On the contrary, high partisanship is the link that connects these institutions with public purposes that people might endorse.

Put differently, what politics needs is not less partisanship, but better partisanship.

The
PROMISE *of* PARTY
in a
POLARIZED AGE

1

THE PARTY PROBLEM

There seems no escape from the vitriolic partisanship enveloping American politics. President Barack Obama, who promised post-partisanship, generated more polarized approval ratings within a year than any other new president in polling history.[1] The president preceding him, George W. Bush, who described himself as a "uniter, not a divider," very effectively divided: at the close of his first term, two-thirds of Republican voters "very strongly" approved of his performance, while two-thirds of Democrats very strongly disapproved.[2] Partisans do not merely oppose the other side—they often *hate* it.[3]

Obama and Bush each sought to overcome the bitter polarization of the 1990s. If they were in some respects very partisan presidents, both Bush and Obama made good faith efforts to attract the center. In office, Obama tempered the idealism of his campaign by hewing to a number of Bush's policies: he retained Bush's secretary of defense and continued Bush's policies in Iraq and Afghanistan—as well as the Wall Street bailout, or the Troubled Asset Relief Program. Bush tried to inject compassion into conservatism and initiated the largest extension of entitlements (Medicare Part D) in memory. But each failed to ameliorate the partisan divisions that beset national politics.

According to the old view—the one students in an introductory course in American politics would have been taught until only a decade ago—American politics was defined by a stable consensus on fundamental values.[4] In the mid- and late twentieth century, this consensus was reflected by the two great parties of American politics, which overlapped so fully they seemed ideologically indistinguishable. Overwhelming bipartisan majorities passed most important legislation. As the political scientist David Mayhew reported, American legislatures were characterized by a "mindset of problem solving," not of ideological combat.[5]

That image of American politics has become laughably—and perhaps lamentably—obsolete. In 1994 the Republican Party won a majority in the House of Representatives for the first time in forty years. Only four years later, the Republican House voted to impeach President Bill Clinton—the first time Congress impeached a president since the turmoil immediately following the American Civil War, and only the second time a president has been impeached in American history. Two years later, the country divided almost evenly in the 2000 presidential election, and in the absence of established procedures for deciding the contested and decisive vote in Florida, the U.S. Supreme Court decided the election with a 5–4 vote. These events inflamed partisan passions to a degree American politics had not seen since the nineteenth century.

One might have thought that the rise of party spirit in U.S. politics mainly reflected the polarizing personalities of Bill Clinton and George W. Bush, and that soon enough the normal, pragmatic, bipartisan pattern of American politics would reassert itself. In all likelihood, normal politics is not coming back. Intense partisanship is the new normal. As the vote to pass President Obama's Affordable Care Act illustrates, important legislation is no longer passed by large bipartisan majorities (no Republicans voted for the bill in either the House or the Senate). Up through 1990, significant legislation could be passed regardless of whether the same party controlled the presidency and both houses of Congress ("unified government") or whether the parties divided control of the executive and one or both houses of the legislature ("divided government"). Today it is difficult to pass *any* legislation when there is divided government. When the 113th Congress (2013–2015) went on summer recess in 2013, only twenty-two bills had been passed by both houses of Congress and signed by the president—the least productive Congress since the 1940s, when political scientists began tracking legislative productivity.[6] Government has become a theater for entertaining partisan true believers rather than a setting for brokering, negotiation, deliberation, and compromise.

Ten years ago, it looked as if hyper-partisanship was an affliction restricted to a small number of political animals—those who run for office, who take an intense interest in campaigns and elections, and whose livelihood directly engages them with the political world. Ordinary citizens who do not make their living from politics continued to agree on fundamentals: they shared a broadly liberal, tolerant, nonjudgmental, pragmatic sensibility.[7] Today, the sense that America itself is divided is increasingly corroborated by scholars who point out that the active, informed, and engaged public generally shares the more emphatic partisan views of elites.[8] We may be "one nation, after all," but our oneness is seen only from certain angles and comes packaged with profound divisions.[9]

At the moment, it is not clear whether the United States is closely divided (evenly split between the parties) or is also becoming more deeply divided. That there is a more profound partisan split among not only political elites but also the attentive public is clear. The worry is that this partisan split will motivate deeper divisions that as yet do not really define the country. Party spirit does not merely reflect divisions already there; it can create divisions. When party spirit runs deep, it can threaten the unity of the political community. The more the political community is severed by party, the fewer values and goals rival partisans share, and the less trust they have in each other, the more the common good becomes unintelligible. When party spirit runs this deep, it can threaten the unity of the political community. If the division goes deep enough, it becomes impossible to deliberate together or to imagine a single ideal of justice that applies to everyone. Justice becomes little more than a grand name for the interests and goals of particular groups, and politics becomes the arena where each group strives to apply its understandings to the rest. Losers to political conflict have less reason to abide by the constitutional processes that delivered their loss. If the losses are frequent or decisive enough, losers may decide that violence or secession is preferable to peaceful opposition and constitutional obedience. The problem with partisanship is found in its potential to destroy the political community.

Perhaps partisanship should not get all the blame—after all, often partisanship only reflects social divisions that are already manifest. But just as often, partisanship creates divisions and obscures the unity that is really there. In Obama's second term, there were any number of policies that might have solicited a majority in the House of Representatives—for example, entitlement reform, immigration reform, support for increasing the debt limit in a timely and undramatic way. But this majority would have consisted of a majority of the Democrats (who were in the minority) and a minority of the Republicans (who were in the majority).[10]

This latent bipartisan majority is disempowered by the party system. The fifty Republicans who might break ranks to support these policies cannot risk the punishments they might suffer—not least, party support for a challenger in the next election—and so they stay silent. Democrats too cannot stray too far from their party leadership without suffering repercussions. As a result, Congress cannot come together even when a majority of its members might like to. To take a different example, President Obama shied away from proposing a specific plan for immigration reform in 2013 because he knew that if the plan had his name on it, Republicans would be compelled to oppose it.[11] Party spirit does not simply reflect divisions—it inflames them. Often, it causes them. In the process, it threatens to destroy the very possibility of the common good.

The Ethical Gap

This is why party spirit has been viewed traditionally as evil, and it accounts for the condemnation of party and faction throughout the history of political thought. Political philosophy historically has largely consisted of the search for justice, understood as a rationally defensible conception of the common good. The grand project of political philosophy is to articulate such a conception, for if none exists, then some fear that no standard by which to assess the health or rightness of a regime could exist: all politics can only be a struggle for power where no one group could be said to be truly better or more righteous than any other. The possibility of justice, in this view, depends on overcoming incomplete, partisan conceptions of the good.[12]

The traditional teaching—that parties are evil—remains with us. But alongside it, political science has come to see parties and partisan contestation as essential to modern democracy. It took a long while to see parties as integral to representative democracy. While factions have always been a part of politics, the ancestor of the modern political party first arose with the empowered legislatures of modern representative government. In England, the Whigs and the Tories came together during the Exclusion Crisis of the 1670s. In a sense, they should have disappeared when the questions that inspired them were settled by the Glorious Revolution of 1688. Curiously, they did not disappear.

Their persistence in eighteenth-century Britain generated a great deal of concern about the pathologies of "party spirit"—the more vivid eighteenth-century term for what we now more antiseptically call "partisanship," or "party identification."[13] In language very similar to the anti-Beltway sentiments that abound today, Lord Bolingbroke castigated the government for its alienation from the people. While he wanted a permanently organized party to oppose the court, Bolingbroke ideally hoped to see party contestation give way to a unifying, nonpartisan "patriot king."[14] The first powerful defense of party as a permanently necessary institution came in 1770, when Edmund Burke laid out the elemental logic of partisanship: "When bad men combine, the good must associate; else they will fall, one by one, an unpitied sacrifice in a contemptible struggle."[15] But the defense of partisanship as a permanent feature of politics could not overcome the traditional understanding that political unity required agreement. The American Founders were more comfortable with the traditional antipartisanship of Bolingbroke than with Burke's defense of partisanship. Washington's warning in his Farewell Address of the "baneful effects of the spirit of party" is aligned with a constitution that never mentions parties.[16] Yet partisanship arose almost immediately in the first session of Congress—as soon as it became evident to representatives that important principles were at stake—and Jefferson himself (who had insisted, "If I could not go to heaven but with a party, I would not go there at all") soon enough founded the first opposition party, which became the governing party with his narrow victory in 1800.[17]

The parties that Burke defended were elite affairs and existed mainly as legislative cliques. It was in the nineteenth century, with the radical expansion of the franchise, that parties became public things. Van Buren's Democratic Party sought to extend partisan feeling beyond the legislature to everyday citizens in order to recruit support from a mass electorate.[18] The phenomena of mass parties stimulated a second wave of philosophic reflection about parties and partisanship in the late nineteenth century. Figures like Woodrow Wilson, A. Lawrence Lowell, and Frank Goodnow—the founders of political science as an academic discipline—opposed the patronage parties that developed in the nineteenth century, and thought carefully about how to use parties to reform democracy.[19] In general, they hoped American parties could become more like their British counterparts. The ideal came to be known in the twentieth century as "responsible party government," where parties would offer voters a real choice between alternative policies and goals, and would command the power to carry out their programs once in office.[20] By the time the American Political Science Association published its report "Toward a More Responsible Two Party System" in 1950, this ideal commanded such generalized assent that it constituted almost a dogma in American political science.[21]

Support for parties and partisanship among political scientists flowed from a fundamental appreciation of the constant conjunction of parties and modern representative democracy. Today, the importance of parties in democracy is usually cast in terms of the essential functions they serve. Parties do important work for citizens, for candidates, and for officials working in the formal institutions of government—they do so much work, in fact, that it is nearly impossible to imagine democratic government functioning in their absence. For instance, parties simplify choices for citizens and equip citizens to make meaningful choices. Imagine trying to make sense of a ballot that simply listed dozens of individual names under a variety of offices—sometimes the party label is all one has to go on when casting a ballot. For that matter, partisan passions in the electorate help spur people to take an interest in politics—and to vote. Party organizations

recruit candidates and help fund them; they bring a variety
of views together under a common general purpose and give
national meaning to hundreds of separate races taking place across
the country every year. In government, parties organize both the
governing majority and the opposition. When they do this effectively, it becomes possible for voters to hold the whole legislature or even the whole government accountable even though
they only vote for one representative (if voters do not like the
direction of government, they can vote against the party that
controls the legislature or the government as a whole). When
they work well, parties connect millions of citizens, each with
his or her own interests and point of view, with the formal offices of government. In certain moments, parties can unite numerous and disconnected offices across the national and state
governments in a "large and definite purpose."[22] They do this
in the U.S. system by connecting the different branches of government (when the same party controls the executive and the
legislature). Parties can relax the tendency to gridlock issued by
the constitutional separation of powers, as well as by the separate ambition of each officeholder. It is only because of the
party organization in government that presidents and legislators do not have to construct a new majority for each and every
bill.[23] Parties do not succeed at doing all these things all the
time. But they do enough of the time, and no open society over
the past three centuries has succeeded without parties and partisanship. The great defender of parties, the political scientist
E. E. Schattschneider, was not exaggerating when he wrote in
1942 that "modern democracy is unthinkable save in terms of
the parties."[24]

Yet the traditional view that parties are evil retains its force,
especially in the way we think of good citizenship. As a quality
of both citizens and legislators, partisanship remains suspect: it

looks to many like a form of bias, prejudice, or simply prejudgment that the best citizens will avoid. It is a mental short-cut that substitutes for paying attention to politics, a divisive form of team spirit that distracts us from the common good. Independence often seems a more admirable political posture than partisanship. Ideally, citizens should be impartial, like judges, and objective, like scientists. They should make up their minds based on the facts, not act on standing loyalties. This makes for a tense combination: on one hand, parties and partisanship are a crucial part of any democratic system; on the other, citizens and perhaps officials often seem better when they are more independent and less partisan. There is a gap between the functional importance of parties in modern democracy and the ethical standing of partisanship. The partisan qualities the political system seems to need are not qualities we can easily admire.

The modern world contains any number of similar tensions, where qualities that have good consequences for the overall system do not seem admirable at the individual level. For instance, one might argue (as some political scientists have) that certain kinds of corruption have unintended beneficial effects on political systems, but this would not mean that it is commendable to buy votes or take bribes. To take another example, economists since Adam Smith have shown how individuals following their self-interest create a productive economy and an efficient allocation of goods and services, but this does not mean we should admire either selfishness or greed. Petty computer hacking may have the effect of making systems more reliable and secure by revealing weak points in the network—but this unintended beneficial effect does not mean we should praise computer hackers. What we admire depends not only on the effects that actions have on overall social systems, but also on intentions and qualities of character.

The tension between the functional necessity of parties and the ethical standing of partisanship as an attribute of citizens and representatives complicates the problem of partisanship. It may account for some of the uneasiness many feel about the partisanship they see in others—or in themselves. And it may help explain the appeal of identifying as an independent rather than as a partisan. As Martin Wattenberg says, "The primary reasons for non-partisanship are . . . normative values."[25] While the number of those who strongly identify with a party has increased in recent years, so has the number of independents: pure independents and independents who lean toward one party or another have risen from 25 percent in 1960 to 37 percent in 1980, and to 40 percent in 2008.[26] Just before the 2000 presidential election, more Americans for the first time since modern polling began in the mid-twentieth century identified as "independents" than as either Democrats or Republicans.[27]

For some, independence is a temporary resting place while they sort themselves away from one party and toward another.[28] For others, the status of independent has its own allure that may cause them to deny or hide their own partisanship. In *The Myth of the Independent Voter,* Bruce Keith and his colleagues argue that many of those who identify themselves as independents but who lean toward a party are in fact "undercover partisans." When prodded, they admit that they lean toward one party or the other. In their behavior, they tend to be loyal to one party—even more so than those who identify as "weak" Democrats and Republicans. These "closet partisans" are responsible for most of the growth in independents since 1960—and they share very little with "pure independents," who lean to neither party and are generally apathetic, alienated, uninformed, and inactive politically.[29] For closet partisans like these, perhaps independence is the veil that makes private partisanship publicly respectable.

Is the Problem of Partisanship Asymmetric?

But not all are embarrassed about their own partisan loyalties. Republicans, and especially conservatives, have been particularly emphatic in their partisanship, to the point of insisting they will punish anyone who is willing to compromise with Democrats. If partisanship is a problem, perhaps it has more to do with the Republicans than with the Democrats. Republicans have moved farther to the right than Democrats have moved to the left over the past three decades, according to the DW-NOMINATE index of congressional roll-call voting.[30] Qualitatively, Republicans are more concerned with ideological purity than Democrats. Pragmatic "Main Street" Republicans are likely to be dismissed as RINOs—Republicans in name only—a breed that true conservatives would rather see extinct.[31] By contrast, the Democratic Party retains its catchall flavor; while the Democratic Party is center-left, its tent continues to cover a great variety of ideological views. The Republican Party, on the other hand, looks more uniformly conservative. Moreover, the tactics that the Republican Party uses in office appear to be less compromising and more destructive of the trust that governing requires, especially in times of divided party control of the executive and the legislature. Two veteran congressional analysts, Thomas Mann and Norman Ornstein, argue that the problem of partisanship, which is "even worse than it looks," is in part caused by the Republican Party, which "has become an insurgent outlier—ideologically extreme; contemptuous of the inherited social and economic policy regime; scornful of compromise; unpersuaded by conventional understanding of facts, evidence, and science; and dismissive of the legitimacy of its political opposition."[32]

Conservative Republicans may see their own unity and aggressive tactics as necessary to interrupt a status quo that they want to change fundamentally. To the extent that anything positive is said about partisanship, it tends to come from the Republican side. Whereas many retiring members of Congress commenting on the political scene upon their departure lament the increasing polarization of the parties, former Texas congressman and House majority leader Tom DeLay praised it. In a defiant and intelligent apology for party spirit, DeLay—who was known to his opponents as "Mr. Corruption" for giving committee chairs to members of Congress who could raise the most money for the Republican Party, and known even to his allies as "The Hammer" for the discipline he imposed on wayward members of the party—scorned those who would "elevate compromise to a first principle."[33] DeLay insisted that one must always compromise *from* principles, and principles are always partisan: they are liberal or conservative or otherwise reflect a partisan understanding of the goals and purposes the political community should embrace. Partisanship is a symptom of democracy's "health and its strength," DeLay insisted, "especially from the perspective of a political conservative."

The defense of partisanship, for DeLay, is essentially a defense of conservatism. The default tendency of modern politics, as he sees it, is liberal and progressive. The logic of progressive liberalism is never satisfied—it needs a task, or something to reform. The quest for inclusion, for extending equality, and for making freedom more effective is never finished. As a result, liberalism has "a voracious appetite for growth."[34] Because liberalism is the default public philosophy of American democracy, partisanship functions to make room for conservatives that they would otherwise lack.[35]

DeLay's argument harkens back to a longer tradition of legitimating partisanship on account of the space it gives to a conservative opposition. Edmund Burke's seminal defense of party was meant to legitimate the permanent presence of conservatives in parliamentary politics.[36] Tocqueville too thought that democracy's egalitarian idea was irresistible.[37] More concretely, the New Deal coalition was the most successful governing coalition in the past century of American politics. The Reagan Revolution may have interrupted liberal progress—but it did not issue in a rival public philosophy or a new durable governing majority. This may be why types like DeLay think liberalism is the dominant public philosophy: in their view, to be a commonsense centrist, a pragmatist, or a centrist is to lean liberal. To contest the spirit of the age—to be a partisan—is to be conservative.

This view of things serves conservative interests—by depicting a dominant but complacent opponent, it rallies people to the cause. But the problem of party spirit likely goes deeper than this account suggests. Although in some respects—particularly in Congress—Republicans have been more unified, less compromising, and perhaps more aggressive, the causes of intensified partisanship run deep. Structural factors suggest that vital partisanship—a combination of ideological unity within each party, growing ideological distance between the parties, and parity between the parties—is a stable feature of American politics that affects both parties. The increasing tendency of partisans to live among the like-minded means that congressional districts are increasingly dominated by voters of one party: the moderate district, like the moderate representative, is disappearing. In time, the Democratic Party may come to mirror the Republican Party in its internal unity and uncompromising posture.

But to suppose that liberalism occupies a dominant place reflects a distorted picture of the dynamics of American politics. Racism, nativism, sexism, and oligarchy define the tradition of American politics alongside its egalitarian liberal tradition, and it is not clear that liberalism always had or always will have the advantage. Even progressive legislation in the United States has a way of being perverted to reactionary ends: the Sherman

Anti-Trust Act was first used against unions. The legacy of the United States Supreme Court overturning hundreds of progressive state social and labor laws was enough to turn generations of defeated liberals against the Court, and nearly destroyed the Court during the New Deal. In the history of the country, liberals have had a decisive majority in the House of Representatives for only a couple of years (in the late 1930s). From the perspective of a liberal, there is nothing inevitable about liberalism, democratic equality, or the progressive wing of the Democratic Party. Liberals too have to fight amid political circumstances that are sometimes very hostile to their values and goals. Partisanship makes room for both liberals and conservatives, and ideally also for others who cannot easily fit within the liberal-conservative dichotomy.

If anything, the problem with liberals is that they are reluctant to admit that they are in a partisan contest—and to fight it effectively, they need to become less embarrassed about their own partisanship. Liberals tend to believe that their convictions do not reflect particular social groups or partial conceptions of the good; rather, they believe they are simply being reasonable and rational. As a result, they expect others will come to the same views as theirs through nothing more than reasoning about evidence presented by the unprejudiced activity of the senses. They see their goals as given by common sense, and their policy preferences as supported by social science. And they see themselves as willing to change their preferences according to what the evolving consensus of social scientists would justify.[38] They might be more effective if they could see themselves as more partisan, and as engaged in a partisan fight. If liberals have not come to this understanding already, they will: there is no reason to expect that reason alone will cause everyone eventually to agree with them.

If this analysis is right, the partisan contest that has made the government so dysfunctional in recent years will be with us for a long time. If anything, it is likely to become more pronounced, not less. The party problem is not going away. The question is not how to overcome partisanship or escape it: it is, rather, how to manage it and live with it. The erasure of partisanship, personally and politically, may have its benefits. The golden age of bipartisanship, during the decades after World War II when each major party covered every inch of ideological ground, allowed the United States to pursue a coherent foreign policy across four decades. But this consensus also came at a price, most notably in the bipartisan consensus to keep racial equality off the national agenda.

Partisan polarization in the contemporary era also exacts a cost, one that hardly needs to be detailed amid the repeated crises that flirt with default or government shutdown. As Mann and Ornstein argue, parliamentary parties—disciplined and devoted to convictions about public policy—can bring a separation-of-powers system to its knees.[39] But the intensified partisanship of the moment also has its benefits, too little noted: for one, parties can clarify important public choices that cannot easily be avoided. Expanding entitlements, maintaining the Defense Department at present levels, cutting taxes, and balancing the budget do not form a coherent package. Today's parties are rigorously presenting the choice between additional entitlements and additional taxes (among other choices): while this may be an unwelcome choice, it is not an unnecessary one.

This does not mean that partisanship should have no limits or that it carries no dangers. The traditional warnings about the dangers of party spirit stand among the most urgent and important insights into politics and human nature ever formed, and we dismiss them at our peril. The pathologies of party spirit are real, and difficult to fully escape. Any defense of party spirit must take full stock of these dangers and pathologies. But it would be a mistake, in light of the pathologies partisanship invites, to suppose that we should overcome it altogether.

Partisanship has its place. In recent years, several of us in political theory have tried to show why partisanship has a place in democracy (and democratic theory). As I mentioned, the traditional task of political theory has been to delineate a conception of the common good that, being rationally defensible, applies to all—and therefore overcomes partisanship. By contrast, a number of political theorists—my friend and colleague Nancy Rosenblum most notably in her book *On the Side of the Angels,* but also Lea Ypi and Jonathan White and others—have tried to defend partisanship not only as a feature of democratic politics but also as a quality of good citizens. The fundamental argument of Rosenblum's book, for instance, is that we should appreciate party identification as a moral quality of citizens and resist the pull to "holism," or the belief that the unity of the political community implies a common interest that makes partisanship unnecessary.[40]

Because political theory has for so long derogated or overlooked partisanship—notwithstanding its crucial functions in modern democracy—it has been important to simply defend the importance and moral standing of party and partisanship. But our appreciation of partisanship should not extend to its every manifestation. As is all too apparent, partisanship invites a range of all-too-common pathologies: blind loyalty, enmity, distrust, and perceptual distortion. What politics needs—what we need from political theory—is neither blanket condemnation nor appreciation, but an account that shows what is good and what is not. Constitutional partisanship, as opposed to revolutionary partisanship, which aims to transform the regime itself, perhaps through violence, is a nuanced quality. It combines agreement and disagreement, and this combination puts a limit on the kind of partisanship we can admire. The nature of this limit changes depending on the constitutional context— whether one is simply a citizen or an official matters, as does the official role one occupies. To better understand the nuances of constitutional partisanship, as well as to manage the party problem, we need to better understand *how* to be partisan.

Loyalty and Compromise

Ultimately, I defend a kind of party spirit that is worn lightly, one that is open to facts and revision, and tolerant of—even appreciative of—opponents. But it still involves a kind of loyalty. Loyalty is an ambiguous moral quality; it can seem to blind us to facts and critical judgments about our friends or our team. But loyalty is a necessary element of effective democratic citizenship; the loyalty that characterizes party spirit at its best is grounded in memory and patience. Partisans are the custodians of a shared memory: they identify certain events of the past— public commitments, legislative enactments—as achievements, and come together, and stay together, to protect these achievements. Policies and programs unfold over years, and it is difficult to know in the short run what works and what does not. Leaders who stumble today often recover tomorrow. Partisans are patient with their own leaders and their own policies—without this patience, neither can succeed.

Party loyalty should not blind people to inconvenient facts and disturbing evidence; it should not generate a "perceptual screen" that filters out all information embarrassing to one's own party, or warrant epistemic closure that makes it impossible to contemplate one's own party's errors and misdeeds. But it is a loyalty nonetheless, and it sustains a kind of commitment that goes beyond what plain reason can underwrite. To be fully aware of this is to know that one's own political commitments are unlikely to constitute the whole truth. Party spirit at its best is tempered by political humility, which allows us to see our own commitments as imperfect approximations. Most political action requires that we act as if we know more than we can know. To grasp that our commitments assume more than available evidence can fully support is to see our political opponents in a different light—not as defective, or mistaken, or evil, but as perhaps motivated in good faith by a reasonable conception of the common good. That might make compromising with them more palatable and respecting them more natural.

Almost all partisanship is a compromise—not always with rival partisans, but always with our fellow partisans.[41] There is no way to stand in a group (even a group of merely *two*) without trimming our convictions. One democratic virtue of partisans is found in their willingness to be part of a group that aspires, in principle, to be large enough that it generates a legitimate claim to rule. The compromise of partisanship involves a combination of high partisanship and low partisanship, or a mix of principled commitments and ambition for office.

Principled conviction is noble, but it usually lacks the pragmatic and rhetorical capacity to enlist large numbers of others such that winning office becomes a real possibility. Certainly there are partisans of this sort—like the conscience parties of the Netherlands, for instance. But they are called conscience parties because they are not interested in office, not at any rate if winning imposes any kind of compromise or concession on their principles. Their motives are pure: wholly idealistic or ideological.

At the other pole are office seekers who are primarily or exclusively concerned with winning. For these partisans, politics is entirely about strategy. Principles may be useful, but their value is always instrumental. It may be prudent to look as though one has principled convictions, but this too is simply an appearance adopted for convenience. Ultimately, these partisans will say whatever needs to be said in order to win (credibility will impose some consistency constraints on what they can say, so they may sound ideologically consistent over time; but this is just the sound of things). Ideology and principle are just the veils that make private ambition publicly palatable.

The best partisans possess principled convictions and more or less exact understandings of the common good, and these convictions motivate their interest in office. But because they are also interested in office, they might be willing to trim their principles to accommodate and to attract others.[42] There will be some limit to how much they are willing to reconcile their own convictions to accommodate others, and locating this limit is what debate within a party is usually about. It is the willingness to engage in that debate that marks off the democratic virtue of partisans, at least in the ideal: by trimming their own convictions to accommodate their fellow partisans, they are willing to participate in the "process" of creating a group that is large and stable enough to possess democratic legitimacy.

The most principled will reject the compromises that come with partisanship. We might imagine them as partisans—bearers of a cause, perhaps the true cause—without a party. In their righteousness, they believe they should rule (they stand *for* something), but cannot bear to associate with those who disagree (they cannot stand *with* others). Perhaps they regard all of the existing parties as too corrupt. Or perhaps they think the rival parties collude to protect what is evil (like the great American parties prior to the Civil War). In their refusal to stand with others for the sake of generating a legitimate claim to rule, these types are not really partisans at all. They might be activists, and try to illuminate the corruption and evil at stake. They might be rebels, and take to either violence or nonviolent protest.

They might turn away from politics in disgust and tend their backyard gardens. When parties are evil and corrupt, all of these options (with the possible exception of violence) may be more admirable than partisanship.

The first part of the book (Chapters 2, 3, 4, and 5) makes the case for party spirit within the terms of political theory. As I have noted, political theory for the most part—both seen through the history of political thought and in contemporary political thought—is hostile to parties and partisanship. My view, elaborated in Chapter 2, is that every political community is in some sense a partisan community. This recalls a more traditional understanding of politics, one rooted in Aristotle's political science; indeed, the defense of party spirit constitutes a critique of a certain modern aspiration for a politics founded on reason, as Chapter 3 explains. But the defense of party spirit is not a matter of grafting some element of ancient politics onto the modern regime (in any case, traditionally, party spirit was viewed as seditious). On the contrary, party spirit is at home in modern politics—even in the ideal of deliberative democracy, as Chapter 4 shows.

The first part culminates in Chapter 5, which elaborates a new kind of party spirit that is worthy of defense. Unlike some defenders of partisanship, I defend partisanship as a kind of loyalty, a commitment that goes beyond what might be rationally justified in the moment. Explaining this understanding of partisanship is the project of Chapter 5. Partisanship as loyalty does not mean cultivating a blindness to embarrassing facts, or seeing the political world through a perceptual screen that exaggerates everything favorable to one's commitments and diminishes everything that is inconvenient. This kind of epistemic closure is typical of partisans—and, for that matter, friends. But party spirit does not need to foreclose on an accurate understanding of the political world. All party loyalty calls for is a certain kind of memory and a particular sort of patience.

The second part of the book (Chapters 6 through 9) maps the new party spirit that I defend onto the institutions of American democracy. What motivates the dogmatic and uncompromising partisanship of the moment seems to be a Progressive reform that was originally thought to weaken parties—the party primary election. Chapter 6 explains the logic of this reform and argues that contemporary efforts to reform the reform by instituting a nonpartisan blanket primary in fact are not really nonpartisan. They need a certain kind of party spirit to succeed. Legislative partisanship is the central subject of Chapter 7. Although the representative legislature is the home of modern partisanship, party discipline threatens to undermine the dignity of legislation. Even in the legislature, Chapter 7 argues, party spirit should be temperate and acknowledge the moral force of a nonpartisan ideal of the common good. Partisans need to know that partisanship has limits. These limits are more obvious and more urgent in the executive and judicial branches, which are the subjects of Chapter 8. The problem with partisanship today is that it encounters fewer limits; the norms of constitutional propriety that seemed to contain party spirit in the past have lost their hold; and partisans seem to have lost their veneer of civility and mutual respect. Party spirit of the moment seems to amplify the legislative impedance that comes with a separation of powers, and threatens to render the government incapable of governing. This is the subject of the concluding chapter.

There is a tension between the first part of the book, which defends and explains party spirit, and the second, which argues for the importance of a "nonpartisan" moment in politics, especially as partisanship moves beyond the legislature to the executive and the judiciary. This tension should call attention to the fact that the defense of party spirit in the first part of the book is by no means absolute: it is attentive to the threats and pitfalls that party spirit is rarely without. One cannot defend partisanship however it happens to be expressed. On the contrary, the ideal of party spirit that I defend is a corrective to the partisanship that defines the moment in American politics. It is something lighter, more open to revision, and more aware of its own incompleteness than partisanship as we usually experience it.

Amid the intensification of party spirit in American politics, it is tempting to embrace the nonpartisan wish—to hope for a politics cleansed of partisan contestation, where reason and common sense rule. Frustration with contemporary partisanship makes the ideologically indistinct parties that dominated American politics in the postwar era look more attractive than they generally seemed at the time. Both the nonpartisan wish and nostalgia for the age of bipartisan consensus represent a constriction of the political imagination, perhaps even a desire to escape politics. What we need is not less partisanship, but better partisanship. So long as we care about what is right in the world we inhabit and in the world we bequeath, partisanship will have a place. To be sure, it is not the greatest thing the political world exhibits. But it has its claim; describing and defending that place is the aim of this book.

2

THE PARTISAN THREAT

"Antipartyism," as Nancy Rosenblum says, "is rife today."[1] The immediate origin of this depreciation of parties, at least in U.S. politics, is Progressivism. For Progressive reformers of the late nineteenth and early twentieth centuries, parties betrayed the promise of democracy. They corrupted government of the people by substituting for it government by party bosses and special interests. The lasting reforms of the Progressive Era—the secret ballot, the direct primary, direct election of U.S. senators, the initiative, the recall—all aimed to circumvent the parties and directly empower the people.[2] They introduced the ideal of the independent citizen who could think and vote free from the influence of party. Because Progressives embedded their understandings so successfully in institutions, their ideas continue to shape ours. If antipartyism is rife today, it is partly on account of how the Progressives reshaped politics.

The suspicion of party in some ways goes deeper than the Progressive Era, to the nature of the political community and citizenship, which require some kind of unity. In this respect, every political community needs to view partisanship with suspicion. At its worst, partisanship threatens to divide the political community against itself, and in the process obliterates the common good, both as something we can imagine and as a practical goal that justifies legislation. This threat inspires the traditional teaching that partisanship is evil. In the traditional view, all political regimes were partisan, but they could not become aware of their own partisanship without destroying their sources of political unity. Therefore partisanship, in the traditional understanding, must remain a secret or fugitive force. Modern politics, by contrast, seems more open to partisan contestation. Many contemporary democratic constitutions make a formal place for parties and partisanship. Even those that do not, like the U.S. Constitution, depend on parties to make them work. Everywhere, regular and open partisanship is a feature of modern democracy.

Yet modern politics generates its own distinctive sources of antipartisanship that are in a sense even more severe than traditional or ancient politics enjoins, because the modern conception of politics is founded on principles of political morality that are taken to be true (and thus beyond contestation), in contrast to the traditional conception of politics, which denied that any political regime could be founded on truth. Modern antipartisanship is mistaken: it is based on an exaggerated sense of the work that moral principles can do in politics, and inflates expectations for a commonsense pragmatic politics that can only, in the end, leave citizens disappointed and confused. Traditional antipartisanship, on the other hand, has a certain wisdom to it. It captures the way parties really can threaten the political community, and yet makes room for parties. To understand the place of partisanship, we need to reconsider how modern political thought remade the relationship between politics and partisanship.

Traditional Partisanship

The traditional understanding of partisanship is found in Aristotle's political theory. The heart of Aristotle's theory is his account of *the regime*. As Aristotle conceives of it, the regime is the answer to the most basic question one can ask about politics: Who rules? Tell me who rules, and I'll tell you what kind of regime we are looking at. *Who rules* is a consequence of two things: how many are involved with rule (the one, the few, or the many) and what ends they rule for (the common good or their own private interest). This typology produces six regime types: where one rules in the common interest, there is a kingship, and where one rules in the private interest, a tyranny; where the few rule in the common interest, there is an aristocracy, whereas the few ruling in their private interest is an oligarchy; where the many rule in the common interest, the regime is a polity, and where the many rule in the private interest of the many, a democracy. In real politics, there are many mixtures of these types, which complicate things further.

But at the same time, in real politics two groups dominate because each possesses a reliable source of power: the many and the few.[3] What distinguishes the few is their property, or money. The many are, well, many—notable for their size. Each group has a kind of power that cannot be easily ignored or suppressed. But just as important, each group offers a distinctive *claim* to rule. Claims convert the fact of power into an argument about why one should have power. For instance, the physically strong may be able to dominate because of their brute strength. But if they are to believe they should rule, they will have to do more than beat people up. They have to make a claim or an argument about why they deserve power.

The oligarchs have money, which is a source of power. But it is also the source of a claim. Their money or property gives them a stake in the regime—a larger stake, in a material sense, than other groups possess. Beyond this, they connect certain qualities of mind and character with the ability to get and to keep property. Acquiring property, the oligarchic claim goes, demands practical judgment and foresight. Maintaining it takes self-restraint. Oligarchs are tough: they deny themselves pleasure today in order to have more money for tomorrow. They can stand against their own desires and temptations. Their way of life ingrains a long-term sensibility and focus on what endures (property) over what dissipates (pleasures). More practically, oligarchs are good at making deals and keeping contracts—they are both shrewd and trustworthy. And their own interest—keeping their property—is intimately connected to the common interest, which must always involve protecting territory. All of these traits translate to politics. The oligarchic character conduces to good practical judgment and deliberation. This is why oligarchs deserve to rule.

The democrats, in the Aristotelian sense, are poor and uneducated. From an oligarchic point of view, they lack not only money, but the virtues that go with it—foresight, self-restraint, and judgment. But they do contribute something essential to the political community: people. They do the work of the community, and without them, there would be no community. The common interest cannot wholly neglect them and still be common. The people may be poor, but they have something elemental: life and freedom. Undistracted by property, they know the value of life and freedom in a way oligarchs cannot. Oligarchs can come to think that property is the point of life, or that life cannot be worth living without wealth. Democrats are not prone to such distorted understandings. They value life and the security that protects it. Since pleasure is not such a threat for them, they can enjoy their freedom in a way oligarchs cannot. They are attuned to real goods like bodily security and freedom. The private interest of the democrats also has an inner connection to the common good, since politics needs the work, the strength, and the cooperation of the people if it is to be stable and prosperous. Finally, Aristotle points out, the democrats may be in a sense more intelligent than the oligarchs, since the many are often better judges of officials than the few.[4] Just as the oligarchs possess an understanding relevant and essential to politics, so do the democrats. And this understanding, apart from the power that the people may together exert, constitutes the democratic claim to rule.[5]

To the democrats, their claim to rule looks convincing and complete. To the oligarchs, their claim looks the same. For both, a material condition gives rise to a way of life that in turn generates certain understandings that constitute a claim to rule. Nothing about these claims makes them look incomplete or partial from the inside. Democrats do not look like bearers of partial claims to themselves, nor do oligarchs to themselves. The partisan contest looks, to each side, like a contest between right and wrong, justice and injustice.

Yet what seems entirely right on the inside looks different when standing at a distance. This distance is provided by political philosophy, which examines the claims that fuel the political contest without having a stake in showing any of the claims to be true. To the philosopher, the claims each group advances look more partial than they seem from the inside. They are partial, first, in the sense that they reflect a group's particular interest: most judge badly, Aristotle notes, "concerning their own things."[6] They are partial also in a second sense—at best they are only partly true. It is not that each side to the partisan contest is wrong, but that each side exaggerates. The moneyed, for instance, have a point. They do in fact possess certain qualities that are relevant to ruling well. And the democrats have a point as well. But the moneyed think that because they are superior in one respect (wealth), they are superior in every respect. The people also advance a real claim. But they too exaggerate, and suppose that because people are equal in some respects, they should be equal in every respect. Aristotle agrees that each party gets it right. But he also thinks each party gets it wrong. "All fasten," Aristotle says, "on a certain sort of justice, but proceed only to a certain point, and do not speak of the whole of justice in its authoritative sense."[7]

Aristotle's use of the term *justice* is revealing. Traditional partisanship is fueled by ideas about justice, or a sense of what people deserve. In Aristotle's view, people do not simply have "preferences" about "issues," as we conceive of good citizens having today. Nor do they merely have "interests," as we assume everyone possesses today. They have claims. Claims, as opposed to preferences, involve arguments about who deserves what; they are connected to ways of life and understandings of character that are nourished by and sustained by these ways of life.[8] More specifically, a political claim is an argument about who deserves the best things. Among the very best things is the honor that comes from holding, or having people like oneself hold, the ruling offices. Each group wants to rule not merely to protect its material interests but to claim the honor of office. The honor conveys a judgment that the qualities of mind and character that define a group's way of life and distinctive understanding of what it is to live well are in fact excellent and worthy. What is at stake in the political contest is not simply a set of rival interests that might be brokered or negotiated, but a publicly affirmed understanding of how to live, of the sort of human being or human character that is most worthy.

Traditional partisanship is motivated fundamentally not by selfish interests but by pride. Because what is at stake is an understanding of how to live, no political regime can easily understand itself as partisan in the sense that it stands for a partial or incomplete conception of how to live and needs complementary ideas that it cannot alone generate. Settled regimes depend on an understanding of themselves as whole, complete, and good, and thus worthy of the permanent allegiance of their citizens and even the support of those they oppress. The modern pluralist insight that any established regime is partial because no social world can accommodate the full human possibility is something traditional partisanship cannot admit. Citizens must be unaware of their own—and their regime's—partiality.[9]

The partiality of the traditional regime—the incompleteness of the conceptions that animate oligarchy or democracy—is illuminated and exposed by political philosophy, which shows how every actual regime is less complete and less just than it thinks it is. In this respect, political philosophy is a subversive force: it shows the regime to be less than it thinks it is. Yet its starting point of Aristotelian political philosophy is not hostile or oppositional. It begins with a sympathetic appraisal of public opinion and of the claims that arise in political life. It does not begin by undercutting popular self-understandings and widely held claims, replacing them with unfamiliar scientific terms that strive to be neutral among competing claims to rule. It does not, for instance, treat the claim to rule as just another desire, nor does it reduce claims to preferences or interests or otherwise assume that nonpolitical concepts drawn from economics or psychology are necessary as a first step toward clearly explaining political things. It takes political claims in the same terms that the democrats and oligarchs understand them—as claims. In this way, it starts with common opinions about what people deserve. The political philosopher tends to rival claims with a sympathy for each, in an attempt to discern the way in which they might be true. Alas, as we have seen, the dominant claims that are presented by rival parties as the whole truth turn out, on examination, to be only part of the truth. In this way, traditional political philosophy reveals the dominant claims of politics to be partial, or incomplete in a way that the partisans themselves do not recognize.

On their own, the democrats or the oligarchs would produce a very imperfect regime. The danger when either group is dominant is that it will make the regime a more extreme form of itself, exacerbating its own injustice. Oligarchs tend to make things more oligarchic, as democrats will make things more democratic. In the process, they accentuate their flaws more than they amplify their virtues. They also deepen the offense to the group that is excluded from rule. The point of a political education—the civic purpose of partisanship—is to cultivate an awareness of the partiality of the regime so that it can lean against its dominant tendency. Doing this requires complementing the dominant tendencies of the regime with opposite tendencies. Regimes need to include what must remain fugitive: the partisan opposition to the regime itself.[10] Ideally, politics would be ruled by those with the most complete virtue and the most comprehensive understanding (a type represented by the philosopher). Only this regime would escape partisanship, since only it is ruled by a type whose claim is not partial, but is rather complete. In practice, of course, such a regime is impossible—not only because philosophers, who are neither numerous nor rich, lack worldly power, and not only because philosophers, who are more interested in knowledge than in power, would not wish to advance their claim, but also because neither the oligarchs nor the democrats would suffer the offense of giving power to philosophers.

The best is unworldly, and real politics is always, at best, a second best. The second best—the most practical solution to partisanship—is to create a regime that gives some space to both democratic and oligarchic claims: a mixed regime. The perfect mixture of democracy and oligarchy does not see itself as a mixture. It is both oligarchic and democratic, as Aristotle says—and neither.[11] The regime makes room for aristocratic and democratic passions (the passion to distinguish and the passion to assert equality), but these passions do not map onto separate classes that inhabit separate social worlds. The dominant social class—the only social class—is the middle class. The middle class wants the regime to remain what it is, not to convert the regime into a more pure democracy or oligarchy. To the extent that the partisan contest remains, it exists within each citizen as a pull toward competing understandings of the good life. The political clash between rival understandings of justice dissolves.[12]

In the traditional or ancient understanding of politics, parties are an evil because they undermine the regime's understanding of itself and its confidence in its own justice; partisanship is a sort of factionalism that threatens dissension, tumult, and, ultimately, revolution. As they destabilize and overturn existing political orders, rival parties cannot easily be a normal feature of a political order, nor can they be openly embraced by those who seek to stabilize and perpetuate a political order. All settled regimes are partisan, but no regime can see itself that way. Traditionally speaking, parties are like conspiracies, and partisans like fugitives. They may be occasionally tolerated when necessary to combat a tyrant. But partisan resistance, even one motivated by justice, cannot have an open or legitimate place in society. If it is successful, the resistance will need to ensure that its example is not followed casually. Partisanship will again need to become fugitive—sensed, but unseen.

In the traditional or ancient view of politics, all settled regimes are partisan, though they do not see themselves that way. In practice, justice is an expression of the values, understandings, and way of life that characterize the ruling group. Democratic justice prevails where the people rule, and oligarchic justice where the moneyed rule. But neither of these represent *true* or impartial justice; they reflect the interests and ideas of only one part of the polity. The inevitable partiality of the regime is the source of its instability, since the rule of one part generates resentments and injustices that the regime can neither recognize nor rectify. In theory, one might be able to describe what true justice demands; but in practice, true justice will be elusive, since it does not serve the interests or flatter the pride of those social groups that are actually powerful. In practice, justice can be approximated by a mixed regime, a formal arrangement of power sharing in which no powerful group is neglected or insulted and no social group claims an exclusive right to rule. The very best that can be hoped for is a mixing so intricate that rival social groups blend together in an indistinguishable mass that forms a kind of middle-class democracy. But even in the mixed or middling regime, the partisanship of the regime itself is suppressed; it does not and cannot see itself as partisan. Further, any kind of partisanship that would oppose the regime is repressed. Partisanship is a fugitive presence if it is a force at all.

Antipartisanship and the Problem of Faction

The traditional understanding of partisanship is by no means obsolete: it continues to inform contemporary worries about partisanship, and it informed the American Founders' understanding of the problem of partisanship. The famous treatment of factions in James Madison's tenth *Federalist* adapts the traditional worry to the circumstances of commercial society, where the fundamental classes of the ancient polity—the demos and the oligarchs—are fragmented into a multiplicity of interests. Like the classes of the ancient polity, the interests of modern commercial society cannot see beyond their own circumstance to an impartial conception of the public interest. But unlike the dominant parties of the ancient polity, none of the interest groups in a commercial society can aspire to dominate. That, at least, is the goal of the Madisonian constitution. Where Aristotle saw the practical solution to partisanship in the consensus of an all-encompassing middle class, Madison saw it in the diversity of a dynamic and extensive commercial society that, when combined with a good constitution, made it impossible for any group to rule. But if he offered a modern solution to the partisan threat, he saw the threat in traditional terms. For Madison, as for Aristotle, the goal of a good constitution is not to contain or to make room for partisanship, but to overcome it.

Factions, or any "number of citizens, whether amounting to a majority or minority of the whole, who are united and actuated by some common impulse of passion, or of interest, adverse to the rights of other citizens, or to the permanent and aggregate interests of the community," are inevitable under conditions of commercial freedom.[13] As Madison says, the "different and unequal faculties of acquiring property" reveal themselves under conditions of freedom, and because of self-love, the unequal possession of property lends a certain tinge or bias to one's opinions. But it is not only property that stands at the roots of disagreement: more generally we are susceptible to a "zeal for different opinions," whether they involve religion, principles of government, or just about any other speculative or practical point.[14] Lost amid so many self-seeking individuals who so enthusiastically disagree is an appreciation of the common good.

How to empower the common good when so few seem to understand it? Much is made of Madison's refusal to rely on moral solutions to moral problems—that is, he does not rely on religion or moral education or civic habituation to instill in people a concern for the common good they would not otherwise have. He instead designs an institutional solution—large electoral districts, a bicameral legislature with staggered terms, a separation of powers—that leaves the moral problem in place, yet selects for legislation in the common interest. That summary of Madisonian constitutionalism is true insofar as it goes, but it overlooks the fact that some kind of civic virtue is needed somewhere in the system for it to work. In particular, Madison hoped that legislative representatives would overcome partisan passions.

The point of large electoral districts is to make it difficult for petty partisans—those who share a way of life or an economic interest or a religious conception—to discover that commonality and express it politically. Only "diffusive and established characters," he speculates, will successfully attract support in large districts—not petty partisans.[15] Madison hopes his system will produce representatives "whose wisdom may best discern the true interest of their country, and whose patriotism and love of justice will be least likely to sacrifice it to temporary or partial considerations."[16] The system perhaps allows citizens to be more narrow. But they too are expected to prefer such "diffusive" characters over promise-making partisans, which is itself a kind of civic virtue. Ideally, the system liberates both voters and officials to act from a disinterested and general appreciation of what conduces to the common good.

In contrast to the ancient tragic conception of politics, Madison hoped that institutional innovations would liberate public deliberations from factions. The multiplication of interests in large districts and the deliberative space created by representation would empower a politics oriented to the common good. These same institutions would invite a new kind of party—one that is a collection of many "partial considerations"—into a large and untidy package rather than the ancient parties that were bearers of the ideals and interests of a narrow class. The Madisonian party is a new kind of party, but it takes its bearings from ancient standards. Its task is to overcome the corruption and injustice that come from accentuating a narrow interest over the whole, and its respectability derives from the way it distills from many smaller interests an approximation of the aggregate interest of the nation.

The ancient ideal of politics continues to inform contemporary political understandings, and the allure of an ideal politics that transcends partisan claims remains strong. The traditional understanding also informs the notion that the best politicians are never mere politicians, who successfully claim power by expressing and responding to the views of distinct social groups, but are like statesmen, who act from a deeper understanding of justice and truth. Like ancient statesmen, Madisonian public officials need to sift through the partial claims arising from various groups and combine these in a way that forms a workable approximation of the interest of the whole. Catchall parties do not abstract from the particular interests that compose them or take recourse in some algorithm or social scientific method that reveals the public interest; they attend, sometimes too solicitously, to particular interests, and search for ways of combining them, serving them, and representing them that actual people can endorse. When they fail, they do so in ways that an Aristotelian political scientist could understand: they give too much to some interests and understate the claims of others. They corrupt the polity by making it the property of one faction or another.

Factions are an obvious evil in the traditional understanding, but they are an evil that cannot be entirely avoided: they must be attended to, and somehow included, in any stable polity. Madison and Washington spoke about parties in traditional terms, but in their time a new and more modern understanding of partisanship developed. Like the traditional understanding, it cast parties as evil—but it did so in a more uncompromising way, and inflated the hope that reason might more thoroughly cleanse politics of party spirit. If this less-tolerant, modern antipartisanship did not characterize the American Founders, it yet possesses enormous force in common understandings of politics, and fuels an impatience with partisanship that far exceeds anything Madison expressed.

The starting point of modern politics refuses to admit the sources of traditional partisanship: it does not begin with the claims various groups advance, nor does it sift through these claims with reference to a philosophic understanding of the best life. The best regime in practice is not one that blends or mixes competing claims to create a stable tension. Modern politics embraces no distinctive way of life and no particular understanding of the best human type or the ideal human character. Because of this, modern partisanship is always at risk of losing any connection to the claims that are nourished and sustained by particular ways of life. As a result, modern politics generates new and powerful sources of antipartisanship, rooted in the idea that the entire society can escape partisanship—or, put differently, can be enlightened.[17]

Modern Antipartisanship

Ancient politics is rooted in an understanding of the good life— the qualities of mind and character that constitute human excellence. Modern politics sidesteps conceptions of the good life and tries to substitute goals that are less controversial because they are more widely shared: self-preservation and comfortable living. As Hobbes says, it is only rational to prefer life to premature violent death. *That* is something about which everyone should agree, since life is the precondition of every other good. John Locke shares Thomas Hobbes's concern with security, but emphasizes the additional importance of the freedom from the arbitrary wills of others, and of property, or the promise of commodious living. These principles—life and liberty—are not understood to be reflective of any particular way of life. In the classic accounts of Hobbes and Locke, they appear as things people would choose naturally, not expressions of a particular, socially contingent, class-based, and thus necessarily incomplete understanding of the human good. They are rather conclusions of reason. As such, a regime devoted to securing them is not falsely generalizing partial conceptions. It does not fasten on part of justice and present it as the whole. Instead, it is a regime based in true first principles of political morality, principles that are available to anyone capable of the unprejudiced exercise of reason. Modern politics does not seek to generalize the highest goods or virtues about which people will always disagree, but rather to secure goods that all can identify and share. Because these basic goods (principally, self-preservation and commodious living) are the presupposition of pursuing other, possibly higher, goods about which people will disagree, basic goods are in a sense universally shared. A politics that focuses on basic goods, and leaves higher goods for individuals to pursue as they please, substitutes a universal end for contestable ends, and thus forecloses on partisanship even more ruthlessly than traditional politics.

For this reason, modern politics gives rise to an antipartisanship even more severe than traditional politics.[18] The goal of traditional partisanship—affirming a way of life and a type of character—is displaced by modern partisanship. No more is politics about justice in the sense of upholding an idea about which way of life is most worthy. Those ideas are privatized by the modern political formula—they become ideas that individuals are free to form, pursue, and revise for themselves as they please. Politics is about goals—security and resources—that are the precondition of pursuing any particular way of life and cannot motivate profound partisan contestation, since they are universal. By severing the connection between political office and concrete ways of life and the claims these ways of life generate, modern politics undercuts the basis for partisan contestation.

There was a particular kind of party that modern politics had to defeat—a party fueled by creedal passions and seeking to install a new social and political order. These parties, religious and revolutionary, wreaked tumult across Europe in the sixteenth and seventeenth centuries. The point of modern politics was to deflate such parties, which Hume called "parties of principle" and Alexis de Tocqueville later called "great parties."[19] The contest of religious parties culminated in an agreement to disagree—an agreement to take rival conceptions about how best to care for the immortal soul out of politics. The solution to religious war—the principle of religious toleration—required a new political science that could show how politics might be conducted on the basis of ends that all share. By displacing profound partisanship and great or revolutionary parties, modern politics allows for an indifference toward small or petty parties which express differences over material interests and are fueled more by rival contenders for political office than by deep social cleavages. By compressing political contestation to such small differences, modern politics can tolerate petty parties that engage neither the profound questions about how to live that animated ancient politics nor the religious differences that roiled Europe in the early modern period.[20]

Modern politics can be open to a partisanship of small differences but must remain hostile to the profound partisanship that animated traditional politics. Engaging small differences is reasonable, since it presupposes an agreement on rational first principles of political morality. Engaging profound differences is unreasonable, since it reveals an inability to grasp the truth of those same principles. The single exception to the modern hostility to party is what might be called the "last party." The last party is distinguished by its commitment to the rational first principles of political morality at a moment when these principles remain in dispute. Its victory would install rational first principles at the foundation of the regime, and this, in turn would make partisanship as traditionally understood henceforth unnecessary and unjustifiable.

The Whigs, who were led by the Earl of Shaftesbury (who was assisted by Locke), saw themselves as a "last party" of this sort. A century later, Lord Bolingbroke's writings inspired a similar sensibility in the followers of Grenville in the 1760s, later in William Pitt and his circle, and finally in the supporters of King George III.[21] The party inspired by Bolingbroke saw itself as the kind of party whose victory would make future opposition unnecessary: "based on non-partisan principles, it was meant to be the last party."[22] The boldest example of the last party, however, is Marx's Communist Party, which he cast as uniquely capable of advancing the true interests of humanity. As Marx said, "If the proletariat during its contest with the bourgeoisie is compelled, by the force of circumstances, to organize itself as a class, if by means of revolution, it makes itself the ruling class, and, as such, sweeps away by force the old conditions of production, then it will, along with these conditions, have swept away the conditions for the existence of class antagonisms and of classes generally, and will thereby have abolished its own supremacy as a class." The final victory of the proletariat will bring, Marx argued, an end to class struggle and, in a certain sense, an end to politics.[23] Politics will come to an end: the contest of rival interests and rival ways of life will be replaced by nonpartisan administration of human interests.

Marx's philosophy does not inspire millions as it once did, and many assume that the bounty of modern capitalism, combined with the capacity of modern democracy to express, balance, and contain rival interests, has decisively refuted Marx.[24] But the idea of a last party does capture a distinctively modern aspiration that, if more muted, is still shared by the sorts of liberals Marx would have derided. The aspiration to replace the contestation of partial interests and rival ways of life with enlightened (nonpartisan) administration of interests and goals that are universal remains powerful, for contemporary liberals in particular. Robert Reich's apology for liberalism, for instance, is titled *Reason*, as if liberalism is not a fighting faith or a partisan creed but a set of scientific conclusions.[25]

In a more philosophic way, one can see this aspiration at work in John Rawls's *Theory of Justice*.[26] Consistent with the modern formula, Rawls's moderately egalitarian politics does not rely on any contestable or comprehensive conception of the good. Justice, for Rawls, is not rooted in any particular group's understanding of life, but in reason. Of course, in fact, many disagree with the degree of redistribution that Rawlsian justice calls for. In order to advance his understanding of justice against liberals or libertarians (who would argue that a redistributive politics would unjustly infringe on individual freedom), Rawls posits a category of "primary goods." Primary goods are good for everyone, whatever one's religion or conception of the good life or plan of life. They include rights, liberties, opportunities, income, wealth, and the social bases of self-respect. It is simply rational to want primary goods, Rawls says, whatever else one wants. They do not privilege or presuppose any particular way of life or conception of how life ought to be lived. Rather, they are all-purpose tools that can be used whatever one's plan of life. It is only because a set of goods exists that every person wants and would "prefer more of rather than less" that it is possible to speak of redistributing goods without implicitly privileging any particular way of life or conception of the good, and without therefore violating people's fundamental freedoms.[27]

Because certain goods are simply rational for everyone regardless of their particular plan of life, it is possible to imagine a politics that is not partisan in the traditional or ancient sense: it does not affirm some particular way of life or single out certain ends or a certain kind of character as most worthy. Nor does it contain a fundamental contest over rival ways of life. It stands, simply, for goods that are rational for everyone. The category of goods that it is rational for everyone and anyone to want undercuts partisanship in the traditional sense. There is, in short, no reason for partisanship of the traditional sort when politics can be based on rational and universal ends.[28]

Rawls may or may not be right that primary goods offer a non-partisan foundation of rational agreement; what distinguishes modern politics is that there is such a basis for politics.[29] To disagree with the rational basis for political agreement is not to advance a partial claim, much less a reasonable conception of the common good. It is to be mistaken—to have failed in the exercise of reason. Politics founded on a rational basis need not admit or consider or perhaps even tolerate such irrational claims. This is the way in which modern politics generates an even more ardent antipartisan temper than traditional politics.

The conceptual categories that modern political morality offers make it very difficult to value political virtues like partisanship. Either the political virtues look too unprincipled (an expression of merely personal ambition) or they look too principled (too uncompromising and ideological). In both cases, the political virtue falls out of view and cannot be identified or admired. To illustrate this, consider three familiar political types: the power seeker, the moral purist, and the zealot. These types are not meant to constitute an exhaustive catalogue of the forms of political and moral agency available today. But they are familiar and common enough. Together, they show how the dominant modes of being political in contemporary politics impede an understanding of the political virtues.

The power seeker, who is ready to do almost anything to advance himself, is too unprincipled to be the object of any admiration. The purist, by contrast, who is more concerned with moral principle, is easier to admire. But the purist is not really *political*, since he or she is unwilling to compromise. Purists would rather lose on principle than get a partial victory at the cost of compromising their principles. When purists aim for real-world results (rather than just maintaining their moral integrity), they are in danger of becoming zealots who will do anything to get their way, even if it means violence. The movement from the power seeker to the zealot is also a movement from less ideological to more ideological types. The extremes (the power seeker and the zealot) are morally deficient and practically hazardous. The midpoint (the moral purist) is more admirable, but ineffectual. What gets lost is any distinctly *political* virtue—an orientation that blends the pragmatic and the principled. Without an understanding of the political virtues, it is difficult even to conceive of how partisanship might be an admirable thing.

The Power Seeker

Political ambition is a difficult thing to fathom. Why do people want to serve in office so badly that they will sacrifice their privacy, their family life, their work, and perhaps a good portion of their finances to win? In the modern view, the desire to rule is not based on a claim to be deserving of recognition (as traditional political philosophy would have it). The desire comes to look more like a psychological drive for power—an idiosyncratic and inexplicable appetite that some happen to possess. In this view, partisanship—the disposition to stand with a party, a group making a claim to rule—comes to be seen not as a quality of ordinary citizens (who are more defined by decency than by the drive for power). Partisanship comes to be seen as a form of personal ambition—power seeking—that marks an elite against which ordinary citizens must ever be on guard.[30]

One reflection of this is the tendency to think that ordinary citizens, even if they identify with a party, are not real partisans.

In his brilliant account of parties as tools that the ambitious create and use to further their goals, John Aldrich restricts the term *partisan* to describe only office seekers and the staffers who surround them. Voters, he says, "are not part of the political party at all, even if they identify strongly with a party and consistently support its candidates." It is better, in Aldrich's view, to think of voters not as partisans but as "brand-name loyalists." They do not belong to the party any more than fans of the iPhone are part of Apple Corporation.[31] Those who are really part of Apple stand to benefit materially from the company's success. Similarly, since ordinary citizens do not seek power for themselves, they are not the real partisans. The true partisan is, at bottom, a power seeker.

Why deny the term *partisan* to ordinary citizens, many of whom in fact profess an identification (sometimes a strong one) with one or another party? People do not describe themselves as "brand loyalists." They say, "I'm a Democrat" or "I vote Republican." Why not call them partisans, as they call themselves? And if they are not partisans, what would distinguish them from independents, who also perhaps have a brand loyalty—just not for a party? We might infer from Aldrich's account (he does not say so directly) that ordinary citizens who think of themselves as partisans are deluded about the true nature of politics. They believe they have something in common with the political elites who run for office—convictions, ideals, values, a common cause that connects them to citizens and leaders of the past and, they hope, the future. But this belief is a mistake. The mistake comes from thinking of partisanship in the traditional way, as if it is about ideals of community, character, and a way of life. But that partisanship is over—it was at home in the world of traditional politics, not the modern one. Modern politics denies partisanship any great task. Once a constitution reflects the first principles of political morality, there is little of great importance left to do. Modern politics is (and should be) about small things, about which there is no reason for ordinary citizens to care that much. They might have a judgment about which party has been doing a better job, and vote accordingly. But there is no reason for everyday citizens to be overly invested in the party.

Of course, to motivate support, partisans need to convince voters that there is a great task at hand, that the fate of the country depends on the next election. They need to offer a vocabulary in their slogans and stump speeches that casts the campaign as part of a great historical contest. They need to convince voters (and perhaps themselves) of this fiction in order to make their ambition palatable. Looking at the small parties of Jacksonian America, Tocqueville incisively captured this dynamic:

> Ambition must succeed in creating parties, for it is difficult to overthrow the one who holds power for the sole reason that someone wants to take his place. All the skill of the politician therefore consists in composing parties: a politician in the United States at first seeks to discern his interest and to see what the analogous interests are that could be grouped around his; afterwards, he busies himself with discovering whether there might not by chance exist in the world a doctrine or principle that could suitably be placed at the head of the new association to give it the right to introduce itself and circulate freely.[32]

An astute, tough-minded voter will not be fooled by the "doctrine or principle" that parties and partisans peddle. But many voters will be taken in. Partisan rhetoric is what makes the truth about partisanship—individual ambition—publicly respectable. It is what allows scheming politicians to seduce a mass electorate. But it is not what partisanship is really about.

Partisanship is really about power. If this is not an attractive fact, it is an avoidable one—all organizations and all political communities will give way to what Robert Michels called (in 1905) the "iron law of oligarchy." In modern partisanship, Michels writes, "aristocracy gladly presents itself in democratic guise."[33] Parties, like all groups, will be dominated by the few. Michels's iron law works like this: A people wants to rule itself democratically. But it needs to organize itself. Every organization must be led if it is going to act effectively. This gives an opportunity to those people with a particular interest in leading. That particular interest will often compete with the common interest. So the community, which wants to be ruled democratically in the common interest, will be dominated by specific leaders who are motivated by a personal and particular interest. The only way around this is to find people who are willing to lead but who have no personal interest in being a leader: democracy depends on selecting for such self-renouncing types. If indeed they exist, what system could select for them in a consistent manner? More likely, democracy will be dominated by the ambitious—which is not democratic.

In this view—the realist view—partisanship is an expression of personal ambition that threatens the common interest. Partisans might be constrained by constitutional procedures to act in the common interest, but that constraint will never be perfect. Self-serving politicians are a stubborn fact that democracies will in some measure have to tolerate. The political virtue, in the realist view, is the ability to get power and to keep it. There is no reason for ordinary citizens to particularly admire the political virtue. On the contrary, they should guard against it and take care not to be seduced by the rhetoric the political class uses to veil its ambition. Perhaps a cadre of self-serving partisans is something that democratic citizens will need to tolerate. But their partisanship is nothing ordinary citizens should be expected to share.

The Moral Purist

In contrast to the power seeker, the moral purist is more self-overcoming and noble. Purists are motivated by principle, not power. The principles of political morality that define the modern regime inspire and guide the purist, who aims to make those principles more accurately and vividly reflected in the political world. Since principles are founded in reason, there is no justification for compromising one's principles: what's true is true, and what's right is right. Moral purism gives rise to a particular ideal of political heroism: the maverick. The maverick hews to first principles, and works—often outside "the system"—to make those principles real. The maverick is Mr. Smith, who naively goes to Washington to serve the public, who is nearly broken by the machinations of the corrupt machine that surrounds him, and who filibusters in an effort to expose the corruption until he finally collapses of exhaustion.[34] The maverick is Senator Wayne Morse, whose campaign slogan, "Principle above politics," was more than a slogan. Over and again, he broke from his party on principle—he ran for the Senate (and won) as a Republican in 1944, as an independent in 1950, and as a Democrat in 1956. In the 1960s he broke with Democrats who supported the Vietnam War, and in 1964 he was one of only two senators to vote against the Gulf of Tonkin Resolution (which authorized President Johnson to escalate fighting in Vietnam without a declaration of war).[35] This is a type we can admire.

The moral purist is a maverick because he cannot bear to compromise. Adapting one's own convictions is always a sacrifice of sorts—and it is one the maverick refuses to bear. Mavericks have great difficulty belonging to groups. Belonging to any group imposes a cost to our integrity, the very quality the maverick cherishes most. When groups we identify with pursue purposes we do not endorse, our integrity suffers (where integrity is understood as an alignment between what we believe and what we say, or stand for, or do). But it is difficult to get groups to do exactly what we think they should do, and this difficulty multiplies as the group grows in size. The larger the group, the more views and interests it contains—and the less likely it becomes that the group does exactly as we would wish. To belong to a group, one has to lower one's standards. It is easier to maintain your integrity standing alone than when standing with others. This cost will usually rise as the size of the group increases. The more members a group has, the more views and interests it amalgamates, and the less likely that what the group stands for fully correlates with what any individual in the group believes. The larger the group, the lower its standards. For this reason, there is often more integrity in being your own person and standing up for what you know is right than in being a party person.

The cost to one's integrity is most severe when the principles at stake involve matters of moral urgency. When important moral principles are at stake, we should perhaps emulate Henry David Thoreau and remain in a party of one. For Thoreau, the principled wrong of slavery—brought to a concrete point by the 1846–1848 war with Mexico and the prospect of slavery's expansion—prohibited identifying with any party. In moments, Thoreau resents even all democratic government and disparages even the individual act of voting, since it implicates one in rule by the majority: "All voting is a sort of gaming, like chequers or backgammon, with a slight moral tinge to it, a playing with right and wrong, with moral questions; and betting naturally accompanies it. The character of voters is not staked. I cast my vote, perchance, as I think right; but I am not concerned that right should prevail. I am willing to leave it to the majority."[36] Thoreau objects to "gaming" or strategic thinking, at least where important moral principles are at stake. It is only principle, in the end, that obligates: "It is not desirable," he says, "to cultivate a respect for the law, so much as for the right."[37] What matters, for Thoreau, are not laws and constitutions, but principles. Conscience is what illuminates an understanding of moral principle, while politics and partisanship cloud that understanding. To remain truly pure, one has to keep a distance from politics.

Or so one would think. Today, as Morris Fiorina explains, partisan politics in the United States is increasingly dominated by purists. The change was first picked up in the 1960s by James Q. Wilson and Aaron Wildavsky, who showed how "amateurs" (Wilson's term) and "purists" (Wildavsky's) came to replace the partisan "professionals" in American politics. As civil service laws and other reforms decreased the ability of officeholders to distribute jobs and other benefits to their supporters, so politics became a field "left to those with policy or ideological motivations."[38] The old partisan professionals were power seekers who aimed to cobble together any coalition that would deliver them to power. The new purists all too often would rather lose than compromise—as we have witnessed in recent U.S. politics, where Tea Party insurgents defeat in the primary a Republican incumbent whom they view as too compromising, only to see the Republican nominee lose in the general election. Fiorina sees (though he does not use this language) a political virtue in the partisan professionals: they know how to knit people together in a large and durable coalition. And he fears that the new purists, who emphatically lack this virtue, will become zealots.

The Zealot

The moral purist is primarily concerned with integrity: the purity that comes first is his own. Because democratic politics always imposes some compromise, the natural stance of the purist is apolitical. It is when purists get political that things get scary. The political purist projects the moral purity he identifies within himself onto the whole world. It is not the integrity of his own character, but the perfection of society, that becomes the aim. The political purist becomes a zealot when he comes to believe not only in his own righteousness, but that there is no justifiable impediment to bringing this righteousness to the world. Like the purist, the zealot is impatient with those who disagree. He is right, and knows he is right—disagreement must be a sign of corruption or evil intention. But unlike the purist, the zealot does not retreat to the purity of private life. His impatience manifests itself as a willingness to do what it takes to save the world. Whether to undertake violence becomes a merely strategic question: Will it be effective?

If the wrongs are wrong enough, and ordinary modes of protest and persuasion are ineffective, some violence may be "worth it," in that it seems to cause less harm than the great wrongs the zealot opposes. So it seemed in the late 1970s to a brilliant Harvard graduate and mathematics PhD who began sending homemade bombs to scientists and university researchers in order to combat the corruption of technological and industrial society. Ted Kaczynski, the "Unabomber," sent dozens of such bombs over a seventeen-year span, killing four people and injuring over twenty others. Kaczynski had suddenly quit his job as a professor at Berkeley in 1969 and retreated to a cabin in Montana without plumbing or heating, in order to live— in Thoreauvian fashion—more deliberately. By the late 1970s,

Kaczynski decided that it was not enough to save himself. He had to save the world. He wrote a manifesto—but in the frustrating manner that open societies can envelop their own harshest critics, it went unnoticed. Indeed, we only know of his manifesto because of his bombs.[39]

Moral certainty did not make the Unabomber a zealot. It was rather his impatience—his insistence that the ordinary modes of democratic persuasion and change would take too long and be too ineffective. He could not put democracy before his morality. Perhaps he had moral virtue, of a sort; but he lacked political virtue. To many, he had no kind of virtue: he was simply crazy. He might have been, but the readiness to classify him as insane also reflects the way in which his example cannot be fit within the terms of modern politics.

Modern politics was born of an effort to defeat zealotry. Religious zealotry ripped apart Europe in the sixteenth and seventeenth centuries and soaked the ground in blood. Modern political theory tried to arrest the violent tendencies of religious zealotry by refounding politics on reasons that were universally shared—and relegating moral ideas that could not command universal assent to the private sphere. The modern political project tried to separate moral ideas that all could share from moral ideas (of a religious nature) that relied on evidence that is not publicly available. The Gospels may be true—but their truth relies on revelation, which is a form of evidence that can only be taken on faith. A different kind of truth—that premature, violent death is bad, or that commodious living is good—can be verified by each person. Everyone wants to live, and everyone would prefer a certain degree of physical comfort. The goods of the body are publicly verifiable. The goods of the soul are not. Modern politics is based on material goods that can be publicly ascertained and verified. What conduces to the eternal salvation of our souls becomes a private matter about which reasonable people can reasonably disagree. To insist that everyone agree with one's idea about an excellent soul is to insist that one's ideas rely on a kind of evidence that others can access. And since such evidence is unavailable, the insistence that everyone agree seems crazy.

This is the spirit in which Hobbes sought to turn his readers' minds away from the fear of "invisible spirits" and to focus their minds—for political purposes—on a more ascertainable fear: suffering a premature and violent death.[40] As Hobbes showed, we will never agree about the invisible spirits that are the evidence of religious revelation. We might compel assent to this or that set of propositions, if we can bring enough violence to bear. But there is no basis for agreement, since the relevant evidence is, in the end, invisible. It is not evident to the senses; since it is senseless, it is crazy to expect agreement.

The twenty-first century analogue to the religious zealotry of the sixteenth and seventeenth centuries is ideology. What goes by the name "ideology" today is not the fully worked out system of social thought that explains all of political history and predicts the future (like Marxism). It is simply a package of general values brought to politics. From a historical perspective, it is tame. But it still seems to overload our political circuitry, because "values"—like religious convictions—seem to rely on evidence that is not publicly available. Questions of value, especially those that go beyond the minimal concerns with human comfort and prosperity, cannot be publicly corroborated, and conflicts of value introduce controversies that cannot be easily brokered. In a sense, merely to introduce questions of value into politics is to raise the specter of zealotry: Why politicize matters that cannot be negotiated, about which there is little or no publicly available evidence? Value politics seems only to ask for trouble. Modern politics is born of an agreement to disagree, at least about those questions about which there is no reason to believe agreement will ever be forthcoming. Why go *there*, when there are so many things about which we can agree? (Life is better than premature death; prosperity is better than penury; freedom is better than slavery; equal respect and rights are better than subjection.)

To glimpse the possibility of agreement in spite of the variability of human situations and the inevitably of disagreement is a political virtue. To accommodate oneself to others, even when those others seem unreasonable or wrong, is a kind of respect. The political virtues involve accommodating others even when we do not agree with their reasons, do not understand their reasons, and think they might have no good reasons. These virtues are at the heart of partisanship, at least partisanship at its best. But these virtues are largely lost to view amid the political types that dominate the modern political imagination. We can make sense of the power seeker—the person of ambition but without principle. And we can make sense of those who have principles—the purist, whom we so often admire, and the zealot, whom we so often fear. But the genuine partisan—who is both principled and pragmatic, who like the power seeker wants victory and power, but who like the purist and the zealot wants power for a public reason—is almost impossible to discern. If she is principled, we ask, Why isn't she more principled (and more uncompromising)? If she wants power, we think she must be driven simply by personal ambition. The partisan—the ideal partisan—is ambitious, and like all power seekers must be somewhat mysterious to those who are satisfied by private life. But the ideal partisan is ambitious for reasons that go beyond personal gratification. She is ambitious, ideally, because she wants to accomplish something good.

Modern politics makes it difficult to fix this blend of ambition and principle in our minds; we reduce the partisan to one extreme or the other. Yet the ideal partisan is not merely a figure in the fantasies of political theorists—he or she can readily enough be found. Perhaps there is no better example in recent American politics than Ted Kennedy. Kennedy was ambitious, and knew how to get power and keep it (witness his 1990 Senate race against Mitt Romney). But he was also principled, and no one was ever in doubt that liberalism oriented everything Kennedy thought. Yet Kennedy was able to abbreviate his convictions when it was necessary to get something rather than nothing. He was warm and collegial, even with those whose views he disagreed with most. Kennedy was a partisan. He was practical and pragmatic and understood power, and he was principled and never doubted the moral convictions that gave his career focus. He was neither a power seeker nor a purist: he was a partisan, in the best sense.

To fully appreciate great partisans like Kennedy (or like some of his erstwhile opponents, such as Alan Simpson), one has to step outside the terms of modern politics and see partisanship in something like the way the ancients saw it. Modern politics posits certain basic, first principles of political morality—that citizens are free and equal, that government should be founded on consent, that individuals have rights. In the modern understanding, these are not merely a tradition. They are not the property of a particular political culture, but instead present themselves as true, elemental axioms of political morality. This puts sharp boundaries on permissible political contestation. They invite us to think that people who relax principles are solely interested in power—and that people motivated by principle should never compromise. Political virtue, or the blend of principle and pragmatism, gets lost in the middle.

The ancient approach to politics, by contrast, saw a political world beset by partial claims—arguments about justice that had some truth but were not the whole truth. Winning the whole truth for the political world, it could see, was impractical, dangerous, and destined to be defeated. The best thing we can hope for, in the ancient view, is some kind of mixture of partial claims—a compromise. Political virtues get their meaning from this goal, the second best. To fully appreciate this meaning requires that we see our community a bit more like the way ancient political thinkers saw the political community—not as an enterprise founded on moral axioms that can be applied rationally, but as an arena where rival claims compete. The modern political project has never so fully succeeded that it has displaced the occasion for party spirit. Perhaps even the modern polity should be understood in a more traditional way, as a community where political contestation reaches to fundamental questions about the definition of the community itself.

3

THE PARTISAN COMMUNITY

The classic worry about partisanship is that it will destroy political unity. This is why partisanship was traditionally associated with sedition. As we have seen, the partisan threat becomes more acute in the modern regime, founded on rational first principles of political morality. The modern or liberal regime based on an agreement about first principles (of freedom and equality) can tolerate disagreement about small things like questions of technique (how do we fight unemployment?), but contestation about the basic principles of the regime or constitutional fundamentals is more threatening. This threat seems even more potent in a political community that relies almost solely on agreement about constitutional essentials for its unity, as opposed to language, ancestry, culture, or religion.

But this is the wrong way to conceive of political unity. What defines a liberal politics is not an agreement only to disagree within certain bounds (never touching foundational ideas), but to disagree in a certain *way*: according to constitutional procedures, in a certain manner. In particular, it is an agreement to engage in disagreement without threatening to exit or to destroy the constitutional process of disagreement. It is an agreement to disagree without taking up violence. Liberal unity is given by a commitment to voice (disagreement) over loyalty (fealty to foundational commitments, such that they are never questioned) or exit (destroying the polity or seceding). The foundational or

constitutional agreement about process is more fundamental
than the constitutional agreement about principle.

Liberal politics can motivate an allergy to ideological contestation, as if ideology must bring zealotry and political fragmen-
tation. Ideological contestation seems to run too deep when it
extends to the agreement about first principles or "ideals" that
unify the liberal polity. But ideological disagreement is not necessarily the threat it may seem. "Ideology" as the term is used
today simply refers to a package of ideas about policies and political goals that bear some principled relation to one another.
While an agreement about first principles of politics might seem
to leave no room for ideological contestation, this in fact mistakes
how constitutional agreements should function in politics.
They establish the terms of an argument and the mode of an
argument—they do not settle all argument, even ideological
argument. This is because as a political matter, the agreement
about first principles is never complete—some dissent from certain constitutional terms. But also as a philosophic matter, first
principles are more contestable than the modern ideal of politics
would suggest. We cannot know how they might be true—where
they might be applied and where they should be relaxed—without
an argument. Even then, the argument will not permanently
settle things. It is a mistake to think that the liberal or modern
regime is founded on an agreement about ideas; it is founded
on an agreement about how to disagree.

Beware the Spirit of Party

The suspicion that partisanship corrodes political unity is never
far from the surface in America, a nation that often understands
itself as founded on ideas. As one "indivisible" nation, we may
disagree, but we cannot divide. Standing together around a fun-

damental agreement about the values of freedom and equality, we share a common devotion to the Constitution. Alien to America, ideological partisans are said to be at home in places riven by class privileges and historic enmities, plagued by fragile governments, and beset by an insufficient sense of political belonging. America's steady preference for moral unity and commonsense pragmatism disadvantages the partisan who would rile things up. This taste for comity and togetherness has long exposed American partisanship to the charge that it creates artificial divisions the country would be better off without. Partisanship arises not simply because the population divides itself spontaneously into two—or three, four, or five—political groups, but rather because some few ambitious people who desire to hold office find it necessary to divide the rest.

The idea that we are naturally one—that we would be politically unified if it were not for the divisions incited by power-seeking politicians—goes back to the first years of the American republic. Arguing against those politicians who favored dividing into "separate confederacies or sovereignties," John Jay insisted that ethnic, cultural, religious, and geographic unity made political unity only natural: "Providence has been pleased to give this one connected country to one united people—a people descended from the same ancestors, speaking the same language, professing the same religion, attached to the same principles of government, very similar in their manners and customs." Political unity was not an artifice, only an acknowledgment of an underlying moral unity. "This country and this people seem to be made for each other," Jay exclaimed.[1] On leaving office in 1796, George Washington underlined the social and moral unity that supported "the unity of government which constitutes you one people." This unity of "religion, manners, habits, and political principles"—a unity amplified by common and complementary interests—offered the "most commanding motives for carefully guarding and preserving the union."[2]

But the overlapping social, moral, and political unity of the nation was threatened, Washington noted, by partisans who seek to "render alien to each other those who ought to be bound together by fraternal affection." By substituting the "projects of faction" for the "regular deliberation and action of the constituted authorities," these crafty and grasping partisans cause citizens to think that northern, southern, Atlantic, and western interests are fundamentally opposed. By sowing the seeds of disagreement and division, "cunning, ambitious, and unprincipled men will be enabled to subvert the power of the people and to usurp the reins of government." As rival factions contest and alternate in dominating government, they will unleash "disorders and miseries that will gradually incline the minds of men to seek security and repose in the absolute power of an individual." Party spirit, which dissolves an appreciation of our underlying social and moral unity and "kindles the animosity of one against another," leads in the end to despotism.[3]

In this view, Americans are fundamentally unified, but the political expression of their prepolitical unity is ever threatened by the smaller interests and personal ambitions that fuel party spirit. This reflects a broader insight of modern political science, one fully appreciated by people like James Madison and Alexander Hamilton: people need to be illuminated by reason to see their common interests, and equipped by institutions to advance those interests to ensure they do not fall prey to the divisive arts of petty politicians. The reasons and the institutions advanced by modern political science enable people to cooperate for their mutual benefit rather than to indulge those differences of opinions and attachments to rival leaders that have "divided mankind into parties . . . and rendered them much more disposed to vex and oppress each other than to cooperate for their common good."[4] Sober reason is a help, but well-designed institutions are essential to this end. A constitution that disadvantages narrow interests and divisive passions will elevate and direct individual ambition to the common good, and replace divisive partisans with public-spirited administrators who direct what Washington called "the efficient management of . . . common interests."[5] But for efficient managers to succeed, citizens need to resist the allure of partisans. The most crucial step in cultivating a resistance to parties and partisans is to recognize that unity is a social, moral, and geographic fact—not a political construction or imposition. Subscribing to the "imagined community" in which we are fundamentally unified is a civic duty.

The Unity of Liberal Ideas

The image of a moral unity underlying American political unity was unforgettably and forcefully advanced by Louis Hartz in his mid-twentieth-century work, *The Liberal Tradition in America*.[6] Hartz described a people bound by a pervasive, inarticulate, and unshakable consensus on the liberal values of freedom, equality, and capitalism. In America, liberalism is not simply a theory; it is not something thoughtful people might think through, assess, and possibly agree with. It is a way of life. Americans do not need to study the seventeenth-century political theory of John Locke: they *live* Locke. Unlike Europeans, Americans actually inhabited a world of social equality and widespread opportunity akin to the state of nature Locke imagined, and as a result liberalism has an "objective reality" in America that it must always lack in Europe. Liberalism, a vulnerable species in Europe, encountered no natural predators in its new home in America. Without a reactionary opposition rooted in the vestiges of an ancient aristocratic regime, America offered no spur to the development of egalitarian socialism: in America, liberalism flourished almost without impediment (the chief impediment, of course, was also unique to America: slavery). With the final eradication of slavery after the Civil War, Americans were liberals all.[7]

Hartz, for his part, was not of one mind about the "utter dominion" of the liberal idea over the American mind. "Almost" charmed by America's "innocence of mind," he had sympathy for its liberalism and knew that people everywhere rely on America for what is best in the liberal tradition. Yet he also worried that "even a good idea can be a little frightening when it is the only idea a man has ever had." Liberalism's omnipresence in America rendered it "absolute and irrational," characteristics at odds with the spirit of liberalism.[8] Without opposition from left or right, the liberal persuasion in America was absolute; it required no thinking out, no reflective articulation, no thoughtful defense. This impressed the American mind with a curiously intolerant disposition—possessing both a salutary intolerance of all that threatens the liberal nation and an intolerance to the very ideas that are the condition of political self-understanding. To take issue with America's consensus, to interrupt its sense of moral unity, meant falling off the plane of respectable citizenship, either branded an alien or ignored. American liberalism is paradoxical: tolerant and open—but dogmatic about its openness, its tolerance, and its liberalism. As Hartz wrote *The Liberal Tradition,* Senator Joseph McCarthy hunted those he suspected of un-American activities, and the Pledge of Allegiance came to be required of all schoolchildren. That it was felt children had to be indoctrinated to feel a sense of allegiance to an indivisible nation suggests the liberal consensus was far more thin and far more fragile than Hartz acknowledged. As in a marriage where the fear of divorce puts argument off limits, so midcentury America could not engage the controversies and divisions it contained.

The sense that America's unity was more fragile than Hartz depicted indicates that it is better illuminated by Hobbes than by Locke. For Hobbes, unity is an artificial creation, motivated by fear of the ultimate consequences of disagreement and disorder: violence and premature death. For America too at the midtwentieth century (as to some extent always), the fear of disunity motivated a longing for consensus that could only be satisfied by enforcing the appearance of consensus. Unity needed to be enforced against threats both external and internal. In the face of external threats from communism and the shadows of fascism, America needed to stand as one, even if that standing was indoctrinated and enforced. The principal internal division that neither the parties nor the political system in general could engage, of course, was race. With blacks disenfranchised throughout the Deep South, the parties had little incentive to respond to the claims of the black population.[9] When searing conflict lies just beneath the surface of comity and consensus, stable union can seem to require a myth of unity.

This may be true for every polity, but it is true in a very particular sort of way for a nation given to think of itself as held together not by birth and blood, but by an idea. Where John Jay could invoke ethnic, linguistic, religious, and racial unity as support for political union, by the twentieth century, American unity was cast as primarily idealistic: anyone, in this view, can become as American as the descendants of the *Mayflower* so long as he or she accepts the "American creed," a belief in equality, freedom, and democracy.[10] In this comforting conception, America is America because Americans agree that every person stands as the moral equal of every other, that everyone is similarly free to pursue his or her happiness, and that every just government derives its powers in consent.[11] These commitments are an inheritance, but they are taken to be an enlightened inheritance, so that anyone might, by the use of his or her reason, come to accept them.

But rational agreements can be among the weakest commitments. Commitments change as easily as they are made. We lose our resolve as quickly as we find it. Reasons that motivate in one moment are forgotten in the next. More fickle than blood, the mind wavers in its attachments. This is why any nation bound by a mere idea needs some auxiliary support, and why any disagreement that threatens to run so deep as to touch foundational commitments is fearsome. Liberal nations would seem to need a special kind of partisanship, the partisanship of those who in some sense do not really disagree. Insofar as it takes itself to be *the* liberal nation, it seems America cannot make a comfortable home for partisan contestation.

The Incoherent Partisanship of Liberal Consensus

If liberal partisanship is the sort of partisanship that forgoes engaging fundamentals, then mid-twentieth-century America presented a model of liberal partisanship. A greater percentage of citizens identified strongly with the two parties in the 1950s than do today, yet the parties were almost without ideological content. This odd combination was a source of comfort and pride. The authors of *The Civic Culture,* with one eye on the tumult of the 1930s and the ensuing rise of fascism, trained the other on the cultural roots of democratic stability. In their account, nowhere (with the possible exception of Great Britain) was the cultural foundation for stable democracy seen to be more solid than in America. Stable democracy needed partisan feeling—but of an easygoing sort much like the "open and moderate partisanship" the authors found in America. While Americans identified in large numbers with one of the two main parties, they did not view their partisan opponents as fundamentally different in their values. Democrats attributed positive characteristics to Republicans, as did Republicans to Democrats. For instance, both Democrats and Republicans thought members of the other party were "interested in humanity" in about the same numbers. Partisanship was not personal. Most partisans in the United States reported that they would be neither pleased nor displeased—but were indifferent—at the prospect of their son or daughter marrying someone of the opposite party.[12]

The contrast with midcentury Europe, where partisanship was often polarized and personal, was stark. Rival partisans in the United Kingdon, Germany, and especially Italy were much less likely than in the United States to attribute positive characteristics to their opponents. For Italians of the time, partisanship was personal: Christian Democrats were chagrined at the possibility that a son or daughter might marry a socialist or a communist. The passionate partisanship of Italy, for instance, embodied deeper ideological antagonisms that threatened the affective ties between citizens and democratic government. Whereas two-thirds of Americans said they enjoyed electoral campaigns (and most felt *something*—more than half also felt angry at some point during the campaign or felt that the campaign was silly or ridiculous), in Italy citizens were emotionally disengaged. Over half of the Italian electorate reported that they neither enjoyed campaigns, nor got angry during them, nor felt contempt. The authors of *The Civic Culture* speculated that Italians were disengaged from political contests because they were so enormously committed to their own party. Rejecting the legitimacy of every other party, they regarded "their own party, not as an electoral contestant, but as a church or a 'way of life.'"[13]

American partisanship at midcentury did not designate rival ways of life. It was something lighter, more like a bowling league or a social club that avoided touching controversy: if they could, parties avoided standing for anything that might exclude something else. In 1942, E. E. Schattschneider noted that both the Democratic and the Republican Party "try more or less successfully to spread over the whole political rainbow from one extreme to the other. Specimens of nearly all shades of opinion are found in both parties."[14] Like holding companies that do a little bit of everything—sell appliances, make jet engines, write loans, and produce movies—but have no core, so the great catch-all parties of American politics offered voters a little bit of everything. They stood for little except winning elections.

With Europe in mind (especially the dissolution of the Weimar Republic in the 1930s), the relative absence of ideological conflict in America was reassuring, for it seemed to offer a secure footing for liberal democracy. Stability distinguished American democracy (along with British) from much of Europe, Mexico, Japan, and elsewhere. America had dissent—its governments faced open and organized opposition—but never an opposition that opposed too much, too often, or in the wrong way. Government and opposition were both loyal to the liberal consensus. Moderate and open, partisanship in the U.S. seemed just vital enough to keep governments accountable but not so vital as to threaten liberal democratic government itself.

But liberal consensus also made partisanship incoherent: Why be a partisan if parties do not stand for anything? Rather than reflecting convictions or coherent ideological sensibilities, partisanship in midcentury America was a patchwork that reflected the patronage parties of the nineteenth century and the loyalties of regions and social groups. White southerners voted Democratic to protect segregation, but the segregationist vote was *Democratic* because Lincoln fought the Civil War. Many in the Midwest and the North voted Republican for the same reason. Those of recent immigrant stock voted Democratic, as did laborers. Protestants voted Republican. Partisanship, the expression of religion, region, ethnicity, and class, reflected the patchwork of electoral coalitions stitched together by ambitious politicians who sought to rally voters to their sides, not coherent packages of ideas. More of an affective loyalty than a rational decision, partisanship was defined by the authors of *The American Voter* (1960) as an unthinking psychological disposition rather than any kind of decision.[15]

Famously, *The American Voter* found almost no voters who met the Progressive ideal of an independent citizen exercising his own judgment with intellectual integrity. Those who abjured any loyalty to the two main parties and identified as "independents" were found not to be freethinking sorts who worked through issues and political decisions for themselves but rather were profoundly apolitical. They displayed little interest in campaigns, held foggy images of the candidates, and betrayed no knowledge of issues.[16] The ideal of the informed voter exercising independent judgment was shown to have no grounding in the facts. However comforting, this picture was not flattering to partisans. In a way, the apolitical independents were more sensible than partisans: When parties do not stand for distinct ideals or programs, what sense can it make to identify with one or the other? Why take an interest in campaigns or form a discriminating understanding of candidates when they are so hard to differentiate in the first place, and when they are all likely to follow the same general course of governance?

From frustration with the fuzzy "catchall" nature of American parties (and casting an admiring glance at the ideologically distinct, internally cohesive parties of the British parliamentary system), reformers yearned for parties and partisanship that had more integrity. In 1950 the American Political Science Association published a report calling for "a more responsible two-party system" that would offer voters a true choice. Responsible party government requires two things: first, that parties take distinct stands and offer a "true choice"; and second, that once in power they are sufficiently internally unified to deliver on their promises. Only then can a mass electorate hold a distant government accountable; if voters do not like the direction the country is heading in or disapprove of the course the government has charted, they know who to blame and where an alternative can be found. "The fundamental requirement of accountability," the report stated, "is a two-party system in which the opposition party acts as a critic of the party in power, developing, defining, and presenting the policy alternatives which are necessary for a *true choice* in reaching policy decisions."[17] Like the ideal of the informed independent voter, the elegant model of responsible party government stood at a great distance from the practice of American politics. As "loose associations of state and local organizations" rooted in the patronage politics of the late nineteenth century, American parties were incapable of standing for coherent alternatives.[18]

Aside from the shortcomings of the parties, the electorate itself made responsible party government difficult, for an "actual choice" requires real disagreement about something important, and the liberal consensus of midcentury precluded such real disagreement. When popular opinion is one-dimensional and clustered in the center, parties have little incentive to take widely distinctive stands, as Anthony Downs demonstrates.[19] Parties that cater to centrist voters cannot but collide in the center. For parties to offer a "true choice," the partisan electorate, in some measure, has to stand apart. But if the electorate is polarized, each party when it wins produces policies that antagonize its opponents, and the alternation from one party to the other causes a kind of whiplash, as radically different policies are pursued in succession. Such a system, as Downs argues, "will be highly unstable, and . . . likely to produce chaos."[20]

For their part, midcentury advocates of responsible parties did not imagine that parties would be—or should be—separated by an "ideological wall." "There is no real ideological division in the American electorate," the American Political Science Association report noted. Reformers wanted not ideological partisanship or "unbridgeable political cleavages," but a "more reasonable discussion of public affairs," where party differences centered not on ideology but on policy. Yet they also hoped that discrete policies would be connected by some overarching idea: they wanted "coordinated and coherent programs," national in scope. Reformers wanted it both ways: they wanted differences without too much difference. They wanted choice but not too much of a choice; they did not wish for rival programs to be rooted in ideological or fundamental differences over the very purposes government should serve and the political community should affirm. They tiptoed cautiously toward an image of partisanship that could be sustained only by engaging more fundamental disagreement than they (and twentieth-century consensus liberalism) would permit. Haunted by the prospect of *real* difference, of "unbridgeable cleavage," they receded, urging a partisanship that could engage only the most patient of policy wonks, as if the arcane and lawyerly details of alternative policies could excite passions, generate loyalties, or sustain lasting commitments. Wishing for a partisanship of difference but afraid of it at the same time, midcentury reformers settled for pointing in a direction they refused to follow. They were unable to untangle the knot of liberal partisanship, to make sense of how a nation allegedly defined by agreement should disagree.[21]

The Nonpartisan Wish

Today's partisan divide in the United States represents the realization of mid-twentieth-century reformist hopes for more responsible parties.[22] The parties stand for a "true choice," and voters increasingly discern the differences that mark them. But aside from a few voices, the resurgence of partisanship is not greeted with celebration or pride; it does not seem like an accomplishment of contemporary politics, but a failing. Most obviously, the failing reflects a mismatch between the uncompromising nature of today's ideologically distinct, internally disciplined parties and a separation-of-powers constitution that requires compromise. More generally and abstractly, it reflects a political world that is neither perfectly whole nor wholly just.

The persistence of partisanship represents the failure to put politics in service to goals and purposes that are higher than politics. Stubborn partisanship reflects the insufficiency of rational first principles of politics to give structure and direction to the political world. For instance, because we desire commodious living, we may think that politics ought to serve productivity and be guided by the insights of economics. Since we think the use of power should be justifiable to all, politics should be subservient to reason or the insights of philosophy. Because we want a good society, politics should be yoked to the cause of goodness. Our desires for comfort, goodness, and justice—for a decent society where power serves the common interest, where all gain a fair share of the advantages of social cooperation—conspire to demote the standing of divisive political contestation and elevate the cool technical decision making of ethical experts, economists, and lawyers. Since we agree about *ends*—peaceful affluence and justice—we need only to discover the best *means*. This is what technical expertise is all about, finding the best means to solving a problem. Against the pragmatic enterprise of technical experts trying to solve problems, ideological partisanship can seem like a failing.

Because they often share the view that politics should be oriented to purposes and ends higher than politics, partisans also share the desire to get beyond partisan contestation. They want to see the causes they fight for instantiated in policies and institutions; they do not simply want to keep fighting. In some sense, partisans most of all dislike partisan contestation, at least if it is to include the partisanship of those they oppose. Generally, they do not perceive their own side as very "partisan" at all, since it seems to them defensible. To the Democratic eye, Republicans (who are more patient with war than with diplomacy, and pursue policies that advantage those who are already advantaged) appear heartless and mean. Republicans experience Democrats (who prefer multinational agreement to the cool prosecution of national interest, rehabilitation to retribution, distribution to production) as irresponsibly innocent. Depending on where one stands, one's opponents lack either intelligence or compassion, and in either case the partisanship of the other side seems to reflect something more defective in it than in oneself. Perhaps the defect is an understandable mistake. Or perhaps it reveals something worse, something negligent—even evil.

In principle, partisans aim not merely to argue, but to win. The logic of partisanship does not fix only on winning *this* election. To follow the logic to an extreme is to see that partisans strive to put their opponents out of business. This uncompromising claim to rule will fail to describe many actual partisans and much of the avowed strategy and goals of actual parties—in practice, partisans are usually not so purely bent on winning at all costs. Sometimes they simply want to make a point, in the hope that the point will have an influence over time. Sometimes they want to stand on principle, even if the stand brings a short-term loss. Prudent partisans will not wish to extinguish their opponents, but to render them a permanent yet visible minority, since holding together one's own coalition is helped by the specter of a viable opposition. The unruliness and violence of partisanship are most often latent, hemmed in by prudence, weakness, or a sense of common belonging that makes the opposition seem more of an adversary than an enemy.[23]

But partisans in their most pure and most ambitious form do not want contestation to endure but to be settled in their favor. They aim for the moment realized by Thomas Jefferson, who at his first inaugural could declare an end to the nation's first partisan divide: "We are all republicans," he said, "we are all federalists."[24] To enjoy a victory that forces the original point of contestation into the shadows clears the way for new points of contestation to arise. New contests may continue to indirectly reflect the causes that motivated older ones (here, contests are iterative and continually revisit old sources of controversy), or new contests may presuppose the settlement of older ones (in this case, they are cumulative, and possibly progressive). It is comforting to think of our partisan contests as progressive. We no longer fight, as the seventeenth-century Levellers did, about whether the people should rule. We no longer battle over whether blacks and whites are equal citizens, as Lincoln was forced to. Those battles have been settled, and we are better for that. Partisans want progress—the sort of victory that in time becomes the invisible foundation of all future controversy.[25]

Partisans contest things, but ironically, often share the independent aspiration for a politics that transcends partisan contestation. They often aim to neutralize partisanship on their terms. Liberals would like a bipartisan consensus that favors liberalism; conservatives, one that favors conservatism. Both would like to entrench their principles in policies and institutions that no longer excite opposition. For instance, Franklin Roosevelt's victories following 1936 allowed him not merely to pass policies he favored, but to embed policies in the administrative apparatus of the state, thereby removing them from the contingencies of ordinary partisan contests. The substitution of administration for partisanship denuded partisanship of its vitality by the 1970s, according to one scholar of these developments.[26] A similar tendency to convert partisanship into nonpartisan administration is evident in contemporary Europe, where the European Union has functioned to reduce the space for partisan contestation at the state level and has facilitated generalized indifference not only to parties, but to legislatures and democratic politics more generally.[27] Part of the antipathy to partisanship is itself partisan. Partisans do not want to reopen old contests or refight those struggles they have already won.

The full success of a partisan project removes its achievement from future partisan contestation. But few successes (and perhaps no successes) are in fact this complete. All settlements leave residues of the contests that preceded them, which may directly or indirectly inspire future partisan contestation. For instance, Ronald Reagan is remembered as a distinguished president, but also a partisan president: "to like Reagan without reservations, you have to be of his party."[28] The very fact that he is remembered as a partisan is a sign that he did not succeed: he did not place his principles and policies beyond contestation. He failed where Jefferson succeeded—at crafting a winning formula that would endure. He also failed to match the example of such immortals as Washington, who had no party, or Lincoln, who is not remembered as a *Republican* president but as a kind of founder whose refounding of America set the terms that bind both Democrats and Republicans today. But these failures were only made possible because Reagan was an uncommonly ambitious partisan who aimed to join the ranks of Franklin Roosevelt. He aimed for a victory that would not merely frame but be the silent presupposition of all future debates. Reagan was the first president since Franklin Roosevelt to question and confront the New Deal's commitment to use the federal government to extend the promise of American life to those individuals and groups that had been previously marginalized; in time, this commitment extended to laborers, the elderly, blacks, racial minorities more generally, and women. The New Deal settlement, whereby the extremes of socialism would be avoided while the federal government expanded its power by extending its commitments to the previously excluded, was not by any means exhausted at the time Reagan took office. The causes of providing general access to health care and basic protections to homosexuals, both extensions of the New Deal's basic logic, would animate American politics in the 1990s. But Reagan interrupted the New Deal settlement, and in doing so inaugurated a new age of partisan contestation in America. He aimed to question things that had gone unquestioned and to unsettle things that had been settled.

Partisans want victory, and the most perfect of all victories would eradicate the basis of future partisan contestation. At the extreme, such a victory would establish the rule of a uniquely deserving class (the wise, the holy, the people), legislating in the name of universal interest and true principle. Whether it issues in a priestly theocracy legislating in the name of God's will or a socialist republic legislating in the name of universal reason, this ultimate victory would constitute a settlement so deep and so just it would cease to be viewed as partisan, and would be seen as akin to the constitution itself. The complete victory of a perfect party—the "last party"—would set both the boundaries and the terms for the partisanship that follows, which would necessarily be smaller and more trivial than that which generated the founding victory, and perhaps so trivial as to end partisanship itself.[29]

The problem of partisanship is not simply that hyper-partisans may co-opt politics to their own ends and in so doing betray a less political and less partisan country. Rather, because partisans play for such high stakes—by aiming to define the nature of the political community itself—they will try to place their victories beyond the reach of ordinary politics. Given these high stakes, partisans may be tempted to take up not only criticism, but arms—this is the ultimate way of taking a contest beyond the bounds of ordinary politics. The word *partisan* often is used to refer to those who contest the very basis of a regime, such as the principled fighters who took to the forests of northeastern Europe in the 1940s to resist Nazi occupiers. Partisanship is particularly potent—and disposed to bloody violence—when, as Hume noted in the eighteenth century, religious creed and political principle mix; here parties are "more furious and enraged than the most cruel factions that ever arose from interest and ambition."[30] But any partisanship that carries a conviction that one is *right* contains a certain danger. For why should one tolerate the rule of those who are *wrong*? Why should a legitimate victory (that comes from campaigns and elections) be considered better than any victory, however won? In these questions resides not merely a temptation to make partisan victories appear nonpartisan, but an ever-present, often suppressed invitation to violence.

Foundational Agreements

The intimate connection between partisanship and violence is the signal danger of party spirit. The invitation to violence arises because partisanship in its most intense forms contests the very basis of a political community. Partisanship threatens to unravel the agreements that hold us together, or that allow us to hold ourselves together in one political community. Disagreement, with all the dangers it carries, is the first fact of politics: without it, there would be no politics. But we can just as easily say that agreement is the first fact of politics, since without some foundational agreement no regime or constitution could ever get going. For all that we will always disagree about, *we,* citizens of modern representative democracy, often agree on certain fundamental points. We have inherited a series of settlements that were originally hammered out in blood and subsequently came not merely to be accepted, but affirmed as basic political principles. These principally include three settlements: the rejection of monarchic rule by divine right (and the corresponding affirmation of rule by the consent of the governed); the rejection of religious intolerance (and the affirmation of individual freedom, especially freedom of conscience); and the rejection of slavery (with the affirmation of political equality).[31] None of these settlements or subsequent affirmations was arrived at peacefully or quickly. All were worked out—which is to say, fought out— over the course of the sixteenth to the twentieth century, the period that defines modern politics. Together they define our political inheritance and set the boundaries of what counts as "reasonable" in politics.[32] No claim to rule absolutely by divine right, to win the whole truth for politics, or to deserve to subjugate another can constitute a reasonable (or persuasive) claim in modern politics. Our agreement is the residue of earlier partisan fights.

One might hold that these foundational settlements set the boundaries for partisanship. However much partisans contest, they do not—and should not—contest these. These settlements are worth securing; they have brought peace, justice, and riches for many whose ancestors toiled at the end of a lord's lash, who knew neither security nor justice nor comfort. When partisanship runs too deep, it threatens to expose these settlements and, in the process, to weaken the agreement that stands at the base of modern politics.

But foundational settlements do not form an impermeable container for partisan contestation. For one, points of fundamental controversy may arise that foundational agreements cannot decide. Neither the settlement of the Wars of Religion nor the Civil War amendments suggest an obvious way of addressing global warming.[33] This problem is ours, and it should not surprise us if even after sober reflection we disagree with each other. Moreover, foundational agreements are not bearers of one-sided easy truths, which can be readily grasped and applied to individual cases. Our foundational values such as freedom and equality are plain enough, and few who desire to win an election can afford to forthrightly dispute them. But they are not without their difficult applications: How free is free enough? Is there any limit to equality? What inequalities are just? Some will advocate a particular way of extending the familiar values of freedom and equality into new terrain. Others will feel the pull of a contrary impulse, and discern amid the general approval of freedom and equality the competing claims of distinction and authority. Partisans of the most active sort—those who run for office—often have an interest in revealing these potential lines of division, since they want to mobilize voters in their favor. Politicians prefer unanimous support, but where they cannot find it (and they never find it) they opt for divisions that work in their favor. Individually, they may succeed or fail, but in the divisive process of soliciting support they rouse us, invite us into the public world, and prod us, indirectly, to reengage foundational agreements by extending their application to a new age. Contemporary partisanship is indirectly nourished by the long-ago struggles over our foundational agreements. When it goes badly, partisanship erodes worthy commitments that help define the political community and replaces civic friendship and trust with misunderstanding, suspicion, and enmity. When partisanship goes well, this too revitalizes public life, as it fosters a deeper appreciation of our founding faith.

In *Civic Ideals,* Rogers Smith argues that the right metaphor for the nation is not, as is customarily held, family, neighborhood, club, orchestra, or compact.[34] Political communities are better conceived of as on par with the broad untidiness of a coalition political party: American civic identity should be conceived of "as a partisan, humanly created historical enterprise."[35] To think of the nation itself as akin to a party demotes the ascriptive and mythological elements that are often built into national belonging. Like parties, nations are ambiguous entities: they are valuable, even indispensable, but capable of destruction, exploitation, and inhumanity. Seeing the political community as a political party also recognizes that all political communities are partial: "tendencies to narrow partisanship are inherent in their very existence, even and perhaps especially in nations that proclaim their world-historical significance."[36] Finally, it acknowledges that the moral understandings that underpin national identity are not fixed by reason, history, or nature. They are the objects of permanent contestation; even liberalism, which for Hartz is the unseen and dogmatic source of national unity, in this view is a "national 'fighting faith.' "[37] If it is in some respects privileged, it is also embattled, and its losses are as central to the national story as its victories.

To see the political community itself as partisan changes the place of partisanship in politics. Partisanship is no longer simply a threat to prepolitical unity and mutually advantageous cooperation, but an expression of citizenship. When the political community itself is a site of contestation (rather than a neutral umpire adjudicating rival interests), to be a member of the community is more about participating in the contest over what the community is about than pledging allegiance to unchanging dogmas or consenting to basic foundational agreements. Reason, and moral reasoning in particular, is not without its force in the world, but reason is inadequate to serve up whole truths whose application to political life is beyond dispute. This does not mean that the foundation of our convictions must *always* lie outside reason (as when Franklin says of his turn away from vegetarianism, "So convenient a thing it is to be a *reasonable creature,* since it enables one to find or make a reason for everything one has a mind to do"[38]). It simply means that even the sober exercise of reason alone does not provide simple truths that can put an end to all controversy. No foundational agreement is ever so comprehensive as to put politics to rest. No amount of decency, no commitment to cooperation or reason, is enough to put disagreement about ends to an end. Rather than think of the political community as a fixed container or a marker of unquestioned agreement, it is more appropriate and more accurate to think of it as a site of contestation in which even our foundational commitments nourish disagreement.

In this view, civic identity involves a certain kind of commitment to partisanship. At times, the contest and the division of society will seem more essential than common belonging or unity. Most notably, the contest over the 2000 election extended after the election to affect opinions about the legitimacy of the president. Following the Supreme Court's 5–4 decision in *Bush v. Gore,* 92 percent of Bush voters thought Bush won the election legitimately and approved of the Supreme Court's action, while 80 percent of Democrats thought Bush's victory illegitimate and disapproved of the Court's action.[39] Yet following Bush's inauguration, there was no rebellion, no effort by the thwarted to overthrow an administration they perceived to be illegitimate. Which is more auspicious, the presence of a deep popular division concerning the legitimacy of a presidential administration, or the total absence of political violence? To explain this by saying that we agree about constitutional fundamentals but not on transient electoral contests begs the question, since we disagree about how the Constitution should be applied to concrete cases like the resolution of the 2000 election. What we agree about is not so much the Constitution or its interpretation or application, but something more basic. We agree, while disagreeing about procedures, Court decisions, and the ends politics should serve, to keep our guns in their holsters. The renunciation of violence signals an agreement that is harder to characterize, since it is consistent with pervasive disagreement. It is an agreement to disagree, and peacefully. It represents a certain commitment to partisanship.

The persistence of partisanship, especially of the sort that addresses the basic commitments that define a political community, is a reminder that nonpartisan expertise is insufficient because our agreement about ends is both incomplete and fragile. Politics is resistant to rational agreement about what is good and right because practical reason does not issue in general agreement about moral and political things. Reason either fails to culminate in certain conclusions or it fails to persuade. Whether our reason fails us or whether we fail reason is beside the point: however much we may want agreement, we cannot agree. What matters politically is that our disagreements are interminable: Is abortion a justified killing? Is it a killing at all? Are stem cells appropriate subjects of scientific investigation? Shall medical doctors be permitted to assist patients who wish to die? Has the government gone too far in securing equal rights for women and minorities? Should the well-off be taxed to support the poor in their midst? Should we privatize prisons? Is gun control a sensible reform or a violation of rights? Should the state recognize same-sex marriage? Should government regulation discourage buying SUVs? Ought wilderness areas be opened for logging, mining, and drilling? What levels of pollution are acceptable? Do we face an existential threat? What is necessary for self-defense?

For all of our inclinations to decency, commonality, agreement, we stand divided on questions like these. To those of conviction, the fact of disagreement is an annoyance; more generally, it is an illuminating revelation about the moral and rational capacities of human beings. If we are so decent and so smart, why should we disagree so deeply and so persistently? Partisanship (and even politics) is the embarrassing reflection of the fact that our reason and our decency are inadequate to secure a politics that is both participatory and consensual. When disagreement goes well, it takes only respectful, mild, and peaceable forms. But partisanship is not always so tepid. It possesses a latent potency, an impulse to violence that comes from its high stakes. For it ultimately concerns the most fundamental questions of politics: *Who rules? What is the political community about, and what does it stand for? Who deserves to rule?*

There is no way to permanently avoid these questions except to cede authority over their answers to others. To accept responsibility for taking a part in answering these questions is to be political, and to be political is to be partisan. The question for citizens ultimately is not whether to be partisan, but how to be partisan without entertaining the pathologies and evils that partisanship unavoidably invites.

4

REASONABLE PARTISANS

The partisan community is founded less on ideological consensus than on an agreement about how to disagree. Many, however, believe that while continuous disagreement is part of any vital democracy, politics would go better if the disagreement worked in a more deliberate and less partisan way. Partisanship, in this view, is a distraction from the consequential work of solving public problems. Ideally, this problem solving would take place in a reasoned way—it would be more deliberative and less partisan. Political types like the zealot are not the only ones who resist a moderate and reasoned approach to politics. Partisanship too seems to introduce a kind of team spirit that distorts deliberation, where defeating the other side becomes more important than "hearing the other side."[1] To explore this criticism of partisan politics, it is instructive to consider the ideal of deliberative democracy and its relation to politics. Is "reasonable politics" really an alternative to partisan politics?

As it has been developed by political theorists over the past thirty years, the ideal of deliberative democracy puts the giving and taking of reasons at the center of political life. Only by offering reasons to each other for our positions can we fully respect other citizens as free and equal, in this view. These reasons and terms of argument citizens offer each other need to be of a particular sort. Namely, they should be "reasonable," which is to say that they are "reasons that should be accepted by free and equal persons seeking fair terms of cooperation."[2] Participants in deliberation are taken to be *"reasonable* in that they aim to defend and criticize institutions and programs in terms of considerations that others, as free and equal, have *reason to accept."*[3] This sounds —well, reasonable enough. But what sort of reasons, we might ask, are the kind that others "should accept"? What, in other words, is "reasonable"?

Answering these questions is more difficult because of the way the word *reasonable* proliferates in some accounts of the deliberative ideal. It seems to show up on both sides of the equation: reasonable people will find reasonable propositions reasonable. John Rawls, the philosopher famous for his 1971 classic, *A Theory of Justice,* considered his own theory of "public reason" to be aligned with the ideal of deliberative democracy. But making sense of public reason can be difficult. Consider the following selections from Rawls's essay "The Idea of Public Reason Revisited":

> Our exercise of political power is proper only when we sincerely believe that the reasons we would offer for our political actions . . . are sufficient, and we also reasonably think that other citizens might also reasonably accept those reasons.[4]

> If we argue that the religious liberty of some citizens is to be denied, we must give them reasons they can not only understand . . . but reasons we might reasonably expect that they, as free and equal citizens, might reasonably also accept.[5]

> A citizen engages in public reason, then, when he or she deliberates within a framework of what he or she sincerely regards as the most reasonable political conception of justice, a conception that expresses political values that others, as free and equal citizens might also reasonably be expected reasonably to endorse.[6]

One could be excused for believing that the word *reasonable* is being called upon in these passages to perform an unreasonable amount of work. Often in argument one is told by an adversary to "be reasonable!" This usually translates as "Relax your stubborn and erroneous commitment and agree with me!" When "reasonable" cannot be assigned any definite content, the rhetoric of "reasonable agreement" is simply a tool to bring argument (and partisan contestation) to a close. The "idea of the politically reasonable" threatens in this way to denude partisanship of the contestable convictions that nourish party spirit. The multiplication of the word—where "reasonable" is what reasonable people find reasonable—has led others to abandon the term altogether.

Yet if its content can seem elusive, the idea of reasonableness and the closely associated idea of "public reason" are in their essentials quite familiar. Reasonableness refers to the motivations of those involved in a discussion or argument and the reasons they offer. Reasonable people have a disposition to give (and to be open to hearing) reasons that are made in public, address the public good, and embody a respect for the freedom and equality of every citizen. A disposition to argue using (and to be persuaded by) these sorts of reasons constitutes what Rawls calls the ideal of public reason.

The term *reasonable* proliferates in Rawls's writings on deliberative democracy because he uses the adjective to refer simultaneously to the *motives* of citizens and to the *terms or arguments* they use to advance their convictions. The distinction between motives and reasonable terms is perfectly sensible. One might offer reasonable terms from unreasonable motives. For instance, a minority religion might argue for religious toleration, which is a reasonable position to advance because it acknowledges the equal freedom of every citizen to follow the dictates of his or her conscience. But the group might really hope for and seek a kind of religious domination over political and social life, and only opt for toleration because of its (temporary) position as a minority. The terms are reasonable, but the motives of those advancing the terms are not, because they fail to respect the equal freedom of others.

"Public reason" refers to the idea that some reasons are suitable for public discourse because they express respect for other citizens as free and equal. The ideal of public reason rejects the view that politics is only a process of bargaining, where outcomes reflect pressure, power, and threats. Everyday, ordinary politics may be all about power, but public reason is not merely a form of power. It is not a tool that the articulate and clever use to their advantage and to the disadvantage of their enemies. In fact, it is the opposite. It is a way of overcoming the politics of domination by giving reasons for laws in terms that all people can in principle accept. The crucial qualifier in that sentence is "in principle." There is a world of difference between terms that *all people in fact accept* and *all people in principle can accept.* Public reason does not provide terms that all people can in fact accept. It does not generate uniformity or perfect consensus. Even a community that is committed to the ideal of public reason will disagree about values and policies.

If people continue to disagree, we might wonder what good it is to be committed to terms that all people can *in principle* accept. To be capable of accepting an argument *in principle* simply means that the terms of the argument are consistent with our standing as free and equal citizens. Arguments for higher marginal tax rates or lower ones are likely to be consistent with our standing as free and equal citizens, but different tax rates for men and women or for blacks and whites would not be. Certain forms of legal discrimination would be ruled out—at the extreme, slavery, for instance, as with religious, sexual, or gender discrimination, for example. One might say that this is a fairly low bar, and in some respects it is (though we might note how frequently politics fails to clear this bar). Some might hope that a politics that is fully committed to respecting the freedom and equality of citizens will be essentially consensual. But this seems a mistake, since the terms of public reason leave a wide scope for disagreement. Public reason does not produce consensus. What it does aspire to is a certain kind of moral community—one that stands together by its commitment to justifying force in a way that all can see as reasonable even when it is not universally agreeable.[7] Deliberation privileges talking, listening, and persuading. If it does not result in consensus, its ethos is informed by the possibility that by explaining themselves respectfully and hearing the other side, people might come to agree more than they otherwise would.

Partisanship seems more at home in the politics of power and domination than in the deliberative ideal. Partisans are only a part of the whole, yet they seek to rule the whole. While partisans may talk and listen respectfully, they know that there is an opposition they will never fully persuade. As a result, they aim not simply to talk and to listen, but to win. They would be happy if their arguments produced consensus. But they want the consensus on their terms. Electoral politics is educative, but it is not a seminar—it is not primarily about learning. It is about winning. (To say that partisans want to rule is to say they aim for *party government,* or a government under the full control of one party—theirs.) To achieve victory, partisans need to attract voters. While good discussion may be enough to attract support, in practice partisans will say and do whatever they can (within the bounds of the law) to get votes. They will be tempted to distort and elide and prey on popular fears. They will even introduce new divisions, if the consequence is that they gain more support because of the division. If one party, for instance, figures that by emphasizing the immigration issue it will gain a larger number of Hispanic votes than it loses in the rest of the population, it will try to make immigration more salient in the campaign. The consequence is that we disagree more, not less. Partisans are not oriented to finding reasons all can accept—they want to find reasons that work for them. In this way, parties can undermine the ethos of deliberative democracy.

Parties and partisanship are more at home in what political theorists call "aggregative democracy" than in deliberative democracy.[8] Where deliberative democracy conceives of legitimacy in terms of reasons that everyone can in principle accept, aggregative democracy conceives of legitimacy in terms of numbers. What makes a law legitimate, for aggregative democrats, is that the law has the support of most of the people (or was passed by a majority of representatives who in turn were elected by most of the people). Party and partisanship are instruments of aggregation. They are the tools office seekers use to attract majority support, or enough support to get elected. Whether the majority is fully informed or reasonable is a side question for aggregative democrats. What matters is not whether the vote is informed, but whether there are enough votes. For aggregative democrats, numbers are what confer legitimacy. Deliberative democrats, by contrast, deny that numbers alone confer legitimacy, and conceive of legitimacy instead as justification through reasons that everyone can (in principle) accept. These rival conceptions of democratic legitimacy account for the basic and undeniable tension between deliberative democracy and partisanship. Aggregation and partisanship look necessary when one gives up on the possibility of reasoned agreement; deliberation looks attractive when one refuses to give up.

Aggregation and Deliberation

This description of the tension between deliberative democracy and party democracy can be overdrawn. Parties may contribute to deliberation, for one thing. In big-party systems, a great deal of deliberation goes on within the parties, among fellow partisans. At times this is very public, such as during presidential primary campaigns. In these moments, rival candidates and party constituencies engage in a contest over what the party stands for—what policies it should advance, what goals it should highlight, and what criticisms of the opposition it should place at the center. Sometimes the deliberation goes on in a less public and more elite manner, as when parliamentary parties decide whether to join a coalition, or when legislative leaders strategize about how to hold their majority (or opposition) together. Beyond fellow partisans deliberating with each other, parties may contribute to deliberation more generally. Nancy Rosenblum argues, for instance, that parties and partisanship structure public opinion, clarify issues, and motivate other citizens to take an interest in political questions.[9]

Partisanship at its best can indeed help make politics more deliberative. But just as often, citizens become more inclined to disengage when they encounter intense disagreement.[10] The partisan contest is often more likely to leave those on the side enervated rather than engaged. Some of what parties do for deliberation might happen in their absence. But the indispensable service parties and partisanship render concerns the moment of aggregation, which deliberation cannot do without and which parties supply. Put differently, deliberative democracy needs elections, and elections need parties and partisans to make them happen. Deliberative democracy needs partisanship not because it always assists deliberation—sometimes it does not—but because partisanship does something for democracy that deliberation cannot do: it makes democracy decisive. In its most satisfying instances, deliberation leads to consensus. But these instances are rare and not to be counted on. More often, deliberation leads to disagreement that even more deliberation cannot dissolve.[11] This stubborn residue of disagreement would lead to indecision and inaction in the absence of a force that legitimates one side of the disagreement. That force is partisanship.

This is not to dispute the moral force of the deliberative ideal. Perhaps every normative theory of democracy will be in some way a deliberative theory.[12] As important as numbers will be to democracy, they are never sufficient. Majorities can be wrong—catastrophically so. They can be unjust, also catastrophically. The moral case for democracy must go beyond the claim that the numerous present simply because they are numerous. To believe in democracy, we have to believe that the numerous are also somehow likely to be right, sensible, prudent, or decent.[13] Without any deliberative component, aggregative models of democracy may be good descriptive accounts of what democracy *is,* but they fail to supply a convincing account of what democracy *should be.*

At the same time, every ideal of deliberative democracy is also going to contain some aggregative component. This is both a practical and a moral necessity. The practical necessity arises from the fact that when deliberation concludes, disagreement will remain. There must be some procedure to come to a decision amid disagreement, and this procedure is likely to involve counting: the more numerous side wins. The only exception to this necessity would be a deliberative process that culminated in complete consensus. But there is little or no reason to expect this result. On the contrary, deliberation may increase the scope or urgency of disagreement. Deliberation is a mode of politics, not an alternative to politics. Since disagreement will survive the deliberative processes, deliberative democracy will need some moment of aggregation, such as elections and legislative votes. That is a fact.

But it is not just a fact. Aggregation brings something of moral importance to the deliberative project. It is not merely a concession to the lamentable imperfections of practical life.

Aggregation has its own moral claim: counting people up and giving more power to the more numerous group is an *essential* way of recognizing political equality. When "everybody [is] to count for one and nobody for more than one," we acknowledge the equality of citizens who under conditions of freedom will inevitably disagree.[14] The numerous—a plurality, a majority, a supermajority—have *some* kind of moral claim to legitimacy simply because of their size.[15] In American political culture, we have developed a keen sensitivity to the possibility that majorities can get things terribly wrong and give themselves over to horrific evil. This is not only the legacy of Madison and his famous warnings about the tyranny of the majority; more concretely, it stems from the legacy of slavery and racism, which for centuries existed by popular acclaim. Numbers alone do not produce a claim to legitimacy. But numbers have *some* claim: the size of a group is one ingredient in the mix of democratic legitimacy. Those who complained that George W. Bush's election in 2000 was illegitimate because he lost the popular vote were, in that moment, voicing this very claim. More generally, any electoral system that does not routinely confer power on the most sizable group would seem undemocratic and would lack prima facie legitimacy.

True enough, the fears of majority tyranny are amply warranted. It is often a good thing to differentiate between the *constitutional majority* and a *bare majority*, where the constitutional majority is more sizable, durable, and dispersed. The familiar constitutional checks on the power of a bare majority are often useful: multiplying veto points, ensuring representation of minority groups and views, structuring constitutional rather than plebiscitary majorities, entrenching rights, and so on. But none of these limits on the claim of the most numerous group can eradicate its claim completely; on the contrary, they presuppose a background condition where the numerous have *some* claim simply because they are numerous.

This highlights what is, from a democratic point of view, an argument in favor of partisanship: it expresses a willingness to make a good faith effort to stand with a group striving for democratic legitimacy. Unlike other familiar political types—the moral purist or the zealot—what distinguishes the partisan is this willingness to stand with a group striving for democratic legitimacy. The purist cares more about getting the moral principle right than building a large coalition. The zealot is even more committed to principle, and is willing to burn down the house in order to be true to it. The partisan also cares about principle, at least in the large sense—a conception of the common good. But the partisan is willing to compromise pure principle in order to form a group that is large enough to claim power by legitimate democratic means. This single quality—compromise—is what sets the partisan apart. Compromise is always with a view to a particular goal: collecting a majority, so as to both win and win legitimately.

For this reason, partisans are driven to offer reasons that appeal broadly—if only from strategic or prudential concerns. Rhetoric, which makes principle palatable by connecting general principles to particular opinions and sentiments, is the partisan's ally. Some rhetoric will appeal to interest, other rhetoric to convictions of a more moral sort. But in either case, parties that aim to attract large numbers to their side have to speak to general concerns. They have to form some more or less articulate and better or worse approximation of the common good. The partisan finds his way to the common good by a different path than the purist or the zealot or even the judicious independent. Purists, zealots, and independents work up what they consider to be the most true conception of the common good in solitude, and follow it, even if no one else agrees. Individual conscience is the ultimate test. Indeed, there is good reason to believe that many will disagree with the conception any individual, however righteous, forms for himself or herself. The burdens of judgment are such that a multitude of individual conceptions of what is reasonable or just will rarely align. It is easy to decide things for yourself—it is something else to get others to sign on. Forming a group that is large enough to claim democratic legitimacy, whether a coalition of small parties or a large catch-all party, is not easy. People in such a group will disagree with one another (and often enough dislike one another). The willingness to participate in the process of coming together—standing *with* others rather than only standing *for* principles or policies—is what distinguishes the partisan from other political types such as the ideal independent citizen, who keeps informed and may even work up a "reasonable conception of justice" to ground his convictions, but who in the end acts alone.[16]

As we have noted, this is not to say that partisans are better simply because they might *succeed* at recruiting a majority to their side. Majorities can be good and majorities can be evil. The moral and epistemic grounding of majority rule is subtle and never altogether convincing.[17] In general, we settle for a majority only because it is a convincing mode of recognizing the political equality of citizens. Because it falls short of complete consensus, the domain of majority rule will, under any decent government, be hedged and constricted. But if the moral case for majority rule (or rule by the largest group) is insufficient, the fact remains that the moral case for democracy cannot easily do without it. If we are going to respect the political equality of citizens, then politics must somehow collect—add up—the variety of individual sentiments, interests, and convictions. This can happen in the legislature, when parties that individually fall short of a majority join a governing coalition. It can happen in the electoral process, where a slate of candidates or parties is winnowed through runoffs or primaries. It can happen in the electorate itself, where, aided by the prod of single-member districts, voters take into account not only what they think about a candidate's positions, but also the probability that these positions will appeal to others. A group large enough to claim democratic legitimacy does not exist spontaneously, antecedent to the political process. It must be created.

Partisans are willing to participate in the process of this creation. This may be because they care more about power than moral principle. But even so, they end up serving a moral principle. The observation that parties "aggregate" opinion is a staple of twentieth-century political science—this is one of the primary "functions" that parties serve. This process of aggregation is not to be taken for granted. The aggregation only happens because certain citizens—namely, partisans—are *willing* to make it happen. This is the respect in which partisanship is a virtue of democratic citizens: it displays a democratic sympathy, a willingness to compromise, to give and to take, and (perhaps most of all) to bear the burdens of standing with one's fellow citizens. The associability of human nature—our tendency to privilege our own point of view—means that standing with others is never easy. To be governed, to govern ourselves—democratically—we have to stand with others to suppress the ways we find others disagreeable and learn to compromise. There is a cost to one's integrity that comes from standing with a group; that's why purists and zealots opt out of this process. But it is a virtue democracy can never be entirely without. Democracy, even deliberative democracy, cannot easily be without partisans.

Is Partisanship at Home in Deliberative Democracy?

Partisanship is a necessary component of deliberative democracy. It helps make deliberative democracy *democratic* by bringing to it an aggregative capacity, but the tension between partisanship and deliberation remains even if, in some respects and under some circumstances, partisanship might help deliberation along. Given this tension, deliberative democrats might want to diminish partisanship and look for aggregative mechanisms that do not bring parties and partisanship with them.

Deliberative polling is one example of a process by which we might retain the importance of aggregative mechanisms without giving up on deliberation.[18] Unlike ordinary polls, deliberative polling does not merely add up what a random sample of the population thinks about an issue or a candidate. Instead, it takes a random sample of citizens and exposes them to expert presentations about issues and policies; it creates a deliberative space where they can discuss alternatives. Only after several days of presentation and discussion are the participants *then* asked what they think about issues and candidates. Deliberative polling does not just give a time-slice snapshot of what an uninformed, distracted, and possibly partisan electorate thinks in a moment of time. It shows the general population what it likely *would think* if it had the time and resources to become informed and to deliberate. For this reason, it might have a kind of authority that ordinary polling cannot pretend to possess: deliberative polls should have more weight than ordinary polls because they are a better representation of the kind of public opinion we should care about.

Here is the question that puts deliberative polls to the test: If deliberative polls truly represent the public, why not actually give them real authority, of the sort we presently assign to legislatures? For instance, several years ago a panel of randomly selected citizens in British Columbia was assembled for the purpose of weighing and recommending reforms of the electoral system to the larger electorate. Citizens who agreed to serve on the panel spent a series of weekends listening to political scientists and others make presentations about variations in electoral systems—proportional representation, single-member districts, Hare systems, and so on—with their attendant advantages and defects. Over a period of many months, these citizens discussed and deliberated and eventually made a recommendation to their fellow citizens, which was voted on in a popular referendum (the recommendation lost).[19] If it is deliberation that confers authority (and numbers or aggregation are made necessary only in order for deliberation to be democratic), why in theory should we wish that these citizens who participated on the deliberative panel merely make recommendations? Why should citizens who did not trouble to inform themselves, who did not devote time and mental energy to mastering the intricacies of rival electoral systems, and who did not discuss and deliberate ultimately get to decide?

If deliberative democracy is right that what gives authority to laws is that they are justified by reasons that everyone can (in principle) accept, it is not clear that voters, who may not have deliberated (and may not know what reasons are at stake), should have the final judgment. There is no obvious reason within the terms of deliberative democracy for making the recommendation of those who did deliberate and who engaged in a give-and-take of reasons merely advisory. The logic of deliberative democracy does not stop with deliberative assemblies that merely make recommendations. The same logic would argue that deliberative assemblies ought to be empowered to make authoritative laws. (The main difference between deliberative assemblies and representative legislatures is that the first are randomly selected and the latter are elected; as a consequence, the selection procedure for the deliberative assemblies, unlike representative legislatures, is necessarily nonpartisan.)

As obvious and intuitive as majority rule seems, it is not the only way to structure democratic decision making. We could substitute any number of procedures for majority rule and yet retain a commitment to democratic equality. Lotteries are among the most obvious examples. Rather than elect representatives by plurality or majority, we could substitute a randomly selected sample of the population chosen by lottery. Random selection exemplifies democratic values in a way that elections cannot. In a certain sense, elections are actually less democratic than lotteries. Elections empower a general citizenry to choose the *best;* random selection denies that some citizens constitute the *best,* and is in this sense based on an aristocratic principle (universal suffrage is what instills elections with a democratic principle). This is why lotteries were viewed as more democratic than elections in classical politics. Lotteries more accurately express the idea that all citizens are equal, and as equals are fit to rule and be ruled in turn. Elections, on the other hand, presuppose that some people are more fit than others to discharge the duties of public office.[20] The decision to combine democracy with elections was not compelled by the logic of democracy; it was a historically conditioned decision that was understood to dilute the force of democracy with the aristocratic principle of election.[21]

Since deliberative assemblies chosen by lottery realize the ideals of deliberative democracy—since they are both deliberative and democratic—perhaps they should not be restricted to addressing discrete questions like electoral reform. They could rather be charged with the same questions and responsibilities that elected legislatures now discharge: deliberative assemblies could take up questions like taxation, spending, Social Security reform, campaign finance, and so on. In short, a random sample of the population given the time and resources to become informed and to deliberate should replace Congress.[22] An empowered democratic assembly would be democratic and at the same time would perhaps avoid partisanship. It might even realize popular hopes for a politics that avoided shrill and pointless partisan posturing in favor of practical problem solving. Such hopes have often inspired the deliberative democratic project. John Rawls himself once lamented that contemporary political debate "betrays the marks of warfare . . . rallying the troops and intimidating the other side."[23] "As things are," he wrote, "sensible proposals" concerning Social Security reform, international institutions like the United Nations, foreign aid, and human rights policy cannot gain acceptance. "Even should farsighted political leaders wish to make sound changes and reform, they cannot convince a misinformed and cynical public to accept and follow them."[24] The partisan quest for victory and for securing the spoils of victory stands in the way of "sensible proposals," impedes the best efforts of "farsighted" leaders, and simultaneously "misinforms" citizens.

With an empowered deliberative assembly, we would perhaps need not suffer such ills. The politics of warfare and partisan intimidation, the games that preoccupy campaigns, and the simplified and sensational propaganda that fills the airwaves in campaign season would all give way to calm, reasoned, dispassionate deliberation. We would no longer have to worry about misinformed or underinformed or prejudiced voters, since people would not be called upon to vote. We would simply need to trust that the sample of citizens called upon to deliberate would decide as we ourselves would if we were chosen.

True, any number of complications would beset such a deliberative assembly. It is not clear, for instance, what we would do about those citizens who sacrifice their livelihood in order to participate in a two- or four-year deliberative assembly. Nor is it obvious how such an assembly would guard against powerful and resourceful interests corrupting such citizen-legislators, who very probably had to quit their jobs in order to serve. Finally, it would be difficult to locate reliable sources of information for members of deliberative assemblies that would not be infected by partisan bias or powerful interests. For these reasons, as a practical matter, such a reform is not likely to come to pass (although the record-low approval ratings that partisan legislatures suffer both in the United States and elsewhere render reforms of this general sort increasingly alluring).

But the real problem with this reform is ultimately not that it is unrealistic. It is rather that the reform fails to accommodate the fact of permanent disagreement. As we have noted, deliberation will not eradicate disagreement. Some "reasonable disagreements," such as those concerning religion or what Rawls calls "comprehensive conceptions," will reflect the burdens of judgment and should be more or less walled off from political decision making. Yet the distinctive thing about deliberative democracy is that it makes possible *politically relevant* reasonable disagreement. This kind of disagreement does not depend on importing comprehensive religious, moral, or philosophic conceptions into politics. It might simply involve technical questions, such as how best to sustain steady economic growth. It might involve questions about extending established values to new realms, such as same-sex marriage. It might involve questions about public goals, such as whether economic growth or environmental protection should be prioritized, or whether the needs of workers or the gratifications of investors should take precedence. In all of these questions, as well as dozens of others, reasonable and respectful people will disagree, and the more reasons they offer (speaking and listening in good faith) one another, the more they may disagree. Without deliberation, we could not discover whether a disagreement is reasonable. Yet deliberation alone cannot arbitrate or decide among politically relevant reasonable disagreements.

There is little reason to expect that deliberation will reduce the scope or intensity of disagreements, and there is plenty of reason to expect that at times deliberation will exacerbate the scope and intensity of politically relevant disagreement.[25] Deliberative assemblies consisting of a random sample of the population are certainly *one* way of resolving disagreements of this interminable sort. Suitably informed, they will be equipped to decide how to define public goals and which goals should take priority. But they will not be equipped to defend and protect any single decision over time. For instance, there are numerous complexities involved in the question whether the government should extend health insurance to the uninsured, and there is every reason to think that informed reasonable people will disagree about the goal itself as well as the best means of realizing the goal. But once a decision is taken—against opposition and amid reasonable disagreement—the victors will understandably want to secure their achievement. Losers, in turn, will want to reverse it. Winners and losers will want to stay in office in order to protect (and to attack) previous achievements. If the legislature were selected randomly, there would be no way to secure the achievements won in the past against the reasonable opponents. Future randomly selected assemblies might arrive at different recommendations and decisions, and would have no reason to feel interest, pride, or possession in the decisions of the past.

This kind of instability across legislative sessions would not matter if deliberation led to consensus (or even if it simply diminished the scope and intensity of disagreement). We could assume that deliberative assemblies of the future could simply build on the consensus arrived at by deliberative assemblies of the past, and parties would not be necessary to secure today's victory into the future. But there is no reason to expect that a randomly selected assembly would be invested in the decisions of an earlier randomly selected assembly. Different groups will arrive at different understandings at different points in time. Politics is indeterminate—it is not a science, and deliberation will not always lead to deeper and wider agreement. A nonpartisan assembly chosen at random would have no way to make a decision and stick with the decision across time. Such an assembly might be deliberative. But it would have no memory, patience, or loyalty. These qualities are virtues of partisanship at its best; they are what equip citizens as partisans to give shape to their political community over time—to govern themselves.

But before turning to memory, patience, and loyalty (which are the subjects of Chapter 5), it is crucial first to take up one common defect of partisanship that is especially apparent from a deliberative perspective. Partisanship seems to introduce a dogmatic element into politics—a narrowness of mind and a self-righteousness that make deliberation impossible. Deliberation requires a degree of openness, a willingness to contemplate the possibility that one's own views might not constitute the whole truth. The indeterminacy of politics is such that no one is likely to possess the whole truth about political questions. This points to an additional component of ethical partisanship (beyond the renunciation of violence, which we saw in Chapters 2 and 3): an ability to decide political questions without allowing that decision to overwhelm one's critical capacities. Partisans know how to criticize the other side—that is what they do, and in some sense is their job. But when that is all they do, they turn off their less partisan fellow citizens from politics altogether. People know that few questions in politics warrant absolute certainty. When this is all they encounter—rival partisans, each of whom is certain the other side is entirely wrong and that their side is entirely right—they understandably turn away. Enveloped in their own convictions, such partisans can only see one side of things. They lack what might be called *negative capacity:* they cannot turn against what they believe to inspect it for flaws. They cannot admit even the abstract possibility that the other side may occasionally have a point. Partisanship needs this negative capacity if it is to complement the deliberative ideal without undermining it.

John Stuart Mill's One-Eyed Men

Partisanship is necessary because being reasonable is never sufficient to permanently and justly settle conflict. Partisanship arises from reasonable confidence in our convictions that some principle or cause in the political world is right and something else wrong, something is better and something else is worse. Yet every political achievement carries a cost, and every increment of progress has an ambiguity. One political thinker who grasped this fully is John Stuart Mill, who was in a sense the original deliberative democrat, and yet who was also a remarkable partisan.

Mill himself was a partisan: he was, he says, *always* a "Radical for Europe."[26] He sided with the "numerical majority," which he thought was "everywhere unjustly depressed, everywhere trampled on, or at the best overlooked."[27] As a member of Parliament, Mill supported reforms that extended power to the majority. If he could embrace a partisan cause, he nevertheless retained a negative capacity to step back from his own commitments. His partisan commitments never compressed the scope of his thought, and his philosophy in turn never unhinged his partisanship. He was both a partisan and a thinker, and if he did not disconnect the two, neither did he tether one in service entirely to the other. Although a democrat and a liberal in politics, in writing and reflection he entertained and worried over the possibility that majority rule would extend not merely to legislation but also to custom and opinion, crushing all that opposed it and eradicating the sources of contestation that might temper and correct a democratic future. He defended democracy but also saw its dangers.

The image of partisanship Mill offers comes into focus in the pages of *On Liberty*, where he defends the ultimate importance of free expression by an appeal not only to humane skepticism (we must tolerate dissent because we can never be completely assured that received opinions are right) but also to the dialectical nature of practical truths. Mill takes it as a "commonplace" that "a party of order and stability, and a party of progress or reform, are both necessary elements of a healthy state of political life." More generally, Mill sees a number of "standing antagonisms" that inform political life: democracy and aristocracy, property and equality, cooperation and competition, luxury and abstinence, liberty and discipline. We could package these "fractional truths" together (though Mill does not) into two coherent groupings, and say that liberalism and conservatism form an overarching standing antagonism. What matters to Mill is that each side gets its due: "Truth," he says, "in the great practical concerns of life is so much a question of reconciling and combining of opposites, that very few have minds sufficiently capacious and impartial to make the adjustment with an approach to correctness, and it has to be made by the rough process of struggle between combatants fighting under hostile banners."[28] As Mill says, "No whole truth is possible but by combining the points of view of all the fractional truths."[29]

In his own life, Mill found the romantic poets a necessary antidote to the overly analytic education he received from his father, and it might be tempting to interpret him as advocating a yin-yang notion of paradoxical truths: truth is the reconciliation of opposites. But the author of *A System of Logic* (1843) would not so complacently betray the canons of consistency. Mill is not making a metaphysical point about "many-sided" paradoxical truth, but rather a political and psychological point. The truths he is addressing are practical and political truths: they are about what we should do. And the reason we have to combine opposites when it comes to knowing what we should do is not that the truth itself is paradoxical, but that our own limitations make it difficult for us to appreciate more than one side of the truth. In the modern age, Mill is saying, political people are ideological: they see one side of things, and are certain the side they see is the whole of things.

This is even the case with the foundational principles of political modernity: freedom and equality. Mill himself was a partisan of democracy in nineteenth-century Europe, yet he also thought the ideal of human equality could be "detrimental to moral and political excellence."[30] He was sympathetic to political equality—and worried about its effects. Equality itself is one of Mill's fractional truths: in some respects every person is the equal of all other persons, in some respects the equal of only some others, and in some respects the equal of no other. Is the principle of human equality *true?* Yes. But only partly true. Figuring out how to apply it in practical life demands a "capacious" practical intelligence that few possess.

It is difficult to hold both sides of a standing antagonism in mind because the vectors of the arguments for each side point in opposite directions. To be "inside" the argument for progress is to ride a train of thought that is headed in a particular direction. It is very difficult intellectually to ride that thought train and to simultaneously ride a separate train moving in the opposite direction. Each side of Mill's "standing antagonism" constitutes a political orientation—or what Gutmann and Thompson call, in a different context, a "mindset."[31] Setting one's mind gives one a particular vantage on the political and social world. That vantage point illuminates some things and hides others. This is the predicament of political understanding in the modern world: the best see only part of things, from one angle. The worst often see nothing at all.

From a progressive vantage point, for instance, one can see certain truths (or partial truths). Progressives cannot view the past with a sort of pious reverence; they regard the past critically.

Tradition, as such, has no independent value: some things we inherit from the past need to change, some things should stay. In place of ancestral authority, the progressive mindset places authority in critical reason. It insists that social order can be maintained in the absence of pious reverence for the past. Order can depend on a popular appreciation of the benefits gained in exchange for compliance and obedience; in short, it can be founded on consent.

Conservatives, by contrast, worry that reason is too fragile to serve as the basis for social order. Political stability requires the auxiliary support of the passions—in particular, reverence. Since people are inclined to revere ancient things, conservatives would hesitate to subject all tradition to rational scrutiny. Ancient sources of order—a royal lineage, a constitutional settlement—should be preserved even if they are flawed (what isn't?), simply because they are ancient. Furthermore, the conservative mindset would hesitate to presume that we can know enough to fully evaluate the utility of tradition. It regards tradition with reverence, as if tradition might contain understandings we cannot fully appreciate. So the inclination that comes from the conservative mindset is . . . to conserve, even if we cannot supply a full account of why we should.

The standing antagonisms Mill mentions might be reconciled, at least logically. What makes them difficult to reconcile is not logic, but psychology. The rivalry between equality and distinction or between progress and order has less to do with the meaning of the concepts themselves than with, as Mill says, "the types of human character which answer to them."[32] Different human types are disposed to see (and to be blind to) different things. If they were not blind in some respects, they would see less. Every capacity is also incapacity. Our own particularity—our nationality, our upbringing, our temperament, our age, our financial standing, our intellectual bent—equips us "for perceiving some things, and for missing or forgetting others.[33]

Mill illustrated this point in separate essays on "the two great seminal minds of England in their age," Jeremy Bentham and Samuel Taylor Coleridge.[34] Mill describes each as a "great questioner of things established." But that was all they had in common: "Each of them sees scarcely anything but what the other does not see," Mill says.[35] Bentham, of course, was the radical. He could see what needed to change, especially in the law. Coleridge defended tradition. For Bentham, a good moral understanding required building up a utilitarian system of morality from scratch—as if all the philosophy of the past was a collection of so many errors and delusions. Coleridge assumed that the antiquity or prevalence of an opinion is "a presumption that it is not altogether false.[36] Bentham neglected tradition in favor of reform, while Coleridge opposed reform in the name of conservation.

If Bentham and Coleridge shared nothing in their philosophy and politics, the point of Mill's essays was to transcend the narrowness they could not. Mill appreciates each of them— their genius and their defects. This—taking them together—is where the real value of each is found. But to offer this value, each had to be deficient: the genius of each, however, is inseparable from his limitation. Mill describes Bentham, for instance, as a "one-eyed man." "For our part," Mill says, "we have a large tolerance for one-eyed men, provided their eye is a penetrating one: if they saw more, they probably would not see so keenly, nor so eagerly pursue one course of enquiry."[37] Partisans are necessarily ideological, in Mill's view. Their insights are generated within a self-contained system of thought that is both the source of their insight and their limitation. Inside the system, certain conclusions or insights become apparent and make sense that seem strange or absurd from the vantage of those in rival systems of thought.

The necessarily ideological nature of partisanship is a reflection on human types—on the psychological dispositions of individuals. Some are prone, by their own idiosyncrasies, to conservatism, others to progressivism. It may also be that the ideological nature of partisanship stems from the job that parties in the early modern world had to accomplish. The liberal or progressive party had to overturn the rule of religion generally, and the rule of an entrenched elite of priests and nobles in particular. Accomplishing this great task required an unyielding philosophy: early modern liberals had to believe they were right. We can see something of this confidence in Jefferson's opening paragraph of the Declaration of Independence. Jefferson does not try to have it both ways or to strike a mean between two extreme views: "on one hand, the rule of kings has served Great Britain well in many ways; on the other, it is failing in the colonies." He leads instead with a declaration of "self-evident" truths, as if they could not possibly need argument or demonstration: "governments are instituted among men, deriving their just powers from the consent of the governed." There is no indication that the principle of consent is limited or partial. Nor is there any sense that Jefferson's party—the revolutionary party in America, or the democratic party more broadly—sees certain things but misses others. Jefferson, whatever he thought, could not afford to introduce any doubt. Without certainty, the revolutionary cause would have been lost. The same might be said for Mill's time—when the democratic revolutions continued to roil Europe.

Perhaps the revolution continues. Only a generation ago, same-sex marriage was unthinkable. Today, it is a given among the young: a turn or two of the demographic wheel, and it will be unremarkable. We may not in the moment be able to glimpse which cause the revolution will next touch—that is the work of partisans (and ideologues) who see further, if more narrowly, than the rest. Yet at the same time, the democratic revolution has touched and transformed many aspects of social and economic life; in certain nontrivial respects, the revolution has been won. We are all democrats. We all believe in the political equality of men and women, people of all races, and increasingly people of all sexualities. Given the accomplishments of the democratic revolution—the overturning of monarchic rule, the rejection of religious intolerance, the rejection of slavery, the affirmation of sexual equality—it may no longer be the case that we need to be ideologues in order to see the value of the revolutionary cause on one hand, or the reasons motivating its opponents on the other.

In his day, Mill thought that the main benefit of partisan ideologues was to the onlookers to the partisan clash. This more impartial view was what Mill was trying to cultivate in his companion essays on Bentham and Coleridge, side by side. "It is not on the impassioned partisan," Mill says, "it is on the calmer and more disinterested bystander, that this collision of opinions works its salutary effect."[38] Perhaps today, we can all adopt something of the perspective of the bystander. Perhaps we can be partisan without being ideological.[39]

Partisan Righteousness

As it happens in our own politics, it rarely happens that bystanders learn from the clash of ideologues and build for themselves a more enlarged and impartial view.[40] In our own politics, dispassionate onlookers are turned off from the "clash" of rival partisans. The clash produces ambivalence more often than judicious compromise. It is easier to pick a side when people—nonideological, less-political people—are surrounded by those on the same side. But when people are exposed to those who vigorously disagree, they try to sidestep the disagreement in order to preserve social harmony. They become disengaged.[41]

Disagreeing with ideologues, who seem to believe they possess the right answer, is intimidating and unpleasant. It seems easier to avoid the fight altogether.

But in the circumstances of the moment, it would seem a mistake to rigorously divide neutral observers and committed partisans, as if these referred to wholly separate sets of people. Such a division asks too much of observers and too little of partisans. The division between "impassioned partisans" and "disinterested observers" can run through the same person. We can commit to a point of view, and develop a partisan loyalty to the cause and the party we think on the whole gets things more right. But there is no reason we have to give ourselves over completely. The political contest today is different than it was in early modernity—it does not require the singularity of focus that defines the revolutionary drive. In standing with a party, we can preserve an observational self that looks at our own commitments from a distance without imperiling the cause.

The best partisans stand for something, but in other moments see that theirs is not the only reasonable place one can take a stand. They possess a *negative capacity* that ideology disables. A negative capacity allows us to see ourselves from a distance, to turn on the commitments and loyalties that define our political orientation and see them more critically. Partisans do not need self-validating systems of thought in order to win—and they can afford to resist the narrowness that so often comes with conviction. In current political conditions, for all that is at stake in our public deliberations, it is a mistake to believe that decisiveness—a willingness to endorse a particular course of action—depends on narrowness.

The best partisans hope their side wins, yet know that victory should never be total. The most admirable partisans are brave enough to stand up publicly for what they see, yet are capacious enough to know that what they see is not the whole of things. This partisanship is capable of reflecting with some detachment on one's stand, perhaps even able to entertain one's political enemies in grudging good cheer. Mill's image of partisan contestation—of "combatants fighting"—is drawn from war. Early modern politics amounted to a war, and if its work is not done, it long ago won the war. This is why partisanship today can be constitutional. It does not aim for wholesale revolution, and it forsakes violence. Rival partisans are adversaries, not opponents.[42] Even when opponents disagree on constitutional fundamentals—and they will—they can agree in general about how such disputes should be settled. They forsake violent revolution, for one. This means, concretely, that they peacefully transfer the powers of the offices they have held when they lose elections.

This peaceful transfer of power indicates that partisans themselves can see partisanship as a permanent and legitimate feature of democratic politics. Theirs is not a fight to end all future fights. They do not see themselves as a "last party," a party that carries the whole truth about social and political life, the victory of which would bring an end to the need for further contestation. Partisans at their best agree to the prerequisites of partisanship: a system of open competition. The single procedural principle that ethical partisans never transgress is the prohibition of violence. Ethical partisans keep their guns in their holsters. Violence might in some contexts be justified—but once we resort to violence, we leave the ethics of partisanship and enter the ethics of war.

Giving up on the idea of a last party should temper the inclination to violence. The best partisans combine two points of view: one that is up close, engaged, and feels the power of conviction, and another that looks on from a distance and sees one's own commitments as partial. This should relax the self-righteousness and pride that nourish violence. The renunciation of violence also finds support in the idea of partisanship as a willingness to stand with a group that is striving to acquire democratic legitimacy. On this understanding, a party is not an entirely principled thing. It is a patchwork association, appealing to principle, but in a loose enough way to appeal broadly. As such, it is not a source of moral truths so pure that losing comes to seem intolerable.

A skepticism about our own convictions does not diminish them or restrict partisan contestation to small things. Much ordinary political contestation is nourished by a deeper and usually unseen contest of fundamental alternatives. This contest is shrouded in nonrevolutionary times. Indeed, partisans' agreement to compete via nonviolent means within the terms of a constitutional settlement itself helps to shroud those deeper differences that nourish partisan contestation. Yet, as Tocqueville noticed about even the partisanship of Van Buren's day (which seemed so utterly devoid of principle), when one attends carefully to the "secret instincts" and "innermost thoughts" of motley and unprincipled American parties, one discovers that they are "more or less linked to one or the other of the two great parties that have divided men since there have been free societies." One works to extend the popular power, the other to restrict it. This does not mean that either party wishes to make democracy or aristocracy prevail wholly, Tocqueville insists, only that "aristocratic or democratic passions . . . form as it were the sensitive spot and the soul of them."[43]

An ambiguity about founding principles is built into liberal democracy. The ambiguity stems not merely from the fact that founding principles can empirically conflict with each other, as with the liberty-equality "trade-off." Rather, it derives from the qualified or partial basis of the claims of liberty and the claims of equality themselves. Thus any foundational or constitutional settlement should leave "contingencies, remainders, resistances, and excesses" that nourish and inspire partisan contestation.[44]

At any moment, certain political questions become *our* questions: they connect to interests, elicit passions, and generate convictions. Are embryonic stem cells an appropriate subject of scientific research? Are concentrations of wealth undermining equality of opportunity? How should the burden of taxation be shared? Professional politicians have an interest in introducing questions like these that engage people and lift their gaze from the more urgent apolitical pursuits that occupy us. At the same time, practical questions arise for us in the particular way they do in part because we understand ourselves as a progressive regime, one that should become fairer, more democratic, more just, and more prosperous over time. But where—if anywhere—do we get off the train of progress? How—if at all—should we slow it down? When—if anytime—should we add to its fuel?

It is difficult to make these judgments exactly, as Mill would say. It is rather easier to give ourselves over to one side or the other—to discern and to *feel* the claims of progress only, or the claims of preservation only. Those who are on occasion internally torn between various pulls, the pull to reform on one hand and the pull to stabilize or conserve on the other, need to see and hear from those who see things in a more one-sided way. Every vital democracy will have party spirit in part because the fundamental sources of disagreement endure. Even our agreements mask disagreements. We agree about liberty and equality and democracy, yet each of these is in some sense unsettled and impossible to be settled. What matters is not that things are settled, once and for all—but that we engage our disagreements in constitutional modes (not violent ones), resist ideological self-righteousness, retain a critical capacity about our own convictions. This critical capacity is consistent with affirming a partisan identity with a certain loyalty, as Chapter 5 shows.

If nonideological, self-critical partisanship seems a long way from the partisanship that we actually witness in political life, it is because many current manifestations of partisanship are pathological and hyperbolic. Partisan contestation is not existential conflict, nor is it likely that one side in a contest lacks all flaws while the other has it all wrong. Partisanship as it is needs to be improved, especially since it is not going away, at least in U.S. politics, anytime soon. This is especially the case with the loyalty that partisanship involves. What we need is not a mode of partisanship that transcends loyalty, any more than we should wish for a politics that escapes partisanship. What we need to understand is how to be loyal partisans. What we need is not less partisanship, but better partisanship.

5

LOYAL PARTISANS

Good citizens are expected to stay informed; to vote; to write letters; to "get involved." That is all true, insofar as it goes. But all these "actions" are solitary. They invoke the image of the lone citizen exercising his or her reason, communicating his or her impartial conclusions about public things to officials. Yet the most effective political action requires citizens and their officials to stand together, at least for a while. The cool light of reason might motivate us to stand by those who share our conclusions. But this gathering may not be very large or last very long. Effective political action requires more than this; it requires loyalty.

Partisanship at its best is a kind of loyalty—but not any kind of loyalty. I have said that ethical partisanship involves a "negative capacity," an ability to reflect critically on one's own views. Yet loyalty all too often undercuts this capacity. Loyal friends might feel they cannot think critically of each other, as loyal citizens might feel the same way about their country: *love it or leave it*. This is what loyalty is often like, true enough. It is as if our loyalties compel us to think nothing but good thoughts about our country, our cause, our group, or our friends. But it is a profound mistake to think this is what loyalty must be like. Loyalty can be—and partisan loyalty should be—far more supple than that. It is possible to be loyal and to see the object of our loyalty as it is, with all its faults. Politics needs loyal partisans, yes—but it needs loyal partisans who can see clearly and think for themselves. At its best, partisanship is affirmed by a choice, and retains an openness to both "bad facts" (facts that are embarrassing to one's commitments) and revision. Party loyalty, at its core, need not bring a distorted perception of the world. What it asks for is not that we suspend our critical judgment or clear perception of things, only that we exercise a certain kind of memory and patience.

Among elected officials, party loyalty is a given. Very few politicians switch parties—since the turn of the nineteenth century, fewer than two dozen U.S. senators have switched parties during their service. Of course, it is almost never in a politician's interest to be disloyal, even if one's party faces a landslide defeat in the next election. Few things will kill a career faster than party disloyalty. For politicians, this is not just a matter of conviction; their careers often depend on steady loyalty. If any senators today were considering a party switch, they would only need consult the case of Arlen Specter, the Pennsylvania Republican who was elected as a Republican in 1980 and—one year after switching to the Democratic Party—was defeated in a primary election in 2010. Specter was never a perfect fit with the Republican Party's social conservatism. After he betrayed his own party by voting for President Obama's stimulus bill, Specter faced a difficult primary campaign and probable defeat. In a final effort to save his career and to align himself with a party that might offer a better fit, he switched to the Democratic Party. "The Republican Party has moved far to the right," he noted; "I now find my political philosophy more in line with Democrats than Republicans."[1]

One might think that the Democratic Party would have been so grateful to Specter for helping it toward a commanding, filibuster-proof majority that it would have protected him from any challenger. But political ambition being what it is, and the party organization being as weak as it is, the Democratic Party could not prevent two-term Democratic congressman Joseph Sestak from challenging him. Yet in the end, it was Specter's disloyalty that killed his reelection chances. Until a month before the election, Specter led in the polls. Then Sestak aired an ad that showed Specter saying, "My change in party will enable me to be reelected." Specter complained that his quotation was taken out of context (and it was: the full quotation emphasized Specter's ability to serve the public rather than his mere ability to get reelected).[2] But the damage was emphatic. After the ad aired, Sestak pulled into the lead, and four weeks later Sestak beat Specter in the primary (he subsequently lost to Pat Toomey in the general election). As one Pittsburgh voter said, "I'm not real comfortable with Specter switching over. I think it was mostly for his own status."[3]

Disloyalty can end a political career. Yet many officials are loyal not only because they are ambitious (and do not want to pay the price of disloyalty). They are ambitious because they are loyal—they want to advance the principles that define their party. Gordon Brown was not a loyal member of the Labour Party because it offered him the highest probability of being elected to Parliament, and prime minister. He was Labour because his convictions meant he could be nothing else. The same can be said about other party leaders, like Dick Armey or Tom DeLay or Nancy Pelosi: they were ambitious because they were partisans, not partisans because they were ambitious. This is even more pointedly the case for nameless and unremembered candidates who run and lose, often against nearly hopeless odds. Could someone possibly run as a Democrat in Utah's third congressional district for only strategic reasons—a district that has only been represented by Democrats for six years of its thirty-year

history? These candidates are loyal to their party in spite of the
fact that their party renders it almost impossible for them to win.

Party loyalty pays in part because voters like to see consistency—it gives them some assurance that what a candidate
says is what a candidate, once elected, will do. But party loyalty also matters because many voters themselves are loyal
partisans. Some scholars would insist that voters are not really
partisans—they are merely brand loyalists. Brand loyalty might
be cast as the lowest form of loyalty, since it is passive. Its central
power comes through *exit:* it lacks *voice.* A loyal Coke drinker
might switch to Pepsi if Coke changes its formula, just as a loyal
Labour voter might vote Liberal if she is frustrated with the
direction of the Labour Party. Yet part of the claim for loyalty
at its best is found in its commitment to voice over exit—to arguing, planning, reforming, protesting, and voting.[4] Without
loyalty, one can leave one's country, party, and friends for better
options elsewhere. True loyalists "love it" but cannot so easily
"leave it": so they stay, and *argue.* And vote.

Partisan loyalty is more like patriotism than it is like our
preference for Hertz over Avis. Perhaps we could call patriotism
a brand loyalty too, but doing so would distort the object of
our loyalty: countries are not merely brands. Neither are parties. Unlike brands, they involve a struggle and a contest over
principle. Partisan identities connect to other social identities
rooted in class, region, and religion. They are linked not only to
philosophic ideals of social and political life, but to concrete
ways of life. The managers of mere brands aspire to this kind of
profound connection to their customers, but can only simulate
it, because brands belong not to social groups, but to corporations. Party loyalty connects to identity, to who we are. To grasp
the promise and the pathology of party spirit, we need to understand it not simply as a strategy, but also as a deep loyalty.

The Pathologies of Loyalty

The seminal description of modern partisanship from the first wave of mass survey research—*The American Voter*—suggested that party identification is an inherited condition acquired in the household that by adulthood becomes a "durable attachment." Partisan identities can seem on par with religious or even ethnic identities; they are groups we belong to before we know what groups we belong to. We do not choose them—they constitute us. As a quasi-ascribed attachment, partisan loyalty carries pathological consequences. It distorts perception by forming a "perceptual screen" that amplifies events favorable to one's own party and discounts unfavorable events.[5] This screen is especially powerful in political evaluations, where we have to make up our minds about things that are essentially contestable and involve underlying disagreements about policy.

Some moral duties are grounded in reasons that apply to everyone. If I have a duty to assist a stranger in need, so do you. If I have a duty to respect other human beings, the same is true of everyone else. Loyalty, however, is not that kind of duty. It is grounded in the unrepeatable particulars of a concrete situation. "Loyalties invariably entail commitments that cannot be grounded in reasons others share," says a recent defender of loyalty. "There comes a point at which the logic runs dry and one must plant one's feet in the simple fact that it is my friend, my club, my alma mater, my nation."[6] When there are no reasons left, when every fair-weather friend has gone home, loyalty kicks in—and you discover who your real friends are. Winning campaigns attract all sorts to their victory party. But only the truly *loyal* partisans come to the party when the election is lost. The loyal remain even when times are bad: after a landslide election defeat, when morale is low and the future is dim and no strategic reason can be found to stay with the cause.

The element of loyalty that goes beyond reason—maybe it is even irrational—is loyalty's essence. Everyone is your friend when friendship pays. The true friend, the loyal friend, is still there long after the payment stops. The loyal friend stands ready—to sacrifice, to remain a friend when the reasons run out. The fact that loyalty goes beyond strategic self-interest (that is what loyalty *is*) gives it an inexplicable, sometimes senseless quality. Loyalists remain true to the objects of their loyalty even when no particular meaning or purpose can be attached to it. Loyalty is blind. And often unthinking. It can prompt great selfless deeds. But it can also carry one into evil. This is why group loyalties, notably patriotism but also partisanship, are morally ambiguous. Yet it is also why we cherish it: if it is in someone's interest to stand by my side, I do not need his loyalty. If loyalty were merely strategic, it would boil down to a form of prudence. But because it prompts us to go beyond ourselves, loyalty can involve a kind of nobility. And yet in transcending self-interested strategic reason, loyalty threatens to become immune to reason and judgment. It can become a form of unthinking stubbornness that brings with it a kind of closure—closure to fact, to principle, and to consequences. This is why loyalty presents a "permanent moral danger."[7]

The danger comes from the way loyalty constrains not only what we *do* but also what we *think*. It invites intellectual closure: our loyalties seem to make a claim on what we are willing to consider, even what we believe. Nowhere is this more evident than in friendship. The philosopher Sarah Stroud in an astute and provocative essay argues that "the demands of friendship extend into the realm of belief."[8] Loyal friends *do* what good friends do—they refrain from speaking badly about their friends, for example. "The good friend," Stroud says, "is prepared to take her friend's part both publicly and . . . internally."[9] This is easy, of course, when you think your friend is right. But this is the point, for Stroud: the loyal friend has a duty of sorts to *think* her friend is right. Loyalty, for Stroud (at least in the case of friendship) is not just about doing. It is also about thinking. The loyal face what we might call epistemic demands—constraints on what they are permitted to think and to know.

This comes to a sharp point when a friend is the object of criticism and blame. Suppose, for instance, that someone tells you your friend connived and deceived to outmaneuver another for a promotion. In a case like this, Stroud says, you owe your friend "epistemic partiality." You have a duty to deny that what you are told is true and to think the best of your friend. Here's how epistemic loyalty works: As a loyal friend we first look for ways to discredit the bad information about our friend. We scrutinize the evidence. We question the source (perhaps the person has a stake in the situation that compromises his objectivity). We look for weak spots in the case. If all this does not work—if the evidence should appear incontrovertible, our epistemic duties as a friend are not done. We imagine alternative explanations ("the person against whom my friend connived had already been conniving against him—my friend had no choice other than to quit"). Finally, if alternative explanations are not credible, we search for different conclusions and inferences that might be drawn from the evidence; perhaps there is a positive way to view the story. What others classify as deception, a loyal friend might call effective; what others call cunning, the loyal friend might describe as a reasonable adaptation to a bureaucratic hierarchy.

If all this seems similar to the way partisan loyalties work, it is. Loyal partisans do certain things—most plainly, they vote for candidates of their party, year after year. But they also seem to think certain things. They think well of their own party's candidates and badly of the other party's, almost regardless of the facts. Take, for instance, the amazing partisan gap in the approval ratings of recent presidents. Only 15 percent of Democrats approved of George W. Bush's performance at the end of his first term—while 89 percent of Republicans approved![10] At the time, this startling gap was the "most polarized presidential approval between parties ever measured by Gallup." What was unprecedented for Bush was ordinary by the time Obama finished his first year as president. At the beginning of 2010, 88 percent of Democrats approved of Obama's performance, while only 23 percent of Republicans approved.

Political friendship—and partisanship is a kind of friendship—seems to be like Stroud's characterization of ordinary friendship. In ordinary friendship, as Stroud says, because we need to "maintain a favorable opinion of our friend's character" it should not be surprising "that we would massage our beliefs about our friend's character in a favorable direction and downplay any information which might threaten that esteem."[11] Loyalty seems to make a corresponding demand of partisans. Partisans hesitate to think badly of their partisan friends. Democrats are more skeptical of evidence that Obama has done a bad job; when they encounter evidence that he has faltered, just as Stroud says of ordinary friends, they construct alternative narratives to interpret negative evidence. They search for a different set of facts than Republicans in order to paint a more flattering picture of the Obama presidency. The same is the case for Republicans with respect to Republican officials. Our commitment to friends, as with our commitment to a party, is a constraint on what we can believe.

The danger here should be obvious. Our loyalty might obscure the reasons that motivated it in the first place—rendering it irrational and making us vulnerable to remaining friends long after we should have stopped. If no evidence can puncture our loyalty, we might remain committed to a friend even when the friendship becomes exploitative or destructive. Possibly our epistemic partiality will prevent us from even knowing that it has become destructive. There is a deep irrationality at the core of Stroud's account of friendship that prevents any degree of stepping back to evaluate whether the person you have been friends with is someone you should continue to be friends with.

To clarify this core irrationality, consider the relationship between the origins of friendship and the loyalty one has to someone who already is a friend. Friendship often originates in a choice: we decide we want to be friends with someone—to *befriend* him—and he in turns decides the same of us. That choice has some kind of reason at its core: without a reason to befriend someone, we could not motivate the choice. Why, we might ask, wouldn't the same reasons that motivated the choice to be friends in the first place also inform our assessment of whether to be loyal to the same friend? For instance, if we decided to be friends with someone because we admired his character, and subsequently discovered him to be a deceiving schemer, it seems natural for the original reason for the friendship (character) to inform our assessment of whether to stay loyal. Why would there be a disjuncture between the reasons that motivated a friendship in the first place and the later decision to remain loyal to an already-existing friendship?

Perhaps Stroud would say that friendships often do not originate in choice. We simply fall alongside certain others—they ride beside us on the bus to school, they are assigned to share an office, they live in the apartment next door. And we discover ourselves, without quite knowing how or why it happened, as friends. Subsequently, we together discover that we inhabit a hostile world in which friends are one of the few reliable sources of protection available, and we stay loyal to our friends (allied with them against the hostile world). If we were to ask *why,* the whole thing would crumble—the loyalty, the friendship, the support, and the protection. In short, Stroud might say, friendship simply is irrational—and also useful and pleasant. To enjoy friends and to keep them, we need to submit ourselves to that irrationality and stay loyal pretty much no matter what.

This is perhaps how many friendships start. They begin without anyone quite intending it. We wake up, as it were, and find ourselves as friends with certain other people. They might not have been the friends we would have chosen if we could have chosen (it's hard to fully control who you work with, live beside, or go to school with). But they are *our* friends, however they came to be. And since they are, we owe them (Stroud would say) a certain loyalty. In particular, we owe them the epistemic loyalty of thinking well of them, regardless.

All this might be mapped onto political friends as well. Often people do not choose their party. Party identifications are learned in the home—the best predictor, historically, of party identification was the party ID of one's parents. It is also learned in one's social environment: one sees that most people in the neighborhood, or at church, or at the club identify with this or that party. Partly out of trust, partly to fit in (and to escape the burden of explaining why one disagrees with most people around), one identifies with the party that everyone else seems to identify with. Like everyday friendships, partisanship is an accident of one's socialization. In this view, neither becoming a partisan nor loyalty to one's party is a rational thing.

This account may be true for many friends and for many partisans. Yet even if it is, friendship and partisanship in their best form somehow involve a choice. Perhaps we became friends by accident (we sat next to each other in homeroom). But at some point along the way, if the friendship is a worthy one, we can choose the friendship we already have. The same holds for partisanship. Perhaps we did acquire it unknowingly from our parents. But at some point, if our party really does stand for something we think is right, we can choose the identification that we inherited. And we can also reject it. Partisanship at its best—like friendship at its best—involves a choice. The reasons that motivate that choice should also inform our loyalties. Loyalties may go beyond what self-interested reason would justify. But they can and should be informed by reasons just the same. They do not need to be irrational at the core—and they should not be. Party loyalty at its best is not an attachment that constitutes one's identity from birth; it is a commitment that arises from reasons. When the perceptual screen or epistemic loyalty that partisanship entails blinds us to the original reasons that made sense of party loyalty, we are at risk of acting contrary to our own beliefs, values, and commitments.

Too often, party loyalty seems to instill a kind of blindness; it incapacitates judgment and looks profoundly irrational. For instance, people will support policies that they should oppose in light of their beliefs and interests—out of what seems like blind party loyalty. In one experiment, subjects are invited to evaluate two welfare policies, one extremely generous and one extremely stringent. As one might predict, subjects who call themselves liberals approve of the generous policy, and subjects who think of themselves as conservatives like the stringent policy. But all this changes when they are told that Democrats in Congress support the *stringent* policy: liberals then support it, and conservatives oppose it.[12] Conservatives, by contrast, are more likely to *favor the generous policy* when told that Republicans in Congress also support the policy and that Democrats oppose it. When asked to explain their evaluations, people say that the "details of the proposal" and their "philosophy of government" motivate their views, not what Democrats and Republicans typically believe. In fact, loyalty to party trumps what people actually believe about what the policy actually does. In this experiment, party loyalty seems to involve epistemic closure; it overrides an accurate perception of factual reality. By insulating us from facts and incapacitating judgment and reason, party loyalty becomes inarticulate, senseless, and self-defeating. It looks more like a stubborn prejudice and less like an admirable willingness to stand together for the sake of protecting past achievements and getting something done. If this is what loyalty in politics amounts to, we might be better off without it.

Before we conclude that party loyalty is a source of prejudice and irrationality, we might consider a more sympathetic interpretation of the subjects in this experiment. Liberals and conservatives in the experiment may simply trust partisan leaders in Congress more than they trust their own abilities to assess the details of a large and complicated public policy. The implicit reasoning of a liberal in the experiment, for instance, might go as follows: "Generally I would oppose the more stringent policy—it will exclude too many people who need support. But Democrats in Congress must know something I do not. These things are complicated, and I am no expert. Members of Congress follow the details of these things. There might be implications to the policy that I don't see. I don't know. What I do know is that on lots of other matters, what John Boehner supports I generally do not like.[13] So I am going to take my cues from congressional leaders." In this interpretation, people trust the party to defend their principles. They put less trust in summary descriptions of legislation: perhaps the description is deceptive.

Of course, this does not explain why subjects in the experiment would *say* that their evaluations depended on the "details" of the policies rather than on where their parties stood. Perhaps there is a way in which loyalty allows us to deceive ourselves about things like the "details" of a policy. It might distort our elemental perception of facts—it erects, as the authors of *The American Voter* noted so long ago, a "perceptual screen" that colors facts—making some look more prominent and others perhaps disappear altogether. The problem with party loyalty is not that it involves trust, or even that it occasionally makes us blind to certain things (the faults of a friend). More threatening is the way it might distort everything we see, obliterating what we might call "facticity"—the world of facts that constitutes the bedrock of all reasoning and deliberation.

While this would be a colossal tragedy for politics, some would argue that we should be skeptical about the possibility that there is (or that we have access to) a terrain of facts that inform our loyalties. In matters of friendship and partisanship, the facts of the matter are themselves unclear. All assessments of character are interpretations, and all interpretations are at bottom partisan. When all is partisan, you are either with me or against me: there is no ground upon which a neutral observer can stand. In her account of friendship, Stroud is ambivalent about whether we have access to those facts that inform one's evaluations of friends.[14] On one hand, she holds that friendship does not require us to ignore, distort, or deny basic facts. Friends might interrogate negative facts with more energy, and accept positive facts more readily—but they can acknowledge the same facts as a neutral observer would. On the other hand, Stroud suggests that we should be skeptical about the possibility that we can have certain knowledge of "base-level" facts that bear on our assessment of people's characters.

It is not easy to know, for instance, whether our friend John in fact deceived in order to get a promotion. Proving such a thing would ordinarily require an elaborate investigation. Even then, the proof would likely rely on people's memories (which are notoriously fallible), on the imputation of intentions (always hazardous), and on the presence of observers who themselves did not have a stake in the matter (always rare). In the world of friendship, perhaps there are very few raw data to go on. That is why, although a friend is not *required* to deny basic facts and events, still, "she will look for openings that might permit her to do this."[15] It is not so much that friendship severs us from the data a neutral observer might see as that it acknowledges that such "data" are rarely encountered in their pure form.

One might say the same about partisanship. Political questions are complicated and interconnected, and it can be hard to isolate facts in a wholly nonpartisan way. Even when we can pick out politically relevant facts ("the budget deficit last year was x hundred million dollars"), it is almost never clear how to explain or to evaluate them in a wholly nonpartisan way. What caused the budget deficit and how to reduce it are matters that leave some room for interpretation. Partisans will use this room to explain things in a manner that shows their party in the most positive light. At the extreme, partisans might even deny the possibility of politically relevant facts that can be ascertained in a nonpartisan way. Indeed, rival partisans often lose access to a shared world of facts. For instance, over the course of Reagan's presidency in the 1980's, inflation fell significantly, from 13.5 percent to 4.1 percent. Yet in 1988 more than half of those identifying as "strong Democrats" said that inflation had become worse or much worse over the Reagan years; fewer than 8 percent said the inflation rate had become "much better."[16] Perhaps in this case, Democrats simply could not accept the possibility that some economic facts during the Reagan presidency were good. Still, what is startling is not that Democrats denied that the economy was good (they may have had good reasons to deny that). It was that they possessed such an inaccurate and distorted understanding of the basic facts about the economy. Perhaps party loyalty indeed obliterates facticity. When party loyalty seems to be the cause rather than the consequence of rival perceptions of elemental facts in the political world, political discussion, debate, and deliberation are imperiled; if brute facts are obliterated, basic political rationality—and therefore political action—become impossible. Sometimes it is said that rival partisans inhabit "different worlds." When the common terrain of factuality is obliterated, this is no exaggeration: it becomes impossible to share a political community.

This disaster is a real possibility. Consider the "controversy" over President Barack Obama's citizenship. Only six months after President Obama was elected, in spite of the most incontrovertible evidence that can be adduced, 58 percent of Republicans thought he was not born in the United States.[17] It is truly perplexing to imagine what is going on with a majority of Republican partisans. Perhaps partisan news sources have incapacitated their ability to assess elemental facts. To the extent that the belief is authentic—and those who say they believe Obama is not a natural-born citizen are not merely saying this to pollsters to get some satisfaction by taunting the other side—party loyalty seems to be closing the minds of some Republicans to elemental facts. Insofar as this closure diminishes those partisans' confidence in the basic constitutionality of the Obama presidency, it works to corrode the legitimacy of government and law more generally.[18] The more this corrosion touches, the more difficult it becomes to share a political community.

Loyalty is one thing; blindness to basic facts is another. Perhaps friendship—and partisanship—call for some degree of epistemic partiality. But to be loyal we do not need to close ourselves off to the terrain of elemental facts. There are politically relevant facts, and we can have access to them regardless of where our loyalties point. For instance, when a presidential candidate says there are more unemployed Americans than employed Canadians, it is either right or wrong (it's wrong).[19] When Democrats say the Bush tax cuts caused the federal deficit, they are either right or wrong (they're wrong).[20]

Some facts will be what defense lawyers call "bad facts." They will be embarrassing to our cause, and we will want to explain them away—if we cannot ignore or deny them altogether. Political people will try to convert bad facts into mere opinion— when they succeed too well, however, they convert all facts into opinion. This may be true more generally, since it is hard to maintain our loyalty in the face of bad facts, and it is embarrassing to admit that our loyalties were misplaced. But to succeed too well introduces its own disaster, one far worse than whatever political people are trying to avert. Obliterating facts undermines the basis for justified loyalties in the first place. It dissolves the ground of political action. In the end, it makes it impossible to belong to a common community.

On some accounts, party loyalty must, in principle, be blind because it arises from inscrutable feelings, not convictions. Consider, for instance, how Stuart Hampshire made sense of his commitment to democratic socialism. It is a mistake, he claimed, "to look for a moral theory, or a set of propositions, that could serve as a justification, or foundation, of my political loyalties." He says, "It is difficult to acknowledge the bare contingency of personal feeling as the final stopping point when one is arguing with oneself, or with others, about the ultimate requirements of social justice. But I am now fairly sure that this is the true stopping point."[21] Hampshire cannot make sense of his own loyalty in terms that might make it compelling to anyone else. He rejects the idea that reason could motivate partisanship—loyalty is a matter of personal feeling. And why should what one person feels persuade anyone else? For Hampshire, argument and reason are frosting on the cake: they are what make a personal and unjustifiable *feeling* more palatable to others, but they are not the real substance of the matter. By reducing his partisan loyalty to feeling, Hampshire insulates it from facts—good and bad. His loyalty is immune to reasons and argument: so long as he has the requisite feeling, his mind is closed.

Yet at its best, party loyalty does not start and end with a feeling. One might acquire one's loyalty very young, in the family—but party loyalties at some later point are affirmed by a choice. This choice involves feelings, but ultimately involves *claims*. In politics, various people and various groups make claims on others and on the community in general. These claims are embedded in an understanding of justice, or a view about the recognition, resources, rights, and opportunities one deserves. And they lead to concrete proposals, policies, and programs.

Feelings may be self-validating, but claims and their associated arguments and policies are not. Thoughtful party loyalties—in contrast to Hampshire's emotive partisanship—are not immune to facts. It is possible to get policies and programs wrong, and to encounter bad facts. Bad facts are stubborn features of the social world that reflect badly on one's favored goals, programs, and policies—in short, one's party. It is possible to be both loyal and open to facts, even bad facts. If the bad facts pile up, it might be right to revise one's loyalties. Even in the case of friendship, a friend is not obligated to believe the best no matter what. Keeping an open mind with respect to facts risks that we might discover that the object of our loyalty is unworthy—even, in the extreme case, that we have wasted a large part of our life in devotion to the cause. But a few bad facts here and there are to be expected: nothing human is pure. The best partisans can make their peace with bad facts and see them for what they are: they can be committed, yet epistemically open. They can affirm even when what they affirm is imperfect. Perfect people would not need loyal friends, and perfect causes do not need loyal partisans.

The basis for loyalty is not that our cause represents the "whole truth." It is that very little of what we accomplish can be sustained, and very little of what we think would be good can be accomplished, unless we stand together. Because every cause, even every imperfect cause, is embattled, we need to stand together to protect and secure the achievements of the past and win something for the future. Political action, imperfect as it always must be, requires memory and patience. These—not epistemic closure—are what party loyalty at its best involves.

Politics Needs Loyal Partisans

Political action requires more than dispassionate reasoning about the common good or the policies that might serve it. The common good, the right policy, the best decision, will always be matters of dispute. To have an opinion about political things engages one in a contest with some citizens and against others. To make one's opinion authoritative—to accomplish something in politics—one has to not only be engaged in the contest, but also win. In democratic politics, the contest has a history—it does not start from scratch with every new election. And it has a future—it is never finally won. The history gives rise to the first element of party loyalty: memory. And the future gives rise to the second: patience.

Once something is done in politics—the Democrats pass a health care bill, for instance, or the Republicans pass a tax cut— the opposition will continue to oppose. They will impede and obstruct, dilute and diminish, unravel and undo. The Republican opposition to the Affordable Care Act may seem unusually stubborn to Democrats, but there is nothing surprising about it. Politics offers few permanent victories. For this reason it is never enough to engage in the political contest only for a moment. Nor is it sufficient to stand alone (no matter how right one is). Perhaps a coalition will come together that, in a moment, gets something done. Without some enduring identity—

without *loyalty*—this coalition will soon scatter. It has no memory and no future. Whatever it accomplishes will be vulnerable to an opposition that does stand together—it will be gutted, stymied, and destroyed. Neither the purist nor the zealot—nor, of course, the independent—can create and sustain such a group. Politics requires not only moral conviction, but also memory. For a group to stand together over time, its members need to remember what the group is about, what it counts as achievements (that need protection), and what it has yet failed to achieve. This is why loyalty only to your own moral judgment is not a genuinely political stance. It is denial of politics, born of vanity and idealism, as if the common good will command universal assent. So long as people disagree—and so long as they are free, they will disagree—politics will need party, and party will need loyalty.

Over and again, one hears that politics should not require partisanship—only a pragmatic spirit of problem solving.[22] Of course, politics is about problem solving. But the metaphor can distort what political problem solving means. In politics, we disagree not only about the best technique to solve a commonly identified problem. We also disagree about whether it is really a problem, or if we agree that it is a problem, we disagree about how to rank its urgency with respect to other problems. Political problem solving is not akin to a plumber fixing your stopped toilet. In politics, once you get to the problem solving, much of the fight has already been won.

Speaking of winning, what counts as a success—as "problem solved!"—is often not immediately evident in politics. Policies take a long time to work themselves out. Whether the health care bill of Obama's first term (the Patient Protection and Affordable Care Act of 2010) successfully extends health care coverage while reducing costs could only be dimly appreciated at the time of President Obama's reelection; by some estimates,

the pilot programs the bill authorizes will take a decade to produce results. Long-term plans require some kind of loyalty from
those who are willing to take the risk that those plans will succeed. Politics requires patience, and patience takes loyalty. Patience *is* loyalty. Loyalty does not ask you to close your mind to
elemental facts—only to wait, at least a bit longer than you
might otherwise.

Independent judgment does not produce patience because
the facts one might judge are not yet in. Meanwhile, those who
oppose such plans—whether the Iraq War, health care reform,
or, in an earlier day, Social Security or Medicare, civil rights or
environmental regulation, or deregulation and tax cuts—will
not be patient. Against this opposition, any citizen or legislator,
any executive or administrator who wants a plan to succeed will
need patient support. They need loyalists. Not loyalists who
close their eyes to a clear and distinct perception of the political
world, or who close their eyes to bad facts, but loyalists who are
capable of remembrance and patience.

Partisan Memory

Loyal partisans remember longer—and differently—than those
who have no allegiance. They remember what they take to be
the achievements of the past and understand that without their
party these achievements could not have been. They give their
party credit even after others take the achievements for granted
(or deny that they are achievements at all). They remember
that these achievements—Social Security for Democrats, or
Reagan's tax cuts for Republicans—required a sustained fight
against a concerted opposition, and they know that the opposition has not disappeared. They stand ready to protect the
achievement and to extend its spirit (sharing risks in the case of
Social Security, or rewarding effort in the case of tax cuts) to

new domains. What it means to be a partisan, for ordinary citizens, is to remember.

What partisans remember and the way they remember are part of what constitutes partisanship. Democrats remember the Civil Rights Act of 1964 and the Voting Rights Act of 1965 as the signal achievements of a Democratic president, Lyndon Baines Johnson, who was willing to destroy an enduring Democratic majority—or, one might say, to spend the capital accumulated across thirty years of Democratic dominance—in order to fundamentally address racial discrimination. Civil rights is at the heart of the identity of today's Democratic Party, even though passing civil rights legislation required steadfast support from northern Republicans in order to overcome the equally steadfast opposition of southern Democrats. But the descendants of the southern Democrats who opposed civil rights are now Republicans. President Richard Nixon was the first Republican to explicitly try to recruit southern Democrats upset about the federal government's intrusion in civil rights to the Republican Party. And since 1965 southern whites have largely abandoned the Democratic Party for the Republican Party, while northern liberals have abandoned the Republican Party for the Democrats—so it is not entirely inaccurate for contemporary Democrats to "remember" the cause of civil rights as their own.

Republicans remember Ronald Reagan, who rejuvenated a conservatism that had seemed moribund or quixotic, but in any case hopelessly out of step, for decades. They remember Reagan for his direct confrontation of the spirit of the New Deal (which cast government as the people's tool to confront problems whose scale defied individual remedies), as when he pronounced in his first inaugural address, "Government is not the solution to our problems. Government is the problem." This is the spirit of Reagan, without which no one can credibly claim today to be a Republican. The spirit is exemplified not only in a general posture toward government—one that puts urgent emphasis on its limited powers, as well as its limited capacities—but in a specific policy: tax cuts.

In his first year in office, Reagan signed a nearly 25 percent across-the-board cut in marginal income tax rates, which moved the top tax bracket from 70 percent to 50 percent. It also indexed tax brackets, to reduce the bite of "bracket creep" during periods of significant inflation. In his second term, he signed a comprehensive tax reform bill that further reduced individual tax rates and reduced the top rate to 28 percent. In addition to these reductions in individual rates, Reagan and the Democratic Congress cooperated in broadening the tax base—raising the personal exemption and standard deduction available to everyone, while making miscellaneous deductions more difficult and eliminating some, such as deducting passive losses, altogether. Reagan also substantially raised the payroll tax in 1983, and taxed Social Security benefits for wealthy recipients. In sum, Reagan *reformed* the tax code—raising some taxes, extending the taxable base, and reducing or eliminating other taxes. But he is remembered for tax cuts. In part this is because his own rhetoric privileged tax cuts; in part it is because his tax cuts were visible to anyone who pays income taxes; and in part it is because his fellow partisans choose to remember him this way.

Republican partisans are not creating a false history—against a challenger in 1984 who promised to attack deficits and defend the stability of government programs by raising taxes, Reagan ran on both the record and the promise of tax cuts. The memory is entirely accurate: the creative part comes in placing that memory at the heart of the party's identity. After all, tax cuts are not uniquely Republican. Prior to Reagan, Democratic president John Kennedy passed a tax cut, and another Democrat, President Johnson, sought one. After Reagan, Republican

president George H. W. Bush passed a tax increase that aimed
to place national finances on a stable and balanced footing.[23]
There is nothing uniquely Republican or conservative about tax
cuts—they are a tool of governance that may or may not be in
any given context popular or an appropriate tool for realizing
popular goals, and they are a tool that both Democrats and
Republicans occasionally reach for.

What makes them the property of the Republican Party is
the way Republicans remember them. Tax cuts, especially Reagan's tax cuts, stand for Republicans as a foundational commitment because of the way they point to and symbolize the larger
goals and ideals of the party. For Republicans today, tax cuts
are not merely a technique of governance, but a principle of government. They represent a fundamental break with the trajectory (as they understand it) of the New Deal state, which sought
to use government to insure individual citizens against risks
they could not successfully negotiate on their own. As Social
Security successfully insures people against the risk of poverty
when they are too old or too infirm to labor, so partisans of the
New Deal state—Democrats—would extend this success to
new realms such as health care. Tax cuts force an end to the
extension of the New Deal state by denying the government the
revenues it would need for more extensive entitlements—they
are an effort to "starve the beast," as the Reagan White House
put it.[24] Characteristically, Ronald Reagan put it more gently:
"Well, if you've got a kid that's extravagant, you can lecture
him all you want to about his extravagance. Or you can cut his
allowance and achieve the same end much quicker."[25] To remember tax cuts the way Republican partisans do is not to see
them as a tool that might be used in times of recession to stimulate the economy, nor as a device to make the tax code more
efficient and fair (should high marginal rates distort economic
activity), but to see them as a matter of principle, and to carry

the policy and the principle from candidate to candidate, election to election.

This is what partisans do: they remember. What they remember and the way they carry what they remember to the present is what defines the *party-in-the-electorate*. This idea is akin to the school of political science that explains partisanship in terms of the retrospective judgments of voters.[26] In this view, what voters mean when they identify as a Democrat is that looking back over recent political history, the Democrats seem to have done better than the Republicans. In the 2008 election, for example, voters looked back over the previous eight years of Republican control of the presidency (during four of which years the Republicans also controlled the House and the Senate) and had a simple decision to make: Did things go well or badly during the previous administration? To the extent that they thought things had gone badly—and amid a financial sector meltdown and two difficult wars, this was a common view—they would not only be more likely to vote for the Democratic candidate (Obama), they would also be more likely to identify as Democrats.

Partisan Patience

The retrospective ingredient in partisan identification captures something of how partisanship involves remembrance. But at the same time, it misses the way partisanship looks differently toward the future. When things do not work out as hoped—when unemployment is more stubborn, or legislation is more difficult to implement than they had wished—partisans see these disappointments in a larger context. Most of all, they tend to wait longer to judge something as a disappointment or a failure. At their best, partisans do not give in to the temptation to deny the disappointment altogether—to literally perceive the world differently than nonpartisans. Rather, they are simply more patient: they are willing to wait longer before branding a disappointment a failure, and they know (or they hope) that today's disappointment might be tomorrow's success.

In the case of tax cuts, Reagan's aim was not ostensibly to "starve the beast" but to stimulate growth. Lower taxes allow people to keep more of what they earn or gain through investment, thus giving them an incentive to work and invest. For his part, Reagan was more focused on investment than earned income (indeed, he raised payroll taxes in 1983). More investment, the logic went, would spur more long-term growth (and thus generate additional taxes, partially offsetting the static loss of the tax cut). Tax cuts, the proposition goes, lead to economic growth. This logic was refined by the time President George W. Bush, consciously following Reagan's example from 1981 and rejecting his father's example of 1991, passed two major tax cuts, in 2001 and 2003. These cuts were designed by Glenn Hubbard, the dean of the business school at Columbia University, explicitly around stimulating long-term growth: they focused on the capital gains tax and the tax on dividends. By decreasing taxes on investment, they were meant to stimulate more investment, and in the long run create more economic growth, more jobs, and more government revenue.

Did they succeed? We *might* be able to answer the question now, with the benefit of more than a decade of hindsight. Indeed, Professor Hubbard himself, along with Alan Greenspan, the Federal Reserve chief who publicly backed the cuts in 2003, now shies away from endorsing them. Massive deficits, which "are just future taxes," Hubbard says, have blunted the impact of the tax cuts. But before the record of the Bush years was in— before the financial crash of 2008, the consequent recession, and the devastation of national finances—it was far more difficult to evaluate the impact of Bush's tax cuts. Indeed, even now it may be close to impossible to assess the precise effect of the tax cuts on the economy, since we cannot know what the economy would look like today or five years from now in the absence of the cuts.[27] Bush's tax cuts were a long-range policy—their full success was meant to be realized only after Bush was out of office. Therefore it was difficult and perhaps impossible to credit or to blame him for their effects when he was up for reelection in 2004, or when his party was up for election in 2008 or 2010. An independent retrospective voter could not have amassed enough data or teased out the causal effects set in motion by the cuts in such a way as to form a judgment about the policy's success. This does not mean that retrospective voting was impossible—only that Bush depended for some of his support on partisans whose loyalty made them patient and willing to wait a great deal of time to see his policies succeed. And his opponents depended on a band of partisans who would not be inclined to "wait and see," but who could be counted on to collect the case against Bush before his policies could fully work themselves out, and to vote against him on that basis.

The same might be said of Bush's foreign policy in the Middle East. In the most immediate sense, the 2003 invasion of Iraq was predicated on Iraq's possession of weapons of mass destruction—weapons that were never found after the invasion because they did not exist. The revelation that Iraq had been toothless, or at least was not in possession of *any* weapons of mass destruction, was certainly the most important failure of the Bush administration and, more critical, was a devastating injury to America's international credibility. But Bush's case for invasion was never based solely on WMD. It was also framed in terms of a larger principle: freedom and democracy for a region that too often denied its people both. The larger justification of the Iraq invasion situated Iraq in a more sweeping transformation of the Middle East. There are more and less elaborate versions of this justification, but the basic idea was that representative democracy in Iraq would spur democratization throughout the region. This in turn would render countries in the region more natural allies of the United States. Our long-run interests in the region and the more general human interest in living under a decent rights-respecting government were joined. As Bush said in his second inaugural address, "The survival of liberty in our land increasingly depends on the success of liberty in other lands. . . . America's vital interests and our deepest beliefs are now one."[28]

In this case, as with the case of tax cuts that aim to stimulate growth, some will hold that it is difficult to know in the short run whether the policy has succeeded. Some, like Robert Gates, the secretary of defense who administered the Iraq War under both President Bush and President Obama, have said that judging whether the Iraq War was worthwhile ultimately "requires a historian's perspective."[29] Seven years into the war, as the United States was drawing down its military forces in Iraq in preparation for the December 31, 2011, deadline for withdrawal (required by the 2008 Status of Forces Agreement), whether the war would ultimately be judged a success was a matter of "furious debate" among historians.[30] Several years *after* Bush and the architects of the Iraq War were out of office was arguably too early to know whether the war was a success.

This does not mean that the success of the venture is wholly impossible to judge. A reasonable case may be made that the venture failed to serve the broad goals that were cited to justify it, and perhaps a case too could be made that it was a success. To say that it is too early to know does not mean that it is too early to judge at all or to form an assessment of how things are likely to work out in the future. Rather, the idea is that the judgments we make today are subject to revision in light of events and developments that have yet to take place. "Extensive and arduous enterprises for the public benefit" that require "considerable time to mature and perfect" also require considerable time to fully evaluate.[31]

This of course gives partisans the chance to fill the political air with the kind of partisan fog that threatens any judgment. When the elemental claims made by parties and politicians—for example, "the war will render the Middle East more democratic," or "tax cuts stimulate growth"—are unfalsifiable because the time frame for assessing them stretches beyond electoral time (the frame in which voters can hold the advocate of the policy accountable), politics becomes a matter of partisan faith. Results do not matter because the results are not in, and will not be in before a decision or judgment must be made. All that matters is partisan loyalty, which commits people to a set of expectations that cannot be verified against hard facts. But this overstates the matter. To say that some of the most ambitious partisan projects take a long while to play out—and therefore require patience, especially from those who are sympathetic to the projects in the first place—does not mean that *nothing* about the war can be assessed. For instance, in the sixth year of Bush's presidency, as Iraq descended into civil war,[32] voters overturned Republican majorities in both the House and the Senate. It was abundantly clear by that point that the Bush administration's initial rationale for the invasion was disproved and that its initial prognosis for the cost and duration of the war had been wildly and hopelessly off the mark (consider former Secretary of Defense Donald Rumsfeld's 2003 statement that the war "could last six days, six weeks . . . I doubt six months";[33] or Deputy Defense Secretary Paul Wolfowitz's 2003 statement that General Eric Shinseki was "wildly off the mark" in his estimate that Iraq would require "something on the order of several hundred thousand soldiers."[34] It was clear to everyone by 2007 that General Shinseki was right—even to President Bush, who was stewarding the "surge" in Iraq and had by then fired the defense secretary whose office had contradicted Shinseki. It was perfectly possible for voters to hold President Bush accountable for the way he managed the war, regardless of their partisan sympathies and irrespective of the patience or impatience they brought to the grand promise of remaking politics in the Middle East.

Partisans should not render themselves immune to facts and evidence, and in any given moment there is a great deal of evidence one can weigh in assessing the incumbent administration or party in power. The point is not that loyalty should take the place of judgment, only that judgment cannot take the place of loyalty. Any ambitious attempt to realize any reasonable approximation of the common good will take a great deal of time to work out, and those who share an idea of the common good will need to stand together over time if they are to discover what is possible in politics. Maybe it is possible, people once thought, to eradicate poverty among the elderly: it required time to discover whether Social Security could work. Maybe, some once thought, it is possible to desegregate public spaces and make the promise of American life available on equal terms to blacks and whites alike. It required time and sustained commitment to discover whether the Civil Rights Act and the Voting Rights Act could work. Such enterprises cannot be judged in the short run, which is the nature of political things: judging them is not like placing a piece of litmus paper in a test tube and recording that "it turned green." Elemental facts of relevance are hard to come by, causal relations are difficult to tease out, and—most of all—any ambitious policy designed to serve some approximation of the common good will take a long while to play out.

All the while, the opponents of the party responsible for the policy will do what they can to undermine and ultimately to overturn it without waiting to discover whether the policy might succeed. They will search for every sign that the policy was misfounded and use every piece of evidence they can invent and adduce to show that it could never succeed. For instance, as soon as President Obama and Democratic legislators passed health care reform, Republicans vowed to overturn it and to obstruct it in the courts. Fewer than two years after the Democrats passed health care reform, Republicans ran—and won—in the midterm elections pledging to overturn it. Near the close of Obama's first term, one Republican presidential aspirant insisted that on his "first day in office" he would issue an executive order giving all fifty states a waiver from the requirements to comply with Obama's health care plan.[35] Such opponents could not claim that the plan had failed, since its key provisions—such as the mandate that everyone carry health insurance, or the health care exchanges and subsidies that aim to make health care more affordable—did not take effect until 2014.[36] Perhaps more important, though less noticed, the pilot programs and demonstration projects established by the bill that are intended to discover modes of cutting health care costs will not generate results (in many cases) until 2016–2020.[37] A neutral, independent voter who wished to see the evidence before judging the landmark health care reform of 2010 would have to wait about a decade to gather the data needed to assess it. This does not mean that there were not reasons to oppose it from the start: one might be opposed to the individual mandate on principle, or not trust the government to efficiently manage a program so large. The point is not that it is unreasonable to oppose the law until the facts are in. On the contrary, there are reasonable concerns that might motivate some to steadfastly oppose the law, and those who have some sympathy for the law will need to be steadfast in their support. They will have to be patient and will need to support the law, the leaders who passed it, and the party that promised it even before they can know—before anyone can know—whether their support is fully justified. No ambitious plan to tackle large public problems can be ventured without such patience. This kind of patience—call it loyalty—is what partisanship among ordinary citizens should be about.

Muddling Through

Some might object to a partisanship of the sort that makes grand endeavors possible, because they object to a politics that entertains grand plans. They would prefer incremental change and pragmatic tweaks to public policy in a manner more at home with the ethos of "muddling through" than with the ideal of programmatic change.[38] "Muddling through," in Charles Lindblom's classic formulation of the idea, is a way of making public policy that does not require a "comprehensive evaluation of alternative policies," but rather is a mode of adaption to the "here and now in which we live."[39] In the "rational-comprehensive method" of formulating public policy—where goals are specified and agreed upon, various methods of attaining those goals are compared, and the optimal solution is chosen and pursued. "Muddling through," by contrast, only requires that leaders agree on a policy—they do not need to agree "that it is the most appropriate means to an agreed objective."[40] Nor do they even need to agree on an objective. For instance, in Lindblom's example from the 1950s, Congress's agreement to extend Social Security benefits reflected a desire among liberals to strengthen the welfare state and a desire among conservatives to reduce pressure from unions for more generous pension plans. Liberals and conservatives in this case agreed on a policy—but not on a goal. Legislation does not require that leaders agree about the common good, only that they find common ground. The way they find it is by "muddling through."

In this argument, this is also the way they *should* find it. Comparing policies and programs that differ only marginally in search of incremental improvements is appropriate to what leaders and policy makers are able to grasp. The human mind is not capacious enough to entertain large-scale transformation administered from the center without courting unintended consequences that overwhelm whatever benefit the change promises. "Neither social scientists, nor politicians, nor public administrators yet know enough about the social world to avoid repeated error in predicting the consequences of policy moves,"[41] Lindblom says. A politics of incremental change avoids "serious lasting mistakes."[42] In this view, the outcome of a pluralist system "where every interest has its watchdog" is likely to be moderate—something that does not deeply injure or offend any particular interest. The mid-twentieth-century American parties, which agreed on fundamentals and could "offer alternative policies to voters only on relatively small points of difference,"[43] were right at home in the politics of muddling through. Insofar as ideologically distinct parties seek to control every branch of government rather than entertain cross-party alliances on specific issues, they would seem to make the politics of muddling through more difficult—impossible, even. They might please ideological purists, but they seem a threat to the sort of legislation that serves the common good by putting coalitions together piece by piece for the sake of something incremental, concrete, and beneficial. This, the argument goes, is the problem with a partisanship of memory and patience that seeks to serve large goals.

Against this argument, it needs to be remembered that distinctive parties and strong partisanship never obviate the need for a politics of muddling through. The so-called ideologies of American politics today—liberalism and conservatism—are not like the ideologies that characterized the nineteenth and twentieth centuries. They are general and vague labels, not comprehensive systems of thought, and they contain many elements in tension with each other. Conservatives who want to balance the budget and conservatives who want to increase spending on the military will find that their priorities clash and that there is no rank order of conservative values that can arbitrate the clash. They will have to muddle through, adapting their goals to the circumstances at hand. Liberals who want stronger environmental protections and liberals who want to combat unemployment may also find that their priorities clash; and again, there is no philosophical liberal system of thought that can decide which goal should take priority. Ideologically distinct parties cannot avoid a policy making of muddling through.

But more to the point, while muddling through can be a virtue of democratic decision making, insisting that it be the *only* way to make policy puts democracy under unnecessarily severe limitations. It rules out the possibility that some profound problems may require a comprehensive and sustained approach if they are to be effectively addressed. Sometimes persistent problems require big solutions. The mid-twentieth-century parties that were so good at muddling through, for example, were very bad at addressing the problem of racial segregation and discrimination. There was no way to address that problem without offending a powerful constituency, and the politics of muddling through, which gives every powerful interest's "watchdog" a chance to amend, derail, or veto policy, could only reproduce an unjust status quo.

Political scientists of the mid-twentieth century wanted more "responsible" parties in part to make the government capable of addressing large problems with comprehensive policies that would be sustained across a long time. As E. E. Schattschneider said in 1948, "It is now necessary for the government to act as it has never acted before. The essence of the governmental crisis consists of a deficiency of the power to create, adopt, and execute,

a comprehensive plan of action in advance of a predictable catas-
trophe in time to prevent and minimize it."[44] The case for more
responsible parties reflected the earlier Wilsonian hope for parties that could collect the separated powers of the U.S. Constitution and "give some coherence to the action of political
forces."[45] The responsible party ideal points back to the origins
of modern partisanship, where (on Harvey Mansfield's account)
party was intended by Burke to qualify the belief that politics
could be renovated in accordance with reason. In that view of
modern partisanship, the progressive party carries the rationalist aspiration, and the conservative party tempers the rationalist
project by denuding it of its pretension to truth. The responsible party project would seem like an effort to make American
constitutional government more accommodating of progressive
rationalism and the programmatic politics it invites. In a similar
vein, perhaps this defense of partisanship, with its emphasis on
discovering what is possible in politics and pursing long-term
"plans," might too be said to reflect the progressive rationalism
that made "responsible parties" seem so essential sixty years ago.

But this prism exaggerates the alliance between the ideal party
system of responsible party advocates and the defense of partisanship advanced here. The idea is not that politics requires partisan patience because this enables the long-term policies that
social science (or reason) would endorse. Social science (of course)
cannot tell us "what is to be done," nor can it give politics detailed recipes for solving social problems. Party is simply a way for
people to use government to serve a popular purpose. A party
may have to try a bit of this and a bit of that to serve a popular
goal: leaders experiment and explore, sometimes succeeding
and sometimes not. The point is merely that these efforts take
time, and that without partisan patience they are doomed from
the start. More to the point, they cannot be ventured at all, and
government can no longer be an instrument of popular purpose.

The goals of containing communism, reducing poverty, extending health care coverage to the uninsured, or controlling immigration required (as many continue to require) experimentation with different policies. We cannot know with perfect certainty how well any of these is likely to work in advance of trying them, and trying any of them requires partisan patience. Partisanship and patience are necessary not only to progressive programs founded in reason (or social science). They are necessary to any government that tries to serve a popular purpose. The alternative to partisan patience is not conservative "muddle-through" prudence, nor is it the laissez-faire utopia of libertarian dreams. It is political disempowerment.

6

THE PRIMARY PROBLEM

In the 2008 presidential primary election in Texas, voters at one polling place routinely requested *both* the Republican and Democratic ballots.[1] Many wanted to cast a ballot for both Senator John McCain in the Republican primary and Senator Hillary Clinton in the Democratic primary. Some were indignant and many were confused when told that they had to choose only one party's ballot. These voters had put some thought into their choice, and they had decided to endorse a certain kind of general election—for instance, some decided they wanted a general election between McCain and Clinton. They were at a loss as to why they were prohibited from giving practical force to their choice through the vote. In a sense, they simply misunderstood what they were doing by voting in a primary election: they were participating in politics *as partisans,* by contributing to the "basic function of a party"—selecting its candidate for office. They simply did not see themselves acting as partisans in a partisan decision.

From the start, primary elections have been shot through with confusion: on one hand, they are informed by the logic of party and partisanship—their original function, after all, was to decide which person will represent a party in a general election. On the other hand, they reflect the logic of democracy—they were intended to amplify the power of the people and to diminish the power of party elites. These two logics can only be reconciled if the people are partisan; only then can primary elections succeed at both engaging the broad electorate and at nominating a party's candidate with integrity. Primary elections have never succeeded at this act of reconciliation.

Today the tendency is to emphasize the democratic logic of primary elections at the expense of the partisan logic. The most prominent reform of primary elections—the "top-two primary," which California and Washington State use—attempts to almost completely negate the partisan aspect of primaries. The reform addresses the worry that partisan primaries are selecting for extremists. As we will see, turnout in partisan primaries is very low. This, when combined with expertly gerrymandered districts and the tendency of like-minded people to cluster, produces primary electorates that seem to be dominated by ideological purists. In turn, according to this view, purists select extreme candidates as the party nominees to the general election. The general electorate, though it seems more moderate, or at any rate less political, has no choice but to choose an extremist from one party or another. Even officials inclined toward moderate positions must guard against the threat of "getting primaried," it seems.

Yet the "blanket primary" reform is unlikely to succeed. Blanket primaries need parties to help voters make sense of what they are choosing when they vote. But at the same time, blanket primaries strip primary elections of their partisan dimension almost completely. Blanket primaries need parties to have meaning for voters—but they simultaneously act to drain parties and partisanship of their meaning. When partisans cannot choose who represents their party, they lose control of what the party stands for. When parties lose their meaning, it becomes even more difficult for citizens who pay only occasional attention to politics to navigate elections. Ironically, the "closed party primary," which inculcates a partisan identity, might be more successful at moderating American politics by inviting moderates into the party fold.

No institutional fix will likely purify politics of partisanship and ideology, leaving only a pragmatic commonsense residue. The current fashion for nonpartisan primaries and redistricting reform will also likely fail to purge politics of partisanship and ideology. The problem is not that our politics are too partisan, but that so many find the most prominent expressions of partisanship alienating and mystifying. The solution lies not in trying to remove the partisan influence, but in elevating and moderating its expression. That means inviting more citizens, especially those currently drawn to an independent stance, to become partisans. Primaries might contribute to this—this was part of what they were originally meant to accomplish.

The Most Radical of Party Reforms

The first law mandating direct nomination of partisan candidates for office in "primary" elections was passed in Minnesota in 1899. In what one contemporary student of the reform calls a recklessly expedited process of experimentation and adoption, nearly every state had adopted primaries for at least some offices by 1915.[2] (The use of primaries was amplified at the presidential level in a subsequent wave of reform between 1968 and 1972, when, following a disastrous party convention in Chicago in 1968, the Democratic Party made primary elections the dominant mode of selecting convention delegates.)[3] "Foremost among the benefits reformers associated with the direct primary," says one historian, "was the prospect that it would bring out more voters."[4] More specifically, reformers hoped that by replacing the caucus-convention system of nominations with a direct invitation to the broad public to participate directly in party nominations, the power of political insiders and party machines would be undercut. As the Progressive Wisconsin governor Robert Marion La Follette stated in 1901, "If between a citizen and the official there is a complicated system of caucuses and conventions, by the easy manipulation of which the selection of candidates is controlled by some other agency or power, the official will so render his services as to have the approval of such an agency or power. The overwhelming demand of the people of this state . . . is that such intervening power and authority, and the complicated system which sustains it, shall be torn down and cast aside."[5]

While primary elections were meant to dethrone cliques, bosses, and machines, they were not exclusively an antipartisan reform. The pace and extent of their adoption in the early twentieth century were only possible because partisans—both partisan legislators and party officials—also supported them. For the two major parties, primary elections offered a solution to problems spawned by an earlier reform, the Australian ballot, where voters cast their votes in secret on ballots that are printed by the state. The Australian ballot, itself a solution to ballot-box stuffing (possible when the parties printed their own ballots), voter fraud, and voter intimidation, led to a number of disputes about who the state should recognize as the true nominee of a given party. Older, more informal modes of settling intraparty disputes became unworkable as the scale of American political life increased. As a result the parties themselves needed to reform their nomination process. And the reform they embraced was the same one favored by less partisan progressives. Primary elections stood out "as an answer to long-term problems associated with candidate selection" not only for their simplicity, but also because they reflected the deep popular view that "if parties were at the center of political life, they should be highly participatory."[6] The consequence was, as Austin Ranney puts it, "the most radical of all the party reforms in the whole course of American history."[7]

It was also perhaps the most confused. Antipartisans supported the reform because they expected it to diminish the role of parties and partisanship. Partisans supported the reform because they expected it would better equip the parties to nominate candidates. Such a coalition could successfully enact the reform—but it could not make it function successfully. Because partisans and antipartisans had diametrically opposed intentions, success would prove elusive, and successive generations of Americans would attempt to reform the reform over and over again. This confusion is perhaps why so few democracies in the world today routinely invite the general citizenry to participate directly in party nominations.[8]

Disappointment with this radical reform set in almost immediately.[9] Primary elections failed to engage the citizenry, turnout levels were disappointing, and, contrary to their hopes, progressive reformers thought primaries did not elicit candidates of the "best sort." Moreover, primary campaigns proved very expensive, cementing the place of money in politics. For their part, partisans were frustrated by the loss of control over nominations—often with the result that the party would be less competitive in the general election. Primary elections brought to the fore a fundamental question: Who counts as a partisan—and, as a consequence, who should get to vote in primaries? There remains, to this day, no settled answer to the question.

The Lost Logic of the Closed Party Primary

When primaries were first adopted in the United States, most thought that only party members should choose a party's nominees. In the first primary in Minnesota, some thought voters should be asked to swear an oath that they were supporters of the party.[10] Others thought the test should be whether a voter had cast a straight party ballot in the previous general election.[11] But this, like most tests of party loyalty, was unenforceable in practice (in this case, as a consequence of the earlier reform, the secret ballots). Some, like John R. Commons, thought that anyone who merely stated an intention to vote for the party in the general election should be allowed to vote in the primary. Others took an even more open stance, holding that anyone attracted to a particular candidate or the issues on which the candidate stood should be allowed to vote in that candidate's primary. The disagreement about whether primaries should be closed or open reflected the strain between the two intentions for primary elections: Should they engage the whole citizenry as fully as possible? Or should they engage only fellow partisans in choosing the party's nominee?

The tension between these two purposes has given rise to many variations of primary election. At least six are used today in U.S. elections. Moving from more partisan to less, they are the following: in a classic *closed primary,* only registered members of the party may participate in the party's primary election; in a *semi-closed primary,* voters registered as independents may participate alongside registered voters; in an *open primary,* any voter may participate in any party's primary; in a *blanket primary,* all voters get the same ballot (with every party's candidates listed), and the top vote-getter from each party moves on to the general election; in a *top-two primary,* all voters get the same ballot, on which all candidates are listed, and the top two vote-getters (even if they are from the same party) move on to the general election.[12] The closed primary encourages partisanship among citizens by making partisanship a prerequisite of participation. The semi-closed primary creates an incentive to register as an independent, since independents get more choice on Election Day. The open primary conveys an ambivalent message to voters: on one hand, open primaries suggest that party does not matter; on the other hand, they restrict voters to participating in one party's primary (hence the confusion in the Texas primary of 2008). The blanket primary and the top-two primary have a different rationale, one born in suspicion about party and partisanship. Since primaries were initiated in the early twentieth century, the tendency has been to move from closed primaries to open ones, and more recently from open primaries to nonpartisan blanket primaries. The participatory goal of popular primaries has progressively overwhelmed the partisan function of the institution. Something important is lost in this development—while nothing is gained. To understand the loss requires grasping the lost logic of the classic closed primary.

When they were first adopted, primary elections had the consequence of making the state responsible for determining which citizens were partisans. Most states did this by adopting a closed primary, restricted to citizens who had, prior to the election, officially registered themselves with the state as partisans. There were, at the beginning, some exceptions: six states had open primaries, and California allowed candidates to list themselves under rival party labels simultaneously. A couple of states pioneered the use of blanket primaries, where voters may cross over and vote for candidates of different party labels for different offices. But most—as of 1915, the date by which most states had adopted primary elections—opted for closed primaries.[13] The logic of the closed primary persisted, and even the McGovern-Frasier Commission (the committee of the Democratic Party that put primaries at the center of the presidential nominating process and instituted rules to ensure that women and minorities were aptly represented among those delegated to the national convention) insisted in 1972 that Democratic presidential primaries be closed to everyone except registered Democrats.[14]

Parties want to be able to exercise some restrictions on who may participate in their primaries in order to cultivate party loyalty and to restrict tactical voting, where people vote for the weakest candidate to undercut a party's ability to compete in the general election. This practice—called raiding—arises when voters hostile to a party participate in its primary. The prospect of malicious voting was seen from the start: an academic observer at the turn of the twentieth century held that "no opponent of a party has a right to participate in its Primary. The law should protect a party from its enemies."[15] The pro-primary and pro-reform magazine *Outlook* stated in 1903, "A primary is not an election, and it is not unfair to ask the man who wishes to take part in a party nomination to accept, for the time being at least, party membership." In this, the confusion at the heart of popular primaries is clear. Party primaries are obviously elections, run and regulated by the state. Their only odd feature is that they do not select someone to fill a public office, but rather choose the party's nominee who will in turn have a place on the official ballot.

In practice, raiding is not much of a threat because it is difficult to motivate many thousands of voters to raid the opposing party's primary. But there remains a sense that there is something wrong with it. On the eve of the February 2012 Republican primary in Michigan, former Pennsylvania senator Rick Santorum paid for automated telephone calls to registered Democrats, urging them to vote for him against Mitt Romney (implicitly acknowledging that Democrats would view Santorum as the weaker general election opponent for President Obama). Romney castigated the tactic as "outrageous and disgusting" and "a terrible dirty trick."[16] As Romney explained, "Look, we don't want Democrats deciding who our nominee is going to be, we want Republicans deciding who our nominee is going to be." But it was soon revealed that Romney himself raided

Democratic primaries when it was convenient. In the Massachusetts Democratic primary of 1992, Romney voted for Democratic candidate Paul Tsongas. Romney was registered as an independent at the time, but his sympathies were plainly oriented to the Republican Party. As he explained at the time, "When there was no real contest in the Republican primary, I'd vote in the Democrat primary, vote for the person I thought would be the weakest opponent for the Republican." Perhaps his sense that Santorum was pulling a dirty trick was based in his sense that Santorum, as a Republican, should not want the Republican Party to nominate the weaker candidate—at least Romney could say that he always voted in what he took to be the best interest of the Republican Party, something that Santorum in his appeal to Democrats could not quite avow. But Romney's objection was not this nuanced. Rather, he objected to the very thing he had done: partisans participating in the primary election of the party they opposed, with the intention of favoring the weaker candidate.

Yet because the logic of the closed party primary has largely lost its hold, the exact problem with raiding a rival party's primary is hard to locate. It is not necessarily an act of disloyalty, since the whole point of raiding is to advantage one's own party. It may, however, be an act of bad citizenship—since if the raiding is effective, it raises the probability that the candidate one regards as worst will in fact get elected. This points to the more serious problem: the lack of integrity. By participating in the nomination process of a party one does not wish to see win in the end, one acts as if one is a partisan of a particular party when it is not in fact the case—akin to someone acting as if he is your friend (in order, say, to make a sale or do a deal) when in fact he is out to defeat you. Acting without integrity is on its own less than admirable. Broadcast on a large scale, it would denude partisan associations of their meaning.

If partisans cannot control the candidates they nominate, they cannot control what the party stands for. In the 1991 Louisiana governor's race, for instance, David Duke, a former grand wizard of the Ku Klux Klan, managed to become the Republican candidate for governor; he could do this only because Louisiana's nonpartisan runoff primary system deprives parties of controlling nominations. The Republican Party disavowed him. Most notably, the Republican president at the time, George H. W. Bush, said, "When someone has a long record, an ugly record of racism and bigotry, that record cannot be erased by the glib rhetoric of a political campaign. So I believe David Duke is an insincere charlatan."[17] The incident reveals how difficult it is for parties to control what they stand for when anyone can carry the party label into an election. As Justice Antonin Scalia, in opposing the constitutionality of blanket primaries, wrote, "A single election in which a party nominee is selected by non-party members could be enough to destroy the party."[18]

Banding together to promote the selection of candidates who share a group's philosophy and goals is the most elemental action in representative democracy.[19] If the group that bands together cannot decide who gets to run in its name, this basic activity is undermined. Those who care for a party should decide which candidates best express the ideals and policies that define the party: this is the logic of a closed primary. In practice, even "closed" primaries have never been very closed. When anyone is a partisan simply by saying so—as in the United States—there is no effective way to enforce a voter's loyalty to party. Still, in the classic closed primary, one has to be registered as a partisan with the state (often for a certain period before the election) in order to vote. Even in states with modified open primaries (where independents, but not rival partisans, could vote in a party's primary) one's status as an "independent" was sometimes automatically changed to the party in which one voted. One could not both vote in a party's primary and remain independent; it took a special trip to City Hall to reregister as an independent. In this way, closed party primaries encouraged partisan identifications. Anyone with an interest to care about who got the nomination would end up registered as a "member" of the party.

Increasingly, the closed primary no longer makes much sense to citizens. Many believe that closed primaries seem to turn candidate selection over to the most uncompromising partisans, who in turn elect uncompromising officials. Although it is still widely used, the days of the classic closed primary are likely numbered, and the nonpartisan blanket primary—a version of what was once a curiosity of Louisiana politics, the so-called jungle primary, as if to denote its wild character—is among the most compelling reforms of the day.[20] Yet the fashion for open primaries, and for abolishing *partisan* primaries altogether, is likely based on a collection of mistakes—mistakes about the character of primary election voters in relation to the larger electorate, mistakes about the effect of nonpartisan primaries on polarization, and mistakes about the place of partisanship in electoral democracy. The reason that closed primaries have lost their persuasive force, and the reason that they are blamed for producing uncompromising and extremist candidates, is that so few voters turn out to vote in primary elections.

Voters Decline the Invitation

What if we had an election and no one came? This is nearly the fate of many primary elections, especially those in which only local and statewide offices are at stake. But even more engaging elections fail to entice voters to the polls. The signal failure of popular primaries is that so few citizens bother to vote in them.

The 2008 presidential primaries are a pointed example of this. These were as engaging as primary elections can possibly be: with neither party fielding an incumbent, both major parties had intense struggles for the nomination among candidates, and each party fielded candidates with national reputations. Media coverage was intense, and the outcome was uncertain for weeks and months. The primary contest persisted in the Democratic Party through to the last primaries on June 3, and in the Republican contest through March 5 (when eleven of forty Republican primaries remained). The 2008 presidential primary represents the upper boundary of what can be expected for popular engagement in primary campaigns. Indeed, the primary turnout was record-setting. Seven of thirty-seven states holding primaries in both parties had record turnouts in both party primaries. Republicans set records in eleven states, and Democrats in twenty-six.[21] Yet overall turnout averaged across all presidential primaries was only 30.3 percent of eligible voters; the historical record is only slightly higher—30.9 percent, set in 1972.

In 2012 only the Republican Party had a contested field in the presidential race: Mitt Romney, who had been running since 2008, faced real challenges by Newt Gingrich and Rick Santorum. Forty-four percent of eligible voters turned out in the New Hampshire primary, while 41 percent turned out in Florida. These numbers are off the charts for primary turnout. In the Michigan primary, where Democrats and independents could vote in the Republican contest and where all three candidates competed intensely, only 17 percent of eligible voters went to the polls. In general, since 1972, presidential primaries have attracted between 20 and 30 percent of eligible voters.

Primaries always attract fewer voters than general elections (overall participation in presidential primaries ranges between 25.7 percent and 43.7 percent lower than the general election turnout of the same year).[22] Turnout drops precipitously when we look beyond national political contests to statewide political contests. In 2008, twenty-one states had either (or both) gubernatorial and senatorial primaries on a different day than their presidential primaries. The overall turnout in these primary elections was 14 percent—a record low since 1972 (nine of the twenty-one states in this category had record low turnouts).[23] In some years, primary turnout only reaches the single digits— such as 2004, when Democratic primary turnout in Connecticut and New York was 5.4 percent.[24] In the congressional midterm primaries of 1994—an election of real importance, when the Democrats lost control of the House for the first time in forty years—Democratic turnout was estimated at 30 percent and Republican turnout at 34 percent.[25] Vast numbers of American citizens simply tune out primary campaigns and primary elections.

To care about a primary election within a party, one needs to care a great deal about small differences. It is often difficult to discern what differentiates various Democrats, for instance (especially when all the candidates are appealing to the same relatively small constituency). Refined and exact convictions amplify differences that seem small from a distance. People of a compromising temperament or with only general, rough-and-ready ideas about government are less likely to arrive at a settled preference about rival candidates within a party, even if they are paying attention. For this reason, classic closed primaries turn the party selection over not merely to partisans, but to the most committed partisans—people with the ability to attribute vital importance to small differences. In a sense, there is nothing wrong with this. The partisans—the citizens who stay keenly informed, whose judgment is nuanced enough to discriminate across small differences, who are invested and engaged in the party—should dominate the selection of party nominees. But these are the

ones getting the blame for the polarization of American politics. They likely do not deserve the blame, but the fact that
primary elections elicit such low turnout has deprived partisan
primaries of their legitimacy. Primaries seem to be one of the
prime causes of the "disconnect" between the people, who are
pragmatic and commonsensical, and their representatives, who
are hyperideological.[26]

Reforming the Reform

Today's charge against party primaries—that primary voters
would enthusiastically nominate candidates unpalatable to the
general electorate—goes back to the earliest experiments with
primaries.[27] When primaries (in which the broad population can
participate) displaced caucuses (in which party elites dominated),
the judgment of pragmatic party officials was replaced with the
decision of ideologically committed purists and amateurs, whose
main interest is in serving the issue, the cause, the principle, or
the movement. The professional politicos who dominated caucuses cared about pleasing the general electorate because they
wanted to compete and to win. Partisans who dominate primaries (the charge goes) care more about doing what they take to
be right than they care about winning—after all, their jobs do
not depend on victory.[28]

When purists dominate the primary electorate, the general
electorate may face a choice between a Republican who is far
too conservative for their tastes and a Democrat who is far too
liberal. In safe districts, primary voters can indulge their preference for the most committed, doctrinaire, and uncompromising true believers. But even in competitive districts, general
election voters often have to choose between extremists. As
David Kennedy has shown, voters in swing districts who are
frustrated because their representative is too extreme often have

no choice but to replace the representative with another ex-tremist from the other party. "One might get whiplash," he re-ports, "from the wild ideological swings."[29] As Morris Fiorina writes, "The bulk of the American citizenry is somewhat in the position of the unfortunate citizens of some third-world coun-tries who try to stay out of the crossfire while Maoist guerrillas and right-wing death squads shoot at each other."[30]

It seems that primary electorates *must* be unrepresentative, and that their unrepresentative character must be partly respon-sible for the polarization and dysfunction of American politics. The simple fact that primary electorates are so small suggests that primary elections must select for a different category of voters—those who are hyperattuned and keenly invested in pol-itics, and who have the resources to show up to vote at various times of the year. In fact, the evidence that primary electorates are unrepresentative in this way is very weak. We do not know as much about the primary electorate as we should, and the primary electorate itself varies depending on whether it is a pres-idential primary (which gets massive media attention) or a con-gressional or local election primary. Still, some evidence suggests that primary election voters are not very different in their pref-erences from general election voters.[31] It is perhaps a mistake to believe that primary elections are the cause of intensified partisanship.

Still, the partisan primary is losing its legitimacy—not only the closed primary, but also the open primary, indeed any pri-mary that has as its function nominating a party's candidate to the general election. Low turnout creates a legitimation prob-lem, even if those who turn out are not that different in key re-spects from those who do not. Primary elections have simply not succeeded at engaging the broad electorate—even if they might function very effectively at recruiting ordinary partisans to participate in the nomination process, they have failed in their democratic mission. As a result, reforming the reform—reshaping primaries again, to make them irresistible—has become increasingly irresistible.

The reform of the reform aims to succeed at what primary elections have tried to do from the start: get ordinary citizens to participate in the selection of nominees. The more specific aim is to moderate American politics by selecting for less ideological nominees. The current impulse is to strip primaries of their partisan aspect by forcing candidates in primaries to face a broader sample of the electorate. Voters in California attempted to do this in 1998, when they passed a referendum to institute a blanket primary. Any voter could vote for any candidate from any party in every office. The top vote-getter within each party would advance to the general election. Unlike the classic closed primary, a blanket primary is not restricted to voters who register with a party; a voter might vote for the Republican candidate for Congress and the Democratic candidate for governor, and so on. The task of the primary voter in this case is not to participate in a party contest, and thus to think like a narrow partisan; it is to pick out the best person from among all parties for each job.

The California reform was halted by the U.S. Supreme Court, which in *California Democratic Party v. Jones* struck down the blanket primary in 2000.[32] In the Court's view, California's blanket primary violated the right of association by canceling a party's ability to nominate candidates. The Court was motivated by the following kind of scenario: Consider an election where two Green Party candidates run against each other in the primary (and, of course, against a bevy of candidates from competing parties). The losing Green Party candidate might get more votes from registered Green Party members than the winning one—in which case the Green Party loses the ability to nominate its members and has been hijacked by voters who have no affiliation with the party.

In a state where one party dominates, as the Democratic Party does in Massachusetts or the Republican Party does in Utah, it is quite possible that voters who sympathize with the minority party will vote for a candidate of the dominant party in order to have more influence. If the blanket primary were used in a state like Massachusetts, and two liberals were to split the vote of Democratic partisans, it would be possible for independents and Republican voters to vote for a more conservative third Democrat, even if this third candidate gets fewer votes from Democratic partisans than the two liberal candidates. Voters who are registered Democrats would lose control over which candidate gets to run in the general election as a Democrat. The Court worried that in a case like this the Democratic Party would no longer be associated with the goals, policies, and principles that voters who identify with the party would give it. Voters, in the Court's view, lose the freedom to associate as partisans.

The problem the Court identified is not restricted to the blanket primary adopted by California voters in 1998. It also afflicts fully open primaries, where any voter can vote in any party's primary—and the Supreme Court did not explicitly argue that these primaries also violate the right of free association. In open or semi-open primaries, independents and partisans of the opposing party might decide on a party's nominee in spite of a rival candidate receiving more support from registered partisans. Were that to happen, the party would lose control over its nominations, just as in the examples from California's 1998 blanket primary. The Supreme Court's decision followed the logic of the classic closed primary: only in a closed primary can a party be guaranteed control of its nominations. Only a closed primary assured the capacity of people to band together to promote candidates who share their philosophy and goals. Implicitly, the Supreme Court in 2000 argued that freedom of association requires closed primaries. The Court did not seem to notice that the logic of closed primaries had been lost for a long while.

Primaries without Partisans

Some parties in some states still use the closed primary—but few look to it as the institutional solution to the problem of partisanship in American politics. It rather is seen as part of the problem. The solution, by contrast, seems to many to lie in obliterating the partisan aspect of primary elections. What would a primary election look like without parties? The answer is the *nonpartisan blanket primary*. Designed to get around the Supreme Court's objection to the blanket primary, it is the reform presently in use in California and Washington State.

The Supreme Court's problem with the blanket primary, as we noted, is that it interferes with rights of association—it restricts the ability of Democratic partisans, for instance, to decide who will be the Democratic Party nominee. The way around this is to design a blanket primary without any partisan function at all—a primary that does not decide on which person will represent this or that party in the general election, but rather simply decides which two names will appear on the general election ballot. In the nonpartisan blanket primary, any voter can vote for any candidate from any party, and the top two vote-getters proceed to the general election. It is not really a partisan primary at all, just a series of elections in which the top two candidates in the first election proceed to the second. The top two candidates might both be Republicans, for instance—in which case the general election is a race between only two Republicans.

Candidates in the nonpartisan blanket primary are not vying
for the party nomination. In Washington State (where there is
no voter party registration), candidates do not have a formal party
affiliation. Rather, each candidate has sixteen characters following his or her name in which to state a party "preference." Candidates may state whatever party preference they choose, regardless of whether such a party actually exists or whether the
party itself wishes to be represented by the candidate in question. If the comedian Stephen Colbert wished to run in Washington State, he could list "Funny" after his name, or "Republican" or "Dem & Republican" if he wished to affiliate with
both parties simultaneously (as Colbert tried but was forbidden
from doing in the South Carolina primary).

This design survived a Supreme Court challenge in 2008 in
Washington State Grange v. Washington State Republican Party.
In substance, the nonpartisan blanket primary has the potential
to obliterate parties' abilities to define themselves, which was
why the Supreme Court found the blanket primary unconstitutional in the first place. The party organization has no say in the
matter over who affiliates with the party. But technically, the
nonpartisan blanket primary preserves the parties' right of association. By eradicating the very possibility of a party's official
nominee showing up on a general election ballot, technically
the nonpartisan primary does not interfere with a party's right
of free association.[33] Parties may continue to nominate candidates, but these nominations have no consequence for the ballot, since the primary election is just a mode of winnowing a
large field to the top two candidates, who may affiliate themselves with the same party if they please. Party organizations
may nominate candidates if they would like—they are just not
guaranteed a place on the final ballot for their nominees. The
general election ballot simply presents the top two vote-getters,

whether these are from each major party, one major party, or no party.

The problem that the Court identified with the blanket primary remained in intensified form: parties lost control of determining who could run under their names. Yet because the primary does not function to decide who shall be the parties' nominees, technically the nonpartisan blanket primary does not violate the right of association. The reasoning is that parties have no right to include their nominees on the general election ballot (but if the ballot does include party nominees, then rights of free association apply). This reasoning convinced a seven-person majority on the Court to approve of the new nonpartisan blanket primary. In the wake of that approval, California too passed a similar plan in 2010, and other states are now flirting with the idea. The reform is attractive because party primaries *seem* to be causing the polarization that renders American politics dysfunctional. The nonpartisan blanket primary promises to moderate American politics: when everyone in the primary can vote for anyone who is running, moderate candidates have a chance (even if they might not fare well in a primary exclusively dominated by the party faithful). This would seem to be especially the case in districts dominated by one party. Here, the expectation is that the general election will include two candidates of the same (dominant) party. Instead of extreme partisans in the primary defeating moderates, resulting in two rival extremists running in the general election, two candidates will go to the general election, one of whom is moderate enough to attract crossover votes from independents and partisans of other parties.

That is, at any rate, the expectation. Given that the logic of the closed party primary has lost its hold, and given that primaries are getting much of the blame for the polarization of

American politics, this expectation is enough to make the non-partisan blanket primary the fashionable reform of the day. The early evidence, however, suggests that the nonpartisan blanket primary may not succeed at moderating American politics. On the contrary, some studies suggest that the more open the primary election is (to those who have not registered with the party), the more ideological the candidates.[34] This is a surprising—and disappointing—finding, though the research is still preliminary. There is little reason in theory to expect that a more open system will select for *more* ideological candidates. Perhaps there are simply not that many "committed, politically active Independents" who participate in primaries of any sort.[35] More likely, voters have a difficult time figuring out which candidates are "extreme" and which are "moderate." In one experiment, voters "largely failed to discern ideological differences between extreme and moderate candidates of the same party."[36] To achieve its promise, the nonpartisan primary places an enormous burden on ordinary citizens. Primary elections as a mode of party nominations already put a heavy burden on citizens: citizens have to know when primary elections occur, they need to be knowledgeable about what is often a dizzying array of candidates, and they need to place a premium on what are often small differences if they are to cast a meaningful ballot. Add to this burden the task of sorting out the ideological positions and tendencies of a vast collection of candidates, and we have a "reform" that simply asks too much to be effective.

Because parties have lost their gatekeeping functions, voters have little to guide them in sorting through a list of candidates in a nonpartisan blanket primary. The party label in the Washington State primary, for instance, means almost nothing—every candidate has sixteen letters and can list whatever label he or she pleases. Any candidate may express a preference for any party. Yet the number of candidates in the first round of balloting will likely be too large for voters to make any sense of it without party labels. In the June 2012 California nonpartisan primary, five people ran against Nancy Pelosi in the Twelfth Congressional District; twenty-four people ran against Diane Feinstein in the U.S. Senate race. Both Pelosi and Feinstein are established incumbents with formidable support (Feinstein received 49 percent of the vote in the twenty-five-way contest, and Pelosi received 75 percent in her six-way race). Imagine the same race without the names of familiar incumbents like Pelosi or Feinstein: even the most public-spirited voters would not be able to figure out much of anything about the candidates.

The "nonpartisan primary" is not in fact nonpartisan (which is why it is more accurate to call it the top-two primary). It is partisan in a new way. If the top-two primary is not to devolve into an endless jumble of names, party labels will need to appear on the ballot—and voters will need to be able to attribute some meaning to those labels. In the closed party primary, a small cadre of voters could define what the parties stood for: the kinds of candidates they selected for the general election and the winners of the general election who went on to serve in office would together define the party for the larger electorate. Often party primaries were an occasion for partisans to fight among themselves over what their party would stand for. Should the party move more to the center? Should its nominee stand for its principles uncompromisingly? What are the basic commitments nearly everyone in the party shares? These questions were hammered out in the course of a primary contest. The top-two primary does not provide any occasion for partisans to work out answers to these questions, and as a result threatens to drain parties of their meaning. At the same time, the top-two primary desperately needs party labels to mean something, for without them most voters would be at a loss.

As we have seen, parties are often referred to as brands, but brands are generally owned by a corporation that defines them and takes care to preserve the value of what they convey. No one owns parties—except partisans, and in the American context, anyone can be a partisan. Parties, especially in the American context, have no dues and no duties. They are more like labels than brands. Labels, by contrast, are anyone's possession, and no group takes care to preserve (or to change) their meaning. For the top-two primary to work, ordinary partisans will need to be able to supply some meaning to these labels. Defining these terms, like defining the related terms *liberal* and *conservative,* has never been easy. Partisanship is less a concrete affiliation with a specific group and more an opinion or an evaluation. The old methods of selection required time; the new ones require time *and* thought. Reforms like the blanket primary ask more, therefore, from civic education than traditional methods of selection like the party caucus or the classic closed primary. If party labels are going to carry any meaning to voters, civic education will need to engage the principles and goals that make sense of the parties. The nonpartisan primary is not a way around party—it needs parties, in a new and more generalized way.

A Civic Education for Partisanship

The closed primary would be a better "reform" in this respect than the nonpartisan primary. The open primary and the nonpartisan primary fail to do away with partisanship—they merely confuse matters by making it look like a dispensable feature of democratic politics when it is just the opposite. As a consequence, primary elections often fail to attune voters to parties and partisanship. Yet without an understanding of parties and partisanship, it is difficult to orient oneself in the political world or to be effective as a citizen. If institutions fail to inculcate a knowledgeable orientation to parties, civic education should. Civic education is a paltry substitution for the kind of practical understanding that comes from habituation, but a civic education for partisanship might be effective—more effective than traditional civic education, which often aims to impart a command of propositional knowledge that is disconnected from action (such as the answer to "What are the five liberties guaranteed by the First Amendment?"). Partisanship is more interesting than the traditional subjects of civic education (like the "structure of government") because it involves a contest—a contest in which students might discover they have a stake.

Effective citizens have opinions. Possessing an opinion is what motivates one to vote, to stay informed, to get involved. There is a deep reluctance to engage partisanship in the civic education curriculum because opinions, it is said, cannot be taught. When they are taught, education becomes indoctrination because what is a matter of opinion is presented as a matter of knowledge. Teaching partisan things in a nonpartisan way is a delicate and, some would argue, impossible task. This is why traditional civic education focuses on the structure of government (separation of powers, federalism), governmental processes (how a bill becomes a law), and the modes of popular participation (writing letters, voting). Yet it is possible to orient students to political opinion without imparting opinion. Such an orientation would aim to convey not simply an understanding of parties, but more crucially, of the ideologies that increasingly define them: liberalism and conservatism.

Today's parties and the ideological packages they are allied with—liberalism and conservatism—are not tidy philosophies. They do not originate in authoritative manifestos or specific philosophers, as Marxism did. They are broad orientations to the social and political worlds that contain many confounding points and seemingly dissonant notes. They give rise to many and various expressions, and the most spirited political arguments often take place within the boundaries of conservatism and liberalism as between them. To engage liberalism and conservatism too directly in a civic education ("liberalism consists in the following three propositions") would impose a false precision on what are loose orientations and would also desiccate them, distorting how they give opinions force. Rather than make liberalism and conservatism the direct subject of civic education, it would be more appropriate and effective to engage them indirectly. As loose popular ideologies, they get their force not from abstract propositions about human nature or society, but from political experience.

Making sense of them requires that we consider our own recent political experience—not the distant events that are the subject of history, nor even the contemporary controversies that make up "current events," but rather our recent political history with a view to elemental questions like, What has the government succeeded at, and what has it failed at, in the recent past? Any account of government's successes and failures over the past fifty years will necessarily be controversial—indeed, partisan. For instance, some will point to winning the cold war as one of the indisputable successes of the past generation. The cold war reveals the capacity of the government to sustain a commitment across several generations and many administrations of both major parties. And some, mainly Republicans, will especially credit President Ronald Reagan with securing its final victory. Others, by contrast, will emphasize securing more effective equal rights for blacks and for women as one of the cardinal achievements of the past half-century. They will single out the Civil Rights Act of 1964 and the Voting Rights Act of 1965 as the legislative achievements responsible for overturning a century of entrenched racial discrimination, and will give special credit to President Lyndon Johnson for risking a durable Democratic majority to pass the legislation. Failures are just as important to understand as successes, and they include the failure of the national government since the mid-1970s to routinely balance its budget, or its failure to decisively win wars in Vietnam and Iraq. Civic knowledge includes an ability to identify the great failures of the recent past, and to say something about their cause.

The nation's successes and failures have both largely been bipartisan enterprises. In neither category do we find a simple story of one party having its way against the sustained opposition of the other. Yet the particular successes and failures one identifies, the manner in which one assigns credit and blame, and the lessons for the future that one singles out all involve a partisan dimension.

Political parties can seem to reflect nothing but the ambitions of office-seeking politicians. Yet as we have seen, their energy ultimately comes from a desire to secure (and to extend) what some regard as the great achievements of the past—against the opposition of others. They are carriers of political memory: today's Democratic Party defines itself by its commitment to Social Security—perhaps the core of the New Deal—and the collective provision of health care insurance; the Republican Party by contrast defines itself by its commitment to tax cuts, which goes back at least to Ronald Reagan and his criticism of what he regarded as the excesses of "big government" (that began with the New Deal). Parties carry what they take to be the achievements of the past into the future.

No science can provide citizens with the civic knowledge they need in a totally nonpartisan way. But by learning about the particular successes and failures of our recent past, citizens can indirectly learn about the partisanship that always divides us. They might even find themselves sympathizing with one view over the other, and becoming partisans of a sort themselves. Partisan sympathies are what illuminate the path from knowledge to action: they are what make us want to see victory for particular candidates and causes and defeat for others. In the contemporary world, most citizens do not learn by doing; they act because of what they believe. And the political world becomes compelling when one knows enough to venture an opinion.

Civic knowledge is not about storing facts disconnected from political purposes and political struggles. Ultimately, it is about holding responsible opinions. Those opinions will by definition be contestable and controversial: they will be partisan. And that is as it should be. Partisanship is not a corruption of our best civic ideals but rather a reflection of them.

7

PARTISANSHIP AT HOME:
THE LEGISLATURE

Partisanship is nowhere more at home than in the representative legislature: this is where modern partisanship was born, and where it continues to be nourished. Legislators who try to insist on independence are often forced to discover (or to reveal) their partisan commitments. Angus King, who was elected to the U.S. Senate from Maine as an independent in 2012, was able to remain an independent for just over a week. During his campaign, King said that he hoped to join with either party on an issue-by-issue basis. But after his election, and after what King called "extensive research into Senate rules and precedence," he decided to caucus with Democrats—as had been generally predicted prior to the election. "This is a place," as Senator Joseph Lieberman, another would-be independent from Connecticut said, "that is still organized by parties."[1]

So long as the legislature is organized by parties, legislators have almost no practical option to escape partisan identity. Even if they have somehow managed to run without claiming any partisan identity, legislators like King have to adopt one if they want any chance to be effective. The parties decide on committee assignments and control the legislative calendar; party leaders decide which legislation to advance or to oppose, and party whips keep the coalition together. This is not to mention the place of party support in fund-raising and organization for the next election.

Partisanship is not just a regrettable side cost of doing legislative work. Getting something done (or preventing something from getting done) in a legislature requires acting in concert. A party of one always loses. The only way to protect what has been accomplished (or to continue to oppose it) is by forming a coalition and remaining in coalition. The logic of legislative action compels legislators to be in a party.

Symbolic and consultative legislative assemblies that cannot forbid or permit, coerce or detain, tax or spend—legislatures that do not legislate—also relax the incentive for partisanship. It is when assemblies have real power, a power legitimated by the electoral connection, that the logic of party becomes all but inescapable. Even when parties are not stipulated as part of the constitutional form (as in the United States), they arise on their own. The party-in-the-legislature is the heart of modern partisanship: parties everywhere else—the party-in-the-electorate, the party-in-campaigns, the party organizations—are outgrowths of the legislative caucus.

Parties are tools legislators design to help themselves get reelected, but prior to that parties are necessary for legislators to pass legislation they care about, to secure their legislative achievements, to oppose what they disagree with, and to dilute or reverse what they want to change. Parties, which originate as a way for representatives to serve legislative goals, are also how legislative causes are made public. Legislators take their causes public by cultivating sympathies and antipathies in the larger society in order to get elected and to stay elected. Partisanship is so natural within the modern representative legislature that the only relevant question for legislators, it seems, is *how to be partisan*.

Partisan by Design: Parliamentary Partisanship

If "legislatures everywhere are partisan," some are by design more partisan than others.[2] In general, parliamentary systems are more partisan (meaning that fellow partisans vote together more often) than presidential systems because the resources by which individual legislators can be rewarded or punished are concentrated in the party leadership. This is most emphatically the case in "closed list" electoral systems, where citizens vote for parties, not persons, and where party leaders control the party lists. If an individual legislator strays from the "party line," the leadership can simply remove his or her name from the list at the next election. Since voters do not cast ballots for individual names, there is no way they can protect mavericks. Of the thirty-six democracies that have been consistently democratic for at least a twenty-year period prior to 2010, *half* used closed list proportional representation systems.[3] Most votes in such systems are matters of party discipline (where party leaders instruct legislators how to vote, in contrast to "open votes," which are sometimes also called "free votes" or "conscience votes").[4]

A similar kind of discipline pervades parliamentary democracies that use "first-past-the-post" single-member districts, such as the United Kingdom. Samuel Beer's 1968 description of party discipline in the British Parliament reflects the astonishment of an American accustomed to fragmented parties: "In the House of Commons were two bodies of freedom-loving Britons, chosen in more than six hundred constituencies and subject to influences that ran back to an electorate that was numbered in the millions. . . . Yet day after day with a Prussian discipline they trooped into the division lobbies at the signals of their Whips and in the service of the authoritative decisions of their parliamentary parties."[5] Even as later students of the British legislature showed that there is often more dissent from the backbenches of Parliament than Beer's enduring image suggests, they still show that members of Parliament "overwhelmingly vote with, not against, their parties."[6]

The beauty of this sort of partisanship—an institutional aesthetic shared perhaps only among political scientists—is seen in the way it facilitates accountability. Without party unity, voters would have a far more difficult time sorting out what their vote is endorsing or rejecting. Parties that take clear stands in campaigns, and that muster the cohesion to enact those plans when they are in power, give voters a clear and easy way to express or withhold their approval at the next election. In the absence of party unity in the legislature, voters would need to track the voting records of individual legislators. Even if that might be possible in single-member districts where voters have only one person to follow, voters would still need to connect these votes with particular laws and policies—and even if that were likely, it would remain difficult for voters as a whole to endorse or reject broad legislative goals. Citizens as a whole cannot hold the legislature as a whole accountable—unless the legislature is organized into coherent and stable groups.

The classic case for responsible party government against fragmented and undisciplined parties—the ideal that was crystallized in the work of E. E. Schattschneider and the famous 1950 report of the American Political Science Association—aims to create this sort of systemic accountability. The report reflected a view that had gained currency since Woodrow Wilson's indictment of the separation-of-powers constitution in 1880: to make government work in the modern age meant harnessing popular power and directing it toward popular causes. The unifying force of such an entity would be party. Implicit though less noticed in this ideal of the modern legislature is its view of the "good representative": one who behaves almost exactly as the party leadership directs. Such obedience is necessary for voters to hold the legislature as a whole accountable. But such obedience drains responsibility and integrity from the role of the representative—this is what puts partisanship under pressure even in the legislature, where it is most at home.

Almost no one believes that a good representative is simply an obedient party soldier. Imagine a candidate running a straightforward campaign as a party loyalist: "Vote for me—unlike my opponent, I will vote as my party leaders want me to vote; I will speak as they instruct me to speak; and I will act only as they direct me to act. Unless dire circumstances force it upon me, I will not express my convictions when they deviate from the party's. I will not deliberate or agitate or machinate. I will do exactly as I am told, today, tomorrow, and every day." Perfect party unity facilitates systemic accountability but reduces legislators to thoughtless levers in a partisan machine. Fully obedient representatives are not true legislators at all; they are merely agents of the party. The more party unity, the less it matters who is elected to fill the legislature, or whether actual people are elected at all. In principle it should not matter whether these "representatives" are actual human beings. Party leaders could instead be given weighted votes in proportion to their share of the popular vote.

Jeremy Waldron, rather against the current in contemporary political theory, has written powerfully about legislation "as a dignified mode of governance and a respectable source of law."[7] The dignity of legislation derives from the ideal of law as something impartial, impersonal, and fair—as a force that embodies the common good, and not merely the partial conceptions and particular interests of specific groups. Few terms seem more fatuous perhaps than *the common good,* which will seem to many like a meaningless invocation of self-serving officials that masks the play of special interests. The more concrete the question, the more obvious the direction that the costs and benefits of a particular policy take, the more elusive the common good. The term seems to have meaning only at the level of generality. Yet even if it cannot be given concrete content (without eliciting a partisan contest), the ideal of the common good is essential to the dignity of legislation. The common good is a point of orientation, not a laundry list of policy prescriptions. Party unity of the sort that prevails in legislatures today, especially in parliaments, dissolves this point of orientation. An individual representative's judgment about the common good is replaced by the representative's fealty to the party leadership.

This is not to say that party unity is ever perfect, even in the most partisan legislatures. The specter of dissent is always on the minds of party leaders, and if dissent is hard to locate in ordinary legislative business (hidden in the votes that are not taken), sometimes it makes itself plain, as in confidence votes. But this truth underlines the point that individual legislators only become true legislators when they allow themselves the real possibility of dissent. Only when dissent from the party leadership is a possibility does it matter that *individuals* serve in legislatures rather than mathematical formulas based on shares of the popular vote. Individual representatives only transform themselves from a loyal army of unthinking supporters into true legislators when they think and speak and act for themselves.

Perhaps this is why popular ideals of representation have never privileged party loyalty. In the American context, we often single out for special praise legislators who stand apart from parties and the majority in order to act from conscience. Even in parliamentary systems today, there is little appreciation for party unity. Across Europe, where parliamentary party unity has predominated, popular trust in parties has withered.[8] A number of countries with closed list proportional systems have created either open lists (where voters can single out individual representatives they prefer) or mixed systems that include single-member districts so that voters can identify the person who is meant to represent them.[9] The loss of attachment to parliamentary partisanship likely has a partly normative cause: the way we idealize the legislative role makes it profoundly difficult to admire the legislator who takes his or her direction from the party leadership.

Partisanship has a bad name, not only among everyday citizens but also among democratic theorists. For instance, in a powerful and subtle work that describes an ideal of the "good representative," Suzanne Dovi holds that we should evaluate representatives by more than whether they appropriately reflect the preferences of their constituents. Even more important, she argues, is the "way in which [representatives] advocate" or "advance public policies on behalf of their constituents."[10] A good representative is not one who would do whatever his constituents desired, in whatever way is most effective; on the contrary, good representatives should be constrained in their advocacy by a sense of what enhances the "fairness and legitimacy of democratic institutions."[11] The work of a good representative is not simply to win on behalf of his or her constituency; it is to win (and lose) in a way that causes constituents to have more confidence in the fairness of the democratic process of resolving conflict. Certain habits of mind and character (or virtues) contribute, in Dovi's account, to representing in a "democratic fashion."[12] These include fair-mindedness, critical trust building, and good gatekeeping. Each of these virtues, in turn, contributes to the realization of certain values that sustain democratic institutions: civic equality, self-governance, and inclusion.

Dovi's core argument is powerful: a good representative should be constrained by a commitment to democracy that comes prior to his or her commitment to constituents or causes. At the same time, it abstracts a great deal from the actual role of elected legislators.[13] Partisanship, which is the first fact of being a legislator—as Angus King discovered—recedes in her discussion to the point of invisibility.[14] Dovi's argument is open in principle to an account of legislative partisanship: since her argument sees advocacy as the characteristic activity of representatives, one might work out an understanding of how *partisan* advocacy (the characteristic activity of most elected representatives serving in legislatures) should be constrained by a prior commitment to democratic norms. Nothing in Dovi's account is inconsistent with an ethics of legislative partisanship. But the fact that her analysis pays so little explicit attention to partisanship is revealing.

An inescapable tension between institutional accountability and individual accountability marks elected legislatures. This "accountability dilemma"[15] means that the same qualities that make it possible for voters to hold the legislature as an institution collectively accountable make it more difficult for them to hold individual legislators accountable. Ethical ideals of the legislative role privilege individual accountability, and understandably: praise and blame depend on assigning responsibility to individuals for individual action. Voting for or against or even abstaining, in addition to the activities collected by what Dovi calls advocacy—explaining, justifying, disputing, organizing, inspiring, agitating, strategizing, and so on—is an individual action. There is really no such thing as a "good representative" unless we can conceive of legislators responsible for these actions as individuals, not as the puppets manipulated by party leaders.

To say by contrast that the legislator is part of a larger partisan machine is to say that the legislator as an individual undertakes no *action* at all. This kind of party discipline may facilitate voters' holding the legislature as a whole accountable. But it also means that the legislator's individual role is not the kind of thing that can be done well or badly, that the individuals in the role can neither be praised nor blamed, and that their individuality and moral responsibility have been dissolved in their party identity. What is so essential for ethical praise and blame—individual responsibility—is undermined by electoral designs that foster systemic accountability through party discipline.

The accountability dilemma is most stark in systems that make it easy for voters to reward and punish the parties controlling the legislator. Here, as in closed list proportional parliamentary systems, legislators advance their careers by advancing within the party. Through work, talent, and seniority, they might come to join the party leadership. When they do, their names come first in the party lists on the ballots. This means that if voters decide to punish their party, these leaders will be the last to go. In the worst cases, "the leaders who stand to gain the most from violating public trust and pillaging state resource stand to suffer the least electoral indignity if their party, collectively, is punished by voters."[16]

This is why much recent electoral reform has focused on creating mixed electoral systems where party lists are combined with single-member districts, so at least some legislators are directly accountable to voters. In this way, electoral accountability aligns somewhat better with the ideal of individual ethical responsibility. How accountable any individual representative is to voters will depend on additional aspects of constitutional design; it is not enough to create a direct electoral connection between representatives and voters, since some systems with single-member districts, like Britain's, give party leaders enormous power. Empirically, most legislators have to answer to party leaders or risk giving up their careers; even in a highly individualistic system like that of the United States, individual legislators can suffer greatly—in committee assignments and fund-raising, for example—by defying the party.

From an ethical point of view, it is essential to hold that legislators should be assessed as individuals. This lends, however, an unrealistic aspect to ideals of representation. From the ideal point of view, we tend to evaluate legislators as if partisanship were an option that an individual legislator might reject. Legislators might be obedient to the party leader, but this itself could be seen as a choice the legislator makes—perhaps with a view to whether the legislator views the party as the most effective instrument of the common good. But in fact, this is not how partisan legislatures work. Partisanship is not really an option that legislators choose—or insofar as it is, it is an option of last resort, since to dissent from the party leadership on a key vote is often a choice to end one's political career.

There seems an inescapable gap between the ethics of individual action and the legislative role. Unworkable ideals (such as an ideal of the good representative as someone who might reject party discipline) have their place in the world. They strengthen our resolve to resist tendencies that cannot be fully defied. But impracticality risks that ideals will be irrelevant—fit subjects for philosophic disputation, but of no matter to what people actually do. The point of every critical ideal is to inspire people to reform their practices so that they may come into closer contact with the ideal; when the gap between ideals and practice is too wide, ideals lose their critical force. Partisanship is so pervasive in legislatures that any ethical ideal of representation that discounts partisanship too severely courts irrelevance. If the very ideal of a "good representative" requires evaluating legislators solely as individuals without much consideration of their partisan obligations, then perhaps we should take the possibility of a nonpartisan legislature more seriously. The nonpartisan legislature is in fact a real possibility. It has been tried, and in an important sense it works. To see it at work, one needs to consider the very special case of the unicameral and nonpartisan Nebraska state legislature.

Nebraska and the Nonpartisan Possibility

Nebraska is the one legislature in the United States that has somehow managed to escape partisanship. Indeed, it is one of the only nonpartisan legislatures in the world. Nearly every empowered and freely elected national legislature in the world is a partisan legislature. Aside from Nebraska, most exceptions to the partisan rule consist of tiny island states with populations under 10,000, such as St. Helena in the South Atlantic or Tuvalu in the Pacific. Some states have experimented with nonpartisan legislatures, like Uganda in the 1980s, or Minnesota in the 1950s and 1960s—only to abandon the arrangements after a short while because parties came to exist in fact even when they were prohibited in name. The Nebraska example suggests that, contrary to the example of nearly every legislature in the world, legislatures do not in fact have to be partisan. In the end, Nebraska does not offer a compelling model. But it—and it alone—shows that partisanship in the legislature (and therefore, by extension, partisanship in modern representative government) is not in fact a necessity. The Nebraska example should open our minds to seriously consider the practicality of nonpartisanship—a possibility that without this example would seem utopian.

Nebraska progressives in the New Deal era comprehensively reformed state government, creating a unicameral nonpartisan legislature. The reform was led by George Norris, a Republican from Nebraska first elected to the U.S. House in 1903, and to the U.S. Senate in 1913. A populist-progressive, Norris saw American politics as marked by a basic divide between the elites, who co-opted government to their own private advantage, and the people—the many—who were too innocent, distracted, and powerless to defend their interests.[17] Norris, who endorsed

Robert M. La Follette (a Progressive) for the presidency in 1924, Al Smith (a Democrat) in 1928, and Franklin Roosevelt in 1932, campaigned for the one-house legislature across the state, and perhaps because of his efforts alone the measure passed in 1934. Norris bundled nonpartisanship with the unicameral legislature. Parties allow special interests to dominate politics, Norris argued. The legislature should be run akin to a business, and "the business of a legislature of a state," he said, "is in no sense partisan."[18]

Nebraska's unicameral nonpartisan legislature commands great respect in the state, even adoration. Among citizens, 76 percent believe that the legislature "does a good job of representing the diverse interests of Nebraska." An equal proportion of legislators agree.[19] Given the powerful incentives toward parties and the seeming necessity of partisanship for legislators, we might suspect that Nebraska presents merely a nonpartisan veneer. Like independents who in fact loyally support one party, so Nebraska legislators must really hold beliefs that align them with a party, identify with a party, and vote as they would if they were in a legislative party. Indeed, the partisan affiliation of candidates for the state legislature in Nebraska is obvious— nearly every candidate is registered to vote as a Democrat or a Republican. Candidates for statewide office also hold views that easily align with the Democratic-Republican and liberal-conservative split. They are partisans when they run for office.

But somehow they forget their partisanship once they arrive in the legislature. Legislative voting does not reveal persistent clusters of legislators who vote together. There is no identifiable Democratic or Republican cluster across different votes and different issues—nor any other durable cleavage, such as urban-rural. This contrasts with Kansas, a very similar state right next door, where legislators vote like partisans in a formally partisan legislature. In Nebraska, legislators "vote with each other across issues almost at random," according to one recent study. Instead of voting reliably as liberals or Democrats or urban representatives, they apparently "focus on any aspect [of legislation] that strikes them."[20] About the only issue where partisanship consistently reveals itself is redistricting—in that moment, legislators seem to remember their party loyalty. Otherwise, independent judgment rules. As one former Republican governor said, "I need 25 votes to pass legislation, and there are 29 Senators who are registered Republican, but it seems like I'm dealing with 49 independent, sometimes very independent people on a particular issue."[21] The Nebraska legislature, in short, succeeds.

The legislators are not closet partisans for whom independence is only a name. There is no de facto party leadership that controls the legislative agenda. And the people of Nebraska have a certain trust in their government. Amid the dysfunction of the national legislature, where party polarization routinely impedes the normal operation of government, the Nebraskan model would seem to offer an attractive alternative. Moreover, it gets around the problem of parliamentary legislatures, where party discipline drains the legislator's role of moral responsibility. At the very least, the Nebraskan case forces us to confront the empirical fact that partisanship, even in the legislature, is not an inevitable fact. It is possible (with a constitution that prohibits party labels on the ballot, legislative rules that allocate power very equally across members of the legislature, and a relatively small legislature—Nebraska has forty-nine senators) to design a well-functioning *nonpartisan* legislature. Perhaps Nebraska points the way other legislatures should follow.

Yet, while a nonpartisan legislature may be possible, it does not escape the accountability dilemma. On one hand, voters can assess legislators as individuals. On the other, voters cannot hold the institution accountable, because each issue generates its own unique coalition. As one former state legislator put it, instead of seeing parties that act in concert, all voters can see is "forty-nine nice people.[22] Legislators have clear commitments when they run for office, but, as Brian Schaffner and Richard Wright observe, they do not connect these "clear ideological preferences on the issues to the bills that they vote on in the legislature. Indeed," the authors say, "it is difficult to imagine how voters could achieve even general policy direction when conflict patterns in the legislature are unstable and unstructured."[23]

A defender of the nonpartisan legislature might claim that this is the point: the task of politics is not to chart a "general policy direction" from a range of highly contestable alternatives. The business of government is not essentially partisan, they might hold. Government, in this view, should be conducted "more like a business," as the founders of the Nebraska legislative system said—focused on solving concrete problems at hand rather than implementing comprehensive (and controversial) plans. In the nonpartisan legislature, various issues and policies cannot easily be collected under a common umbrella or linked as parts of a larger program, because the legislative coalitions that come together for one bill cannot be relied on to reappear for another bill.

This is exactly how George Norris, the founder of the Nebraskan nonpartisan system, wanted it. In his view, state politics was mainly about problem solving, and was not essentially controversial. Politics did not give rise to causes that divided people against each other. In the problem-solving mode of governance, each issue has its own particularity and context, and each should be taken as it is. This is often the flavor of local politics: how we solve the problem of an overcrowded intersection may have no connection to what we think of a new recycling program. When politics is a process of solving a series of disconnected problems, partisanship threatens to be a distract-

ing intrusion. It opens opportunities for advocates of more narrow interests to influence collective decisions. The purpose of a
simple, transparent, nonpartisan, unicameral legislature like
Nebraska's is to disempower such interests. In this view, legislation in the general good is imperiled by unnecessarily complicated institutions like bicameral legislatures, whose conference
committees (where differences between bills in the two houses
are ironed out behind closed doors) give special interests an opportunity to defeat measures or obtain special privileges by
pressuring only a handful of people. Disempowering such small
interests would—Norris believed—dissolve the partisan dimension of politics, and people would not need to choose between
alternative "general policy directions."

This notion—that the popular interest is essentially unitary,
and that democratic government would go well if it could be
cleansed of special interests—has long had a powerful hold over
the democratic imagination. One can see it in the simple constitutionalism of Thomas Paine's *Common Sense,* which advocated
for a unicameral legislature; or in the Jacksonian insistence on
keeping government small, so as to preclude powerful but small
interests from finding an opportunity to exert influence and ex-
tract favor; in the populist-progressivism of George Norris and
the Nebraska reformers of the early twentieth century; even
in the wish for bipartisan centrism of the moment. The underlying idea is, as Nancy Rosenblum calls it, "holism": because
the people stand naturally as one, so should their government.[24]
The Nebraska system, like all holistic ideals of politics, conceives of the political community not as a contest—as a partisan
community—but as essentially unified.

Perhaps this assumption fits the circumstances of Nebraska—
but generalizing to all political communities involves a fundamental mistake about the nature of politics. The analogy of political decision making to business decision making reveals the

dimensions of the mistake. The purpose of a conventional business is given: to maximize return for shareholders or owners. That is why certain stakeholders (such as labor) are rarely present in corporate boardrooms, at least in the United States. The efficiency and decorum of business decisions are only possible because all those who might systematically dissent are silenced (for example, those who would trade some increase in profit for more of something else, like job security). This oligarchic principle may have its benefits for the economy, but it is plainly inconsistent with a diverse and vital democratic society. The purpose of a democratic political community, unlike a firm, is never settled: there is no single purpose that must be prioritized over all rivals. For that reason, politics should almost never be conducted *like a business*.

The Nebraska model is nice—too nice. It might be suitable for a municipality or a small rural state, but in any place that contains deep diversity (or even a light variety of ways of living and thinking), we should expect and desire partisan sympathies to dominate the legislature. So long as the political community contains real disagreement, we should want our legislators to be partisans. But perhaps more fundamentally, voting for individuals (disconnected from party, program, and policy commitments) undermines the purposes of political representation, as Nadia Urbinati argues. As she says, "if election were truly a selection between and of single candidates—between and of individual names rather than political group names—representation would vanish because each person would run for him or herself alone and would in fact become a party of his or her own interests." The legislature, she notes, would become an "aggregation of individual wills," rather than a place for deliberating about ideas and opinions that have collective backing.[25] Political representation requires voting for something larger than a person.

The Nebraska legislature, though it realizes the nonpartisan ideal, is not a model for the resuscitation of democratic legislatures more broadly. But even if it cannot serve as a template—at least not for legislatures representing diverse and large communities—its example is instructive. If the nonpartisan legislature is disconnected from the social reality of diverse communities, it expresses the ideal of overcoming diversity in the name of the common good.

The idea of justice invites us to believe that politics can be something better than a mode of accommodating rival groups, each of which would prefer to impose its own interests and ideals unimpeded. The possibility of justice depends in principle on the possibility of the common good. The nonpartisan legislature, where each representative deliberates impartially and in good faith about the common good, better reflects the idea of justice than a legislature of warring parties, each of which seeks to rule unimpeded. The nonpartisan legislature invests legislation with a dignity that partisan legislation cannot achieve, unless after its enactment it becomes so universally popular that it transcends its partisan origins. Legislatures that are partisan on their face, such as parliamentary assemblies whose members are elected on party lists, cannot endow legislation with the same kind of dignity, because the visible and almost undeviating loyalty that each representative gives to the party leadership too severely disconnects the process of legislation from any nonpartisan ideal of justice.

Breaking the party list and creating a tether between a particular territory and a particular representative help establish some slight connection between the legislature and justice by rendering representatives accountable on their own. This does not necessarily make legislators less partisan, but it does make them more individually accountable for their own partisanship.

When a representative toes the party line, the representative—
not just the party leadership—has to answer for it. This answer
links an individual representative's judgment with legislative action, and compels even party loyalty to be explained as a consequence of free judgment. To survive public inspection, such
judgment must be explained as a judgment not about what is
best for the party, but about what is best for the country. The
independence of the legislature in this way preserves the idea
that there might be such a thing as what is "best for the country." It preserves the idea of the common good.

A Speaker of the Whole House

The lesson of the Nebraska legislature is not that every legislature should be nonpartisan, but that even a partisan legislature
should contain a nonpartisan capacity to act, and to look as if it
were acting, for the sake of the common good. This capacity
might be exercised only on occasion—an exception to the partisan rule. But without it, the legislature—the home not only of
modern partisanship, but also of modern democracy—will
likely fail to elicit the confidence of the people, who are naturally less partisan than their representatives and less jaded about
the possibility of a truly common good. Partisanship is the rule
for almost every legislature. But the exception to the rule preserves the idea of a nonpartisan common good. This idea is an
ideal that defies practice most of the time—but not all of the
time.

For instance, the Speaker of the United States House of Representatives is, as speakers often point out, "Speaker of the whole
House." The speakership is not, formally speaking, a partisan
office; it is a constitutional office meant to represent the institution as a whole, which in turn is meant to represent the people
as a whole. This is what gives the office its dignity. But partisan-

ship gives the office its power. Since the "Reed rules" of 1890,[26] the speakership has been the property of the majority party in Congress. By determining who will be Speaker and controlling the organization of Congress, the majority can compromise and even eliminate the ability of the minority party to obstruct legislation. In the best case, the majority can pass its own agenda. But even when internal divisions or the Senate or the presidency impede that affirmative project, the majority can use the speakership to prevent legislation from reaching the House floor. Any number of bills might pass the House with a bipartisan vote (consisting of a majority of the minority party and a minority of the majority party), but these bills rarely progress to a floor vote.

This power to control the agenda has been codified by the so-called Hastert rule, whereby the only bills that will see a floor vote are those that a majority of the majority supported.[27] The Hastert rule has the effect of moving what congressional scholars call the "pivot point" much farther in the direction of the majority party. Consider, for example, a 100-person legislature where each member is evenly spaced apart along a left-right continuum, and where the "right" party has a 51-person majority. The "majority of the majority" rule means that no bill can get to a floor vote unless the twenty-sixth most conservative member supports the bill. Centrist legislation (for instance, that appealing to 45 percent of the majority party and 55 percent of the minority party) would never get to the floor. Voting out the majority party does little to help "moderate" legislation: if the legislature were to flip in the next session to a fifty-one-person liberal majority, the application of the same rule would mean that nothing could receive a floor vote unless it were supported by the twenty-sixth most liberal member. To get to a vote, legislation has to be *either* liberal or conservative; centrist legislation never gets to a vote.

Speaker John Boehner came under criticism in the final months of the 112th Congress for his rigorous application of the Hastert rule: by December 2012, there had not been a single piece of legislation passed over the opposition of a majority of his Republican Party. His fealty to the "majority of the majority" principle threatened to render Congress incapable of dealing with the impasse known as the "fiscal cliff," a financial crisis of Congress's own making that required the body to pass *something* in order to avoid an assortment of tax increases and spending cuts that the Congressional Budget Office predicted would send the national economy back into a recession.[28] Congress as a whole had the capacity to pass something with a coalition of Democrats and Republicans. But many in the Republican Party had taken a vow to oppose all tax increases, and any deal that did not include some new revenues would fail to pass the Democratic-led Senate and win the approval of President Obama. The effect of this combination was that nothing supported by a majority of the majority in Congress would also pass the Senate and be signed by the president. Rigid adherence to the Hastert rule rendered the government incapable of governing.

In times like these, the Speaker of the House needs to rise above his or her partisan identity and act for the sake of the whole by allowing measures onto the floor that the Speaker's own party opposes. Every Speaker in the contemporary era has on occasion allowed bills to the House floor that his or her own party opposed—even Speaker Dennis Hastert, for whom the Hastert rule is named.[29] To accept the Hastert rule as something that can never be broken stretches legislative partisanship to an extreme and mocks the idea of a common good that transcends partisan divisions. In the context of a separation of powers and a bicameral legislature—where party government only obtains when the same party happens to control both houses of the legislature and the presidency—it also undermines the capacity of the government. It would seem better to liberate the speaker-ship from partisan control, to draw perhaps a minority of con-servative Democrats and a minority of moderate Republicans together in a new center legislative party that elects a Speaker who is not beholden to a majority of the majority.[30]

As it happens, Speaker Boehner relaxed his adherence to the Hastert rule just in time to avoid the worst consequences of the fiscal cliff by passing a tax bill in the very last hours of the con-gressional session—and the opposition of a majority of the ma-jority.[31] In the four following months, Boehner allowed three additional major bills to pass in spite of opposition from a ma-jority of his own party. At least two of the bills addressed salient public issues (Hurricane Sandy aid and the Violence Against Women Act). The third involved an allocation to purchase Rev-olutionary War and War of 1812 battlefields. In each of these cases, the Republican majority could not pay the price of sup-porting the bill, often because some ardent constituency in the Republican coalition would object, and Republican members of Congress feared that this would generate a primary election op-ponent. At the same time, the Republicans did not want to pay the price of obstructing popular legislation: the party wanted the legislation it opposed to pass.

The Hastert rule has never been a true "rule." Various Speak-ers have violated the Hastert rule thirty-six times since 1991, including Speaker Hastert himself, who violated it eight times during his speakership (which covered the 106th through 109th Congresses, from 1999 to 2005).[32] Speakers, who owe their position to a vote of their own party caucus, generally have to please a majority of their own parties, and any Speaker who does not will be voted out and replaced. The Hastert rule is a simple matter of prudence. At the same time, Speakers have a responsi-bility both to protect their own party from itself—at times a party cannot do what it wants to do—and to serve the House as an institution that is larger than any one party. Every Speaker will find occasions when he or she has to move legislation in spite of his or her own party's objection. This capacity serves the dignity of the speakership by allowing Speakers to act out the formal constitutional ideal that they are Speakers of the whole House.

A Third Party: The Latent Majority

Speakers need to occasionally represent the whole House because parties in the legislature sometimes obscure and impede what might be called the latent majority. Any number of issues might command broad support within both parties, yet fail to command the support of the majority party. For instance, consider a hypothetical 100-person legislature with 51 Conservatives and 49 Liberals. Any issue that is not agreeable to the twenty-sixth most conservative member of the legislature will not pass—indeed, under the Hastert rule it will not even see a floor vote. Many issues might attract the support of twenty-four Conservatives and twenty-six Liberals. But this bipartisan centrist majority is almost completely disempowered. It does not command a majority of the majority party, and therefore cannot move bills it supports to the floor. Such a majority will lie latent—unable to form, to speak, or to act.

There is reason to believe that such a majority may exist in the current U.S. House of Representatives. This bipartisan majority might support reliably raising the debt ceiling, enacting entitlement reform, addressing inflation in health care expenses, passing comprehensive immigration reform, and constructing a comprehensive tax reform. These are not small issues. But the latent majority, if indeed it exists, cannot express itself in the legislature because it cannot overcome the rule of the majority party (or more specifically, the rule of a majority of the majority party). Relaxing the Hastert rule is one way of empowering the latent majority. But a more direct way would be for a third legislative party to form that attracts just enough members of the majority party and just enough of the opposition party to prevent either major party from forming a majority. To form a majority of the legislature, either of the large parties would have to form a coalition with the smaller Centrist Party. Attracting the support of the centrists, in turn, would entail moving the decisive point in the legislature away from the majority of the majority party, and toward the center.

This is what Charles Wheelan, author of *The Centrist Manifesto,* proposes.[33] The idea is not to form a third party on a par with the Democrats or the Republicans. The Centrist Party would not need to compete in presidential elections or to form a national presence. It would only need to successfully compete in enough moderate districts to effectively prevent either of the major parties from garnering a majority in the legislature. In the 113th House (2013–2015), with 233 Republicans and 200 Democrats, winning merely 16 Republican seats and any number of Democratic districts would be enough to prevent either great party from commanding a majority and would move the center of gravity in the House emphatically to the center. The same purpose could be accomplished with many fewer seats in the Senate.

Most proposals for a centrist third party are decisively antipartisan. Sometimes they take the form of naive holism and embrace the notion that the common interest would be an uncontroversial matter if it were not muddied by the great parties. "Centrists cut an independent path between the extremes—putting patriotism before partisanship and the national interest before special interests," says one advocate.[34] For others, centrism is the way to get past the terms of the New Deal, which set in motion a conflict over the scope of the national government.

The two great parties are dead to the "tectonic shifts taking place in our private, public, and communal sectors," argue the authors of *The Radical Center.* "Our nation's politics are dominated by two feuding dinosaurs that have outlived the world in which they evolved," they claim.[35] These expressions of centrism, like the post-partisan fantasy and like all forms of holism, deny the fact of the partisan community. *"We don't really disagree,"* they say. *"It only seems that way because the traditional parties have an interest in disagreement—without it, they could get power."* Centrism, in this view, is a way to displace parties from politics.

But Wheelan's proposal is much more carefully calibrated than this. The aim of his Centrist Party is not to displace the parties entirely, but to force one of them to enter into a governing coalition in the legislature, for the sake of moving the decisive point in the legislature closer to the middle. Wheelan's Centrist Party is not antipartisan. On the contrary, it aims to secure the most important benefits of the Nebraska system (empowering centrist majorities) without the major defect of the Nebraska system—it does not suppose that politics, ideally, will lack partisan conflict. If there are numerous issues that might unite a bipartisan majority (entitlement reform, tax reform, and so on), there remain plenty of issues that in today's context would likely divide the legislature along familiar partisan lines: gun control, national health care, increasing taxes on the wealthy, and redistributing resources to the poorest, for example. Parties and the ideologies that increasingly define them would still matter.

To succeed, the Centrist Party proposal would need to become *more partisan* to be successful. Centrism on every issue— the midpoint or a compromise position between the ideal points of the two parties—is not a coherent political posture because what it stands for is always hostage to the extremes. If the Con-

servative Party moves to the right more than the Liberal Party
moves to the left, for example, then the Centrist Party moves to
the right also, since the "center" by definition must also move.
As a mere spatial point between extremes (rather than denoting
its own set of independent convictions), the center cannot hold.
A Centrist Party could not easily elicit passions and devotion
because it can offer no steady principles, it can invoke no social
or historical story about itself, and it cannot connect in a stable
way with concrete social groups. It offers itself as the solution to
our present discontents—and perhaps it would bring a respite
from the dysfunction that often characterizes Congress. But its
place would ultimately be ephemeral, unless it can connect to a
set of principles, purposes, and goals that uniquely define it.
The Centrist Party is a solution to a certain kind of predicament
that parties create in the legislature. It promises to reconnect
the legislature as a whole to the common good by empowering
the latent majority. But unless it stands for something that
gives it definition and continuity, it will remain an abstract, if
elegant, solution—and will fail to inspire the loyalties and identifications of real candidates and real citizens.

Once the Centrist Party becomes a real party and stands for
something, many of its positions will start to seem more controversial. Take the classic social issue, abortion. Morris Fiorina,
whose account of the ways that the parties today have disconnected from what most people believe and want, argues that
abortion is not in fact a polarizing issue.[36] Abortion should be
legal, most Americans think, when pregnancy poses a threat to
a woman's life. And most also agree that abortion should not be
permitted when prospective parents prefer their fetus to have
a different gender. Americans split on abortion in other circumstances: financial distress, fetal defect, threat to a woman's
health (not life). As Fiorina says, "When given a stark choice
between classifying themselves as 'pro-choice' or 'pro-life,'

Americans divide fairly evenly, with a slight edge to pro-life. But . . . these simple labels make a mockery of the nuanced views that Americans actually hold."[37] Political people, however, have to translate nuanced views into legislation. A majority, for instance, thinks that abortion should be legal in the case of incest; a majority also does not think that abortion should be legal in the case of financial distress.

Perhaps a Centrist Party could propose a nuanced piece of legislation that could differentiate the two circumstances. If the nuanced legislation is drawn in a manner that minimizes the chance that someone in financial distress will successfully procure an abortion, the restrictions in the legislation might also prevent *some* victims of incest from getting access to abortions. Conversely, if the legislation were drawn to ensure that no victim of incest is denied access, it might be impossible in practice to exclude those seeking abortions out of financial difficulty.

Which kind of errors does one find more tolerable? Would one rather have legislation that prevents access to some incest victims in order to be sure that absolutely no one who feels her fetus has the "wrong" gender gets access? Or would one rather be more certain that no incest victim is denied access even if this means that the policy will be broad enough to permit some people who think their fetuses have the "wrong" gender to get access? As soon as one begins to answer these questions, one will be pulled away from the nuanced middle toward policies like those favored by the more extreme pro-choice and pro-life positions.

The same might be true of many other issues. Everyone wants to put the government on sound financial footing. But what would one rather risk to accomplish that: the prospect that Social Security will be underfunded, or that higher marginal tax rates might depress the animal spirits of the wealthy? One might encounter similar dilemmas in other issues that present themselves as a natural fit for a Centrist Party: immigration, tax reform, or global warming legislation. The only way to discover whether there is in fact a latent majority is for the Centrist Party to try to become a real party. Centrism, which looks so viable in theory, may founder once it tries to become a practical force in politics. At the least, it will not offer an escape from partisan contestation, with all its attendant frustrations.

The importance of centrism, even when it is occasional, stems less from what the country is than from what it wants to be. There is a powerful yearning to stand together as one, to unify around a shared conception of the common good. This reflects the ideal of justice as something fair and right that applies to the whole. We may in fact be divided and disagree about what is right and just—such disagreement is unavoidable under conditions of freedom. But we do not want to be permanently divided, where all politics can ever be is "civil war carried on by other means."[38] This yearning, the desire to stand as one and to make the ideal of justice something real, is what gives bipartisanship its symbolic power. It is also what gives partisanship its disrespectability. Partisan contest is the reality of politics, especially in the legislature. But when partisanship encounters no limit, when it defines the whole of politics and replaces the aspiration to justice with the need for strength, the legislature loses some of its dignity. The prospect of deliberation becomes a childish dream, and law becomes nothing better than the way one part of the country imposes its way on the rest.

When partisanship has no limit, a loss accrues to partisanship itself. Partisanship's moral force comes from its connection to justice. When partisanship is severed from any plausible connection to what is right for the whole, when it becomes nothing more than one part's conception of what is advantageous for it, partisans themselves are diminished. The limit may not be apparent most of the time, but it becomes visible in certain rare moments, such as when a partisan legislative leader, such as the Speaker of the House, allows the agenda to include bills that the majority party opposes. In the days when centrism ruled, partisanship, which was always quietly the rule when it came to electing Speakers and organizing the House, was restricted to important but invisible procedural wrangles: important measures were nearly always passed by whopping bipartisan majorities in final roll-call votes.[39] But today, in an age of party polarization, fewer important measures attract bipartisan majorities in the final roll call. Partisanship, even when legislators are not elected on party lists, can seem like everything. Unless citizens can see that partisanship has a limit, unless there are occasions when the Speaker can act not as a partisan but as Speaker of the whole House, party spirit can undermine both the dignity of legislation and the respectability of party itself.

8

PARTISANSHIP BEYOND
THE LEGISLATURE

What distinguishes politics from every other mode of cooperation is its essentially coercive nature. Even when the state's monopoly on coercive force is incomplete, politics is never wholly without coercion. The polity enforces its mandates with ever-present threats: it can take people's possessions, restrain them, confine them, and kill them. This is why the justification of political power is always an urgent thing: the individual, standing nearly alone, has almost no ability to resist the state's coercive power. It is also why we can never be completely comfortable with partisanship. When one party commands the coercive apparatus of government, the invitation to abuse coercive power seems too potent to resist.

The executive stands at the center of the coercive power of the state: this is the power that enforces laws, at the penalty ultimately of death: the executive *executes*. The general aim of modern political thought has been to contain the very coercive power it justifies, which has always meant containing the executive. An essential part of this containment has been stripping the executive of its partisan character: the early modern conversion of monarchic power to executive power aimed to replace personal or familial partiality with impartial administration of law. In the simplest version of the separation of powers, the executive is meant to faithfully and impartially apply laws whose content derives from a power outside the executive. Enforcing the law is not in principle a partisan activity, and neither the executive nor judicial functions are "political": they are not invested with the responsibility of deliberating about the common good; they apply, enforce, and interpret the results of legislative deliberations. By contrast, partisanship is natural in the legislature, since making laws involves specifying the common good, and every exact formulation of the common good is a matter of reasonable yet unceasing contestation. Yet even in the legislature, as we have seen, partisanship should have a limit.

The limits of partisanship, which are only glimpsed in the legislature, are sharper in the executive and judicial functions of government. In the legislature, the limit of partisanship is a very occasional yet useful act of fealty to the nonpartisan ideal. Executive power clarifies the limits of partisanship as those limits are encountered not only by presidents, but also by citizens, legislators, and judges. High partisanship—the partisanship that is about the broad goals that define a partisan conception of the common good—can be a salutary force, and perhaps there is no way to think deeply about the common good without becoming a partisan in the high sense. But low partisanship—the partisanship that drives a strategic approach to electoral victory—is something else. If low partisanship is necessary (and it is), it can also be corrupting—not only for presidents, but for all. Presidents have to navigate an office where high partisanship is essential and low partisanship must be contained. This is what makes the presidency a particularly difficult office to fill. But the challenge presidents face is one those in other roles cannot entirely avoid. It is difficult to escape partisanship completely, at least if one wants to be politically effective. But it is essential to know its limits, at least if one wants to preserve the possibility of justice and the rule of law. This is just as true for citizens, legislators, and judges as for presidents.

Partisanship and the Supreme Court is itself an extensive subject that would require its own book, but the general outline of partisanship on the Court is suggested by the analysis of executive partisanship. Like the judicial power, the executive cannot avoid interpreting laws in the process of enforcing them. And the logic of partisanship in the executive—an abundance of caution about low partisanship while aligning high partisanship with established procedures—applies to the judiciary as well. Broad matters of public policy that are ineliminably partisan—directing the Justice Department to make a priority of illegal immigration on one hand or civil rights on the other— will be articulated by political appointments at the top layers of the executive bureaucracy. But below that layer of political appointments, the vast bulk of bureaucratic decisions should follow nonpartisan procedures. Somewhat analogously, where precedent runs out and cases must be decided on essentially contestable theories of jurisprudence that have a partisan edge, judges will be, and must be, political. But in most lower court cases nonpartisanship must be the norm. The legitimacy of both the executive and the judicial roles—a dignity supplied by the connection of these roles to the rule of law—depends on marginalizing partisanship.

And yet partisanship is unavoidable in the executive and the highest reaches of the judiciary. The grammar-school summary of the separation of powers suggests that only one branch—the legislature—is "political": *Congress makes laws, while the executive enforces and the judiciary interprets.* But the American system exhibits less of a strict separation of powers than a sharing of powers: the executive, as Madison pointed out, shares in legislative power through the veto; the legislature shares in executive power through its confirmation powers, its power to ratify treaties, and its power to declare war; and the judiciary cannot interpret laws or the Constitution merely by looking within the four corners of the relevant documents—it needs to interpret the intentions or spirit of legislative and constitutional intent, which engages it in a kind of legislation. To a degree, all of the branches are political. All, to a degree, are partisan. To suppose that the executive and the judiciary should be entirely immune from party spirit is a mistake. The indeterminacy of the common good and the insufficiency of reason to determine or apply the common good with any precision mean that both the executive and the judicial functions of any government will be to a degree partisan.

But when partisanship explains any more than the occasional case, both the enforcement of law and the authoritative determination of law lose something of their fairness. In both of these roles, officials need to be able to give an account of what they do that can explain their behavior as nonpartisan. When these accounts seem to citizens nothing more than a veil that shrouds true partisan motives, law in general loses its legitimacy. It is with the executive and the judiciary particularly that we need to "beware the spirit of party." Partisanship in the executive, and even more, on the Court, needs to be nuanced. There is a respect in which any ambitious president *must* be partisan. And there are other respects in which every honorable president must be nonpartisan.

The President as Party Leader

The nuance of presidential partisanship is so tricky because partisanship is so essential to presidential ambition. More than any other political officials, presidents (and often their parliamentary equivalents, prime ministers) have the prospect of being remembered. Legislators will all be forgotten—if not in a day, certainly in a generation. But presidents stand apart. It takes longer to forget them, though some are ultimately forgettable. Ambitious presidents (and perhaps all presidents are ambitious) want to be remembered. And indeed they might be remembered for the good they have done, so long as that good lasts. So presidents will want to do something good that lasts: their ambition directs their gaze far beyond the next election to the horizon where the present meets its posterity. This is what is meant by presidential "vision." Since it is oriented to long-term innovation, presidential vision is intimately connected to, if it is not the origin of, high partisanship. No president can be truly successful or great—and no president will be remembered as such—without standing for principles that are controversial in their moment, installing these principles at the core of a party (that continues to serve them after the president's terms have passed), and institutionalizing the principles in a way that citizens regard as successful, so that in time they come to be regarded as definitive of the country itself (and appear, in the end, nonpartisan). Presidents are not merely partisans in the ordinary sense. They are the leaders of their parties.

James Madison's first proposal to the 1787 Constitutional Convention (called the "Virginia Plan") stipulated that the legislature would elect the president to a single seven-year term.[1] Had that sort of plan been adopted by the convention, the president today would be a creature of the legislative majority, and the presidential office would likely have become partisan in a very similar way to that of Speaker of the House. Something akin to this was the practice between 1800 and 1824, when legislative party caucuses drafted presidential tickets.

Instead, the framers designed the befuddling and occasionally frustrating Electoral College; while they may have expected that indeterminate outcomes from the Electoral College would turn the election of the president over to the House in any case, the Electoral College nonetheless gave the president's power a foundation independent of the national legislature. This independence, combined with the fact that the presidency is the only office that covers the entire country, establishes the president as an official meant to be "above party."[2]

Yet only George Washington and John Adams have fulfilled that expectation (perhaps also Theodore Roosevelt, though as the founder of a party he was not exactly above party). Every other president has been a partisan, and the most successful have been not merely leaders of parties but founders (or refounders) of great and enduring parties. Thomas Jefferson and Andrew Jackson share credit for founding today's Democratic Party; Abraham Lincoln was, in essence, the founder of today's Republican Party. Woodrow Wilson and Franklin Roosevelt refounded the Democratic Party into the progressive and liberal force that it remains. Ronald Reagan endowed the Republican Party with the assertively conservative spirit that continues to define it. And Barack Obama seeks to complete the undone project of the New Deal (national health care), to counter the Reagan Revolution, and to restore the Democratic Party to its New Deal foundations.[3] No president can be great who is not also a great partisan.

The meaning of the partisan presidency was transformed in the twentieth century. From the time of Jackson—who with Van Buren took the party beyond the legislative caucus and gave it to the people[4]—party organization was decentralized: parties drew their national power from localities and states, which compromised their philosophic or programmatic cohesion on a national level. Partisan presidents were tethered to local democracy.

In the twentieth century, beginning with Theodore Roosevelt but even more notably with Woodrow Wilson, presidents became partisan in a new way: they were charged with formulating and advancing a program that would orient the actions of both the national legislature and the executive administration. Party nominees for the presidency were expected to persuade the public of the desirability of their program, to translate public support into the support of a legislative majority, and to guide legislative majorities by advancing specific legislation. Using the presidency to transform eighteenth-century constitutional democracy into twentieth-century party democracy was Woodrow Wilson's idea. In Wilson's view, party government was presidential government, with the president cast as chief partisan.[5]

In the nineteenth century, partisanship empowered local hostility to centralized government. In the twentieth century, partisanship harnessed public opinion to empower a national party program. If Woodrow Wilson first articulated this vision of the partisan president, Franklin Roosevelt fulfilled it. Roosevelt put the presidency at the center of government and at the center of the party; he did not fashion his program to suit his party, but ultimately remade his party to suit his program. In the late 1930's, Roosevelt tried to "overcome the state and local orientation of the party system" and make the Democratic Party more "national and principled in character." Having failed at that, Roosevelt proceeded to strengthen the presidency as the "vital center of government action," and the steward of liberal progress.[6] While this diminished the connection between the national party and localities, it also helped realign the parties in a way that made the New Deal legacy a principal point of contention between them. Later Democratic presidents, like Lyndon Johnson, William Clinton, or Barack Obama, attempted to solidify and extend the achievements of the New Deal. In this respect, Roosevelt's purposes and program lived on through the party he created.

What Roosevelt did for the Democratic Party, Reagan did for the Republican Party a half-century later. Reagan identified the Republican Party with a new kind of conservatism, one rooted not merely in go-slow prudence or a sympathy for commercial interests, but in principle. Against the expansion of the New Deal, Reagan held that welfarist entitlements cultivated passivity and undermined responsibility; against the New Deal's spirit of centralization, Reagan proposed a "new federalism"; and to curb programmatic momentum of the New Deal state, Reagan proposed tax cuts that would deprive the expansion of progressive programs of its fuel. A "program" implies an expansion of governmental action and responsibility. Reagan's conservatism was antiprogrammatic and harkened back to the nineteenth century's hostility to centralized government. But unlike the nineteenth century, the new conservatism of Reagan's Republican Party would depend on a partisan president who gave direction to popular frustration with programmatic government by translating it into an antiprogrammatic party program (affirmatively expressed as a balanced budget with lower taxation). Reagan deployed the Wilsonian image of a partisan president commanding a national majority against the progressive ideal of programmatic government.

The Post-Partisan Fantasy

The bureaucratic nature of the administrative state, combined with the constitutional invitation to see presidents above party, can invite presidents to neglect their role as party leader and to define themselves as efficient, nonpartisan managers of the commonsense common good. Former New York City mayor Michael Bloomberg typifies this sensibility: "Real results," he said, "are more important than partisan battles and good ideas should take precedence over rigid adherence to any ideology."[7] Bloomberg's unremarkable pragmatism found a pointed echo in California governor Arnold Schwarzenegger. "We don't need

Republican roads or Democratic roads. We need roads," Schwarzenegger said in his 2007 inaugural address. "I believe we have the opportunity to move past partisanship . . . to move past bipartisanship . . . to move to post-partisanship," he continued.

A post-partisan or pragmatic orientation to governing may be appropriate for mayors and even state governors. But it distorts the partisan work that any ambitious president must undertake. Post-partisanship would have been forgotten as soon as it was pronounced had it not been for Barack Obama, who embraced the idea at the heart of the term. Both liberalism and conservatism, in Obama's view, had lost their relevance to our political circumstance. Obama was more comfortable contrasting himself with liberals than taking the label as his own (even if his opponents viewed him as the liberal of their egalitarian nightmares). Obama denied that politics is essentially contestatory, engaging a recurring contest that engages new particulars in each new iteration even as it is animated by a steady spirit. He disdained partisan approaches to politics: "The pursuit of ideological purity, the rigid orthodoxy and sheer predictability of our current debate," he wrote shortly after entering the U.S. Senate, "keep us from finding new ways to meet the challenges we face."[8] The impulse of Democrats to defend "every New Deal and Great Society program from Republican encroachment" betrayed, for Obama, the exhaustion of liberal ideals.[9] Liberalism rooted in the contests of the twentieth century is "bereft of the energy . . . needed to address the changing circumstances of globalization and a stubbornly isolated inner city," he insisted.[10]

Obama could not seem to fully own *his* liberalism. "One of the things that makes me a Democrat, I suppose," he wrote, is the "idea that our communal values . . . should express themselves not just in church . . . but also through our government."[11] To hold that the coercive power of the state should enforce communal values of the sort that individuals express within their churches is a profoundly controversial idea. The central ideas here—that citizenship should involve a level of sharing and mutual responsibility more typical of families or certain religious congregations, that government should embrace a deep sense of communal responsibility, that our laws should reflect a willingness to share one another's fate—are not simple pragmatic conclusions. They are contestable (and partisan); they go well beyond what pragmatic reason alone can clarify. Ideas like these will always generate controversy as they are applied to new domains of policy. Ideas like these are what motivate partisanship, not what put it to an end.

Obama confused the low partisan game that motivates small-minded machinations in Congress, always with a view to the next campaign, with all partisanship. He supposed that because the partisan game is tiresome, therefore his political ideals and goals were not partisan. So put off by the political game, Obama could not see the enduring relevance of liberalism and conservatism, and he could not recognize the partisan character of his own convictions. He could not recognize that his own political commitments (which mapped the responsibility entailed by the statement "I am my brother's keeper" onto laws and policies) situated him in a political contest that connects him with the parties to political contests of the past century—as well as, in all likelihood, to the next. Obama's partisan commitments implicated him in an argument he did not want to join. The promise of avoiding an argument is the attraction of post-partisanship, which says that arguments are beside the point of politics. That may be true when it comes to filling potholes. But the more engaging and inspiring purposes of politics require an argument—and a fight. The post-partisan pretense that political argument is unnecessary amounts to a form of free-riding, where we neglect the team that carries our side of the argument from one contest to the next. Hidden in this pretense is an arrogant insistence that everyone should agree with us, without the bother of explaining why.

Perhaps it is more accurate not to take post partisanship that seriously, and to see it as simply a rhetorical strategy designed to appeal to a centrist or apolitical electorate. It communicates sympathy with the popular intolerance of argument and fatigue with low partisan gamesmanship. More of a manner than a set of ideas, post-partisanship makes political ambition palatable to a broad coalition of voters who do not understand themselves in terms of ideology and who are put off by the aggressive certainties of the self-righteous.

Fair enough: political people and especially candidates have to connect to those who do not care as deeply or know as much about politics as do they. The problem with the post-partisan manner is that even the most calculating candidates can come to believe their own rhetoric. When presidents believe their post-partisan brand, they come to see themselves as wholly superior to the partisan game and in the process misunderstand themselves and their cause. When they forget they are engaged in both an argument (at the level of high partisanship) and a fight (at the level of low partisanship), they are more likely to lose both. To an extent, this seems to have infected Obama's understanding of his most impressive and controversial achievement: health care.

Partisan Victory: The Affordable Care Act

Obama cast health care reform as a nonideological solution to an undeniable web of problems: cost inflation, which "threatens the financial stability of families, businesses, and government itself"; insecure and uneven coverage for those who change jobs, lose their jobs, or have preexisting medical conditions; and insufficient or nonexistent coverage for those who lack employer-sponsored coverage.[12] Perhaps out of hope that he might attract some Republican support for the policy, Obama did his best to describe his approach as nonpartisan. He described the policy as a pragmatic bit of problem solving, and designed it according to a plan developed in a conservative think tank (and first employed by a Republican, Mitt Romney, in Massachusetts). As a solution so effective that the problem would henceforth vanish, health care reform would seem more necessary than controversial.

Yet, of course, any health care law that socialized the risk of individual illness would be partisan—indeed, the most partisan legislation in a generation. Health care was only a problem in the way that Obama perceived it to be if one saw the common good in a certain kind of way, a way that has been allied with the Democratic Party since the New Deal. Like Social Security, it expresses in policy the more general aspiration to stand together as a political community and insure one another against certain misfortunes that some individuals cannot insure themselves against individually. Heath care in particular is the completion of a project initiated by Roosevelt, picked up by Truman, by Ted Kennedy, and by Clinton. It has represented for two generations the undone project of the Democratic Party. It is not simply a nonpartisan solution—it is a cause at the heart of the Democratic Party.

Obama, of course, understood this. But he expressed it indirectly, through the words of Ted Kennedy (who was fighting for his life against brain cancer at the moment Obama was working on the passage of what would become the Affordable Care Act). Even then, Obama felt required to insert a distance between himself and Kennedy's partisan voice: "For some of Kennedy's critics," Obama said, "his brand of liberalism represented an affront to American liberty." As if to comfort listeners who might be put off by Kennedy's partisanship, Obama assured his audience that Kennedy's "passion" for the issue was born of his own experience, not rooted in "some rigid ideology." Kennedy's support for health care reflected his "large-heartedness," Obama said, his "concern and regard for the plight of others." This feeling, Obama explained, "is not a Republican or a Democratic feeling. It . . . is part of the American character."[13]

By invoking Kennedy's words on one hand, and denying that they reflected ideological (or partisan) conviction on the other, Obama diminished the force of Kennedy's example. Ted Kennedy's convictions about national health care were not the reflexive conclusions of his personal biography. His personal experience as a man born to wealth and celebrity insulated him, if not from sorrow and loss, at least from deprivation and financial insecurity. This experience might have oriented him very differently (one could imagine his experience supporting a certain kind of conservatism). Ted Kennedy was a liberal and a stalwart advocate of universal health care not simply because of his experience, but because of the distinctive way he interpreted his experience and its relation to the common good. Kennedy understood that the moral case for health care, which was also the most forceful case, was partisan: it was political, not simply personal.

What is at stake, Kennedy wrote (in the words Obama quoted in his speech), "are not just the details of policy, but fundamental principles of social justice and the character of our country."[14] This connection between the details of policy and the moral character of the country is what defines partisanship at its highest and most noble. If it is what makes politics worthwhile, it is also what makes it contentious. Kennedy understood himself to be partisan in this way; Obama, restrained by post-partisan posturing or perhaps by a real desire to govern without partisanship, could only glimpse it vicariously. He could quote the most famous partisan of the Democratic Party and invoke the names of Roosevelt, Truman, Kennedy, and Clinton, and aspire to complete what they could not. But he hesitated to join their ranks as liberals and Democrats. He could offer himself as a leader, but not as the leader of a party.

As months passed, as health care bills were drafted and debated and eventually passed, Obama's reluctance to make the high partisan case for health care restricted the rhetorical resources he could draw from in defending the cause. The White House focused on the pragmatic benefits of the law: the way it would help senior citizens navigate the so-called doughnut hole in Medicare coverage, the inclusion of tax breaks to assist senior citizens in purchasing additional coverage, the extension of coverage to Americans with "preexisting conditions," and the ability of young people to stay on their parents' insurance through age twenty-five.[15] Obama was comfortable discussing how discrete benefits would flow to particular demographics, but he seemed unable to relate these specific policy benefits to a larger ideal of the kind of country these would help make. Without such an ideal, there is no reason to support the policy unless one can identify oneself as one of its beneficiaries. Indeed, the most forceful reason to support the policy is seen in the way it expresses a conception of what the country should be—a necessarily partisan conception.

The conception of the country at the heart of the Affordable Care Act affirms a community where citizens do not leave each other to suffer from treatable illnesses because they lack insurance, where ambulance drivers check on patients' coverage before driving them to the emergency room, where the poorest among us must forgo routine checkups, where we do not insist the working poor should endure ailments for which their wealthier neighbors can afford a cure. It says that this is a country where citizens stand together to shoulder some of the risk against which the poorest among us can least afford to protect themselves. Health care policy is not just a policy; it is a solution to a problem. It is not the tar that fills the pothole. It (partly) constitutes the moral character of the political community. This moral ideal of community has been carried across the decades not only by policy experts, but by a party.

"I am not the first President to take up this cause," Obama said, "but I am determined to be the last."[16] With the policy's "success," Obama will be the last to take up the cause not because every public problem associated with health care will be solved; even the primary problem of the moment, health care cost inflation, may likely persist. Rather, the most complete success of the policy will be seen in the way it shapes our self-image as a country. Success is a solution as a victory—the victory of a party that aims to shape the moral character of the political community. Without a president—a partisan president—no party in American politics can be victorious in this way.

Obama was a partisan president: he tried to enact a party's understanding of what the country should be. He tried to restore the core of the New Deal's image of the national community and conception of government, and thus arrest the Reagan Republican conception that cast government not as the solution to our problems but as the problem. Obama's partisan opponents understood the stakes, which is why they voted against the legislation—and having lost that vote, subsequently voted dozens of times in the House to repeal it. But he could not see himself or his program as partisan. By shying away from the partisan justification of health care—or invoking it only occasionally, through the words of others, like Ted Kennedy—Obama deflated supporters while failing to persuade opponents.

Post-partisanship might maintain a nation that has nothing left to do, but it cannot make a nation. Perhaps it is appropriate when the federal government can do no more than fund defense, existing entitlements, and interest on the debt. But post-partisanship cannot harness the desire of citizens to shape the character of their country.

As we have seen, no ambitious president can disdain the high partisanship that links particular policies and programs with (necessarily controversial) conceptions of the common good. In turn, presidents cannot remove themselves from the low partisanship of tending to campaigns and elections. Presidents need to tend to their own reelection; the White House since Clinton has become the site of a "permanent campaign," and the president the party's chief fund-raiser. Equally important is tending to the president's majority in Congress. Former House Speaker Thomas "Tip" O'Neill's dictum—"All politics is local"—is increasingly backward: *All politics is national*.[17] Yes, members continue to need to tend to their districts, and voters continue to approve of their own members of Congress more than they approve of the institution as a whole. The local and personal element has not disappeared. But congressional elections are increasingly about the national issues that define the parties, and presidents have a special power to clarify the national stakes of congressional elections—especially midterm elections. The president's agenda is also the party's agenda; it is what links or divides the legislature and the executive. Presidents are the source of partisan vision—they maintain and shape the ideals that define a party. To give this vision force, presidents must also take care to lead the party through elections—they supply the leadership for the party organization, they recruit candidates, they raise money, and they strategize. This—the presidential connection to low partisan activities—is where danger abounds.

The Corruption of Low Partisanship:
Bush Dismisses His U.S. Attorneys

Presidents are partisans in a way that no other official can rival. They define their party—and when they succeed, their definition extends its force well beyond their own term in office. Yet at the same time, the power of the presidency depends on a kind of dignity that partisanship undercuts. And the legitimacy of the presidency depends on a kind of impartiality that partisanship corrodes. Presidents need to be partisans in one sense— they need to embrace the high partisanship that articulates the purposes and policies that define a party. But they need to simultaneously be nonpartisan; they need to insulate themselves from low partisanship—the calculations that bear on a party's short-term electoral success. Low partisanship corrupts the presidency because the president is in fact responsible for a range of governmental powers that must be undertaken impartially for their exercise to be legitimate. The presidency is simultaneously the most partisan electoral office—and the least.

The presidency is entrusted with police powers, the legitimacy of which depend on their nonpartisan and impartial administration. This is difficult because the prosecution of crime and the enforcement of law necessarily have a partisan dimension. In campaigns, candidates may promise to make a priority of enforcing certain laws, and elected officials will be held accountable by their success in preventing certain kinds of crimes. Liberal administrations might emphasize prosecuting labor law violations or firms that flout environmental regulations; conservative administrations might put an emphasis on combating illegal immigration or pornography. These priorities reflect both the social groups that support the parties and the larger conceptions that inform partisan understandings of justice. Because conceptions of justice have a partisan accent, the enforcement of law will also, at least in those domains where what counts as a harm is contested.

The high partisan dispute about justice is one thing—one that democracy should not avoid. The more potent danger in the prosecution of crimes comes from low partisanship. To have control over the investigative and prosecutorial powers of the national government is the sort of raw power that can profoundly benefit one's friends and hurt one's enemies. Partisans, at the extreme, will always be tempted by the power to investigate (if not also prosecute and imprison) one's enemies, and by the capacity to protect one's friends. This temptation can corrupt the administration of justice to the very core.

How to balance the fact that even the administration of justice—the quintessentially nonpartisan thing—will be inflected by high partisan goals and values, while insulating the administration of justice from the low partisan sensibility of friends and enemies? This balance was reflected, for instance, in the traditional manner of appointing United States attorneys. The ninety-three U.S. attorneys are appointed by the president with the consent of the Senate, and constitute the nation's chief law enforcement officers. They are political and therefore partisan appointments. Nominees for the position are initially chosen by the senators *of the president's party* from the states in which they will serve; if no senators from a given state share the president's party, then state party leaders (of the president's party) choose the nominees. The nomination process, however, establishes a critical degree of independence from partisan control. By custom, home state senators, even if they are not from the president's party, have the opportunity to veto nominees during the Senate confirmation process. While U.S. attorneys, like all political appointments, nominally serve at the pleasure of the president, they serve for a fixed four-year term, and by custom continue to the end of their term even if there is a change of presidential administration. When there is no change of administration, it was also the custom that U.S. attorneys can elect to continue in their positions for a second four-year term after the first expires. Befitting the balance of partisan loyalties and nonpartisan standards they are meant to uphold, U.S. attorneys enjoy a measure of independence from the partisan process by which they were nominated.[18]

Such was the case, at any rate, before George W. Bush's second term. Until 2006, U.S. attorney vacancies were filled either by the elevation of the first assistant to the U.S. attorney (with a limit of 210 days) or by direct appointment of an interim U.S. attorney by the attorney general (with a limit of 120 days) until a Senate-confirmed candidate could assume the office. But in 2006, language was mysteriously inserted into the USA PATRIOT Act that allowed the attorney general to make interim appointments for an indefinite term—thereby avoiding Senate confirmation and depriving U.S. attorneys of some of their independence. By the end of the year, the Justice Department forced nine U.S. attorneys to resign.

In some instances, the administration simply wanted to reward its friends: for example, the U.S. attorney for Arkansas was asked to resign in order to make way for one of Karl Rove's assistants.[19] In other cases, the reason was partisan in a more corrosive way: political authorities in the Justice Department and the White House wanted someone who would more reliably prosecute their enemies. The U.S. attorney in New Mexico, David Iglesias, was forced out in 2006 because state Republican activists and officials complained that he had not undertaken public corruption prosecutions against Democratic officials and pursued voter fraud prosecutions with sufficient zeal in the months leading up to the 2004 elections. Their complaints reached six-term New Mexico Republican senator Pete Domenici, who pressured the White House to fire Iglesias.[20] The Justice

Department did exactly that. The reason (though Justice Department officials subsequently lied to Congress about this) was simply that Iglesias was not using prosecutorial resources to benefit the Republican Party. This firing crystallizes how unbounded partisanship in the executive can corrupt the rule of law.

"Voter fraud" has been a preoccupation of the Republican Party since the early 2000s. The concern has focused on the possibility that liberal groups fraudulently register noncitizens to vote, facilitate their fraudulent ballots, and perhaps also enable them to vote multiple times. Notwithstanding the intense concern with the issue from Republican quarters, actual cases are difficult to locate, and many see voter fraud as itself a fraud.[21] What some suspect motivates the concern is a crude electoral calculus: the favored solution, voter identification laws, is likely to depress turnout among certain Democratic Party demographics (young, immigrant, poor, and minority voters).[22]

In 2004, after Republican officials in New Mexico repeatedly asked both the attorney general, Alberto Gonzales, and the U.S. attorney (Iglesias) to investigate voter fraud in 2004, Iglesias did not immediately launch investigations. Instead, after consulting with various attorneys in the Justice Department (those with experience prosecuting voter fraud, those in the civil rights and criminal divisions of the Justice Department), he set up a task force to investigate the issue. Iglesias understood the partisan charge that the issue carried, and "to avoid any public perception that the task force was seeking to advance a Republican political agenda," he included New Mexico's Democratic secretary of state on the task force.[23]

Iglesias struck the right balance. He handled an inevitably partisan question in a manner consistent with his responsibility to maintain both the appearance and the substance of impartiality. He did not ignore or dismiss complaints, even if they came from partisans and even if they may have had a partisan motivation. At the same time, he resisted the temptation to bring the full power of his office to bear on intimidating political opponents, even if the complaints came from his political friends. He adopted a course of action befitting a federal prosecutor: he responded to the complaints in a deliberate and careful way, while making a special effort to avoid the appearance of partisan motivation. Most important, he took care to avoid any action in the months immediately prior to an election that might alter its outcome. Iglesias was a political appointee—a loyal supporter of George W. Bush (he headed a New Mexico group in 2000 called Lawyers for Bush[24]) who had long been active in state Republican politics. But his actions as U.S. attorney were not partisan in the crude sense; his actions reflected the stature of his office, which required him to serve not his party but the rule of law.

Iglesias's subtle handling of a charged issue elicited no admirers in his party. Republican activists in New Mexico thought his response was "a waste of time" and "a joke."[25] Republicans in New Mexico complained to the White House, where staffers decided that Iglesias should be replaced.[26] Compounding Iglesias's problems with his own party was a public corruption investigation of a Democratic official in the fall of 2006. Republicans were keen to see Iglesias bring charges before the November election. Karl Rove and President Bush himself mentioned the alleged problem of voter fraud in Albuquerque, New Mexico, in a meeting with Attorney General Gonzales in October 2006.[27] Senator Domenici even called Iglesias at home in late October to inquire about the status of the investigation. When Iglesias told Domenici that he likely would not bring charges before Election Day, Domenici said, "Well, I'm very sorry to hear that," and abruptly hung up.[28] In December 2006, Iglesias was told to resign.

Later, when the removal of nine U.S. attorneys became a controversy, Attorney General Gonzales professed to have taken no part in putting Iglesias's name on the list of U.S. attorneys to be removed, as did numerous other Justice Department officials.[29] Justice Department officials later characterized Iglesias as an "underperformer" and an "absentee landlord," and indicated that he was a bad manager who lacked leadership capacity.[30] These explanations appear to have been lies; in fact, partisan concerns, not performance concerns, were at the heart of the decision to fire Iglesias. Or rather, the administration conflated the two things: they could not maintain a distinction between performing well in the job and using the powers of the position to benefit the Republican Party. The inspector general later faulted Attorney General Gonzales for abdicating his responsibility to "safeguard the integrity and independence" of the Justice Department.[31] The inspector general's report on the matter also condemned the deputy attorney general and the chief of staff for their "troubling dereliction of their responsibility to protect the integrity and independence of prosecutorial decisions by the Department."[32] The principle they acted on— that U.S. attorneys should be removed when they lose the confidence of partisans from their state—erodes public confidence that "the Department of Justice decides who to prosecute [*sic*] based solely on the evidence and the law."[33]

Pointed though they were, the inspector general's conclusions did not reach far enough. The president himself failed to select people who understood the limits of executive partisanship. Lower-level deputies in the Justice Department acted as they did not in spite of the attorney general and the president, but because of them. Even if President Bush himself did not order the attorney general to fire U.S. attorneys, his deputy chief of staff, Karl Rove, interceded with the attorney general to identify places allegedly suffering from an epidemic of voter fraud. The president and his cabinet allowed the administration to become infected with a spirit of crude partisanship. They permitted and possibly nourished a belief that the purpose of the administration was to act for the electoral advantage of the Republican Party.

Bush understood the intimate connection between the presidency and partisanship, but he failed to appreciate that presidential partisanship must be balanced against its opposite. He grasped how presidential greatness requires standing for principles that are controversial in their moment, installing these at the core of a party that continues to serve them after the president's time has passed, and institutionalizing them in policies that citizens come to regard as successful, so that in time they come to be regarded as definitive of the country itself (and thus seem nonpartisan). In practice, attaining this kind of success requires constructing a durable governing majority—something Rove and Bush explicitly aimed for.[34] There is no greatness without winning elections. But Bush allowed himself to be distracted from the high purposes—the values, principles, and policies—that he sought to identify with compassionate conservatism, and to become preoccupied with the crude partisan project of winning elections.

George W. Bush possessed a deep appreciation for the dignity of the presidential office. But he confused dignity with timeliness, formality, and proper behavior within the confines of the Oval Office; in contrast to Bill Clinton, Bush saw himself as restoring dignity to the White House. But he failed to grasp that the substance of presidential dignity is rooted in the rule of law, and that this in turn requires an ethic of impartiality that suffuses the executive branch, most especially those offices that exercise the raw and coercive power of the state. Bush's unembarrassed partisanship, reflected and amplified in his closest aide, Karl Rove, extended to his most important cabinet appointments, such as Attorney General Gonzales. In the end, it corrupted the Justice Department.

The problem was not that Bush was partisan. His partisanship was in many ways astute: significant presidential accomplishment depends on partisanship. The problem was that he was partisan in the wrong way. He allowed crude partisanship, something necessary but also often dangerous and sometimes evil, to define the whole of his partisanship. In the end, even Bush and his appointees knew there was something shameful about the low partisanship that came to dominate: that is why, when first questioned about the removal of U.S. attorneys, they lied.

The Ideal of Nonpartisan Administration

No president can fully embrace partisanship without sacrificing the dignity of the office and corrupting the rule of law. The dignity of the executive is rooted in the ideal of administration: presidents should select for and lead any number of people who are chosen for their competence as much as their party loyalty. The distinction between administration and politics or partisanship was rendered starkly by Woodrow Wilson, a critic of the nineteenth-century spoils system of political appointment. "Administrative questions," Wilson wrote, "are not political questions. Although politics sets the tasks for administration, it should not be suffered to manipulate its offices."[35] In practice, Wilson's distinction is often difficult to draw clearly: the separation between making policy and applying policy is never as distinct in practice as it is in theory. But the distinction is not entirely false. When a prosecutor investigates his political rivals, for instance, the crude Wilsonian distinction makes sense: politics has infected and corroded the administration of law. Without the possibility of maintaining the distinction between politics and administration, executive power and law more generally lose their dignity.

Selecting for loyalty alone is an obvious abuse of public trust, since there is no reason that the loyal will also be competent at what they do. But all presidents will want to select for some measure of loyalty, simply because they are engaged in a partisan fight to implement their principles and policies, and loyal supporters will be more effective than the merely competent. Partisans should not want governmental jobs to simply reward party loyalty, since good and efficient government is the key to implementing the broad conceptions of the common good. In this sense, the administrative state is not an alternative to party government; it is the instrument of party government. Presidents will always select in some measure for those who agree—who share the president's partisan convictions. Yet selecting for programmatic agreement can compromise competence. The deeper danger consists in depriving law and government more generally of legitimacy. To command respect, the administration of law must seem impartial. This points to the delicacy of executive partisanship: on one hand, the presidency is intensely partisan while the leader of his party; on the other hand, the president as chief executive is also entrusted with executive responsibilities that demand impartiality. This invests the executive office with a certain dignity. Presidents need to know when to be partisan and how to be partisan, but they also need to nourish the dignity of their office by distancing governmental administration from partisanship.

Nowhere is this distance more critical than in the elements of executive power that directly involve the coercive power of the state. For instance, as commander-in-chief, the president controls a potent army that no citizen can resist. Also, the president appoints the attorney general, the chief law enforcement officer of the nation (some would say that the president is the chief law enforcement officer, since the attorney general's office is statutory, while the president's is constitutional).[36] As such, the executive is responsible for investigations and prosecutions—occasions that compel people to testify and often lead to prison sentences. To legitimate these awesome powers, presidential power must retain a kind of dignity that requires keeping partisanship at a distance.

Presidential dignity is not just a matter of theater—pomp necessary only because the United States lacks a ceremonial office like a monarchy that can symbolically unify the nation. It rather derives from the impartiality that is necessary to the rule of law. It is for this reason that executive branch employees (approximately 2 million people work in the executive branch of the U.S. government, including about 2,500 people on the president's immediate staff) are restricted in their partisan activities.[37] Most of these are civil service employees covered by the 1939 Hatch Act, which bars federal employees from engaging in certain kinds of partisan activities. The most restricted employees are those who, because of their access to weapons, information, and the compulsory tools of the criminal justice system, wield enormous power. For instance, employees in the Criminal Division of the Justice Department, the Federal Bureau of Information, and the National Security Administration are restricted from holding offices in party organizations and from volunteering on a campaign or making donations to candidates. They are permitted to be partisan—they can register to vote as a Republican, Democrat, or whatever, but they cannot be partisans in the active sense. Perhaps some should even refuse to register as partisans. Even the act of voting may be suspect (not as a matter of law under the Hatch Act, of course, but as a matter of ethical norms).[38]

Should Military Officers Vote?

In 2008, General David Petraeus, who at the time commanded all U.S. forces in Iraq, was asked whether he would be willing to continue his command in Iraq if a Democrat were elected president in November. "Look," the general said, "I haven't voted in elections in some time, actually. And it's because I feel that senior officers in particular should try to be apolitical."[39] Petraeus exemplified an older norm of military honor that developed with the professionalization of the military in the nineteenth century; from the Civil War to World War II, the custom among officers was to avoid all signs of partisanship, even voting.[40] As General George Patton said, "If I vote against the administration I am voting against my commander-in-chief."[41]

Yet in the decades following World War II, the nonvoting norm was relaxed. There seems to be no argument or collective decision that motivated the shift: "no definitive explanation exists for the military's increasing politicization."[42] One cause may be the enhanced status of voting as a right and duty of citizenship. Today, legislation mandates that the military take steps to ensure that all service members are not disenfranchised when they are stationed away from their legal residence. Also, the breakdown of the postwar consensus after Vietnam gave military officers more of a stake in elections. In the country at large, the demographic groups disproportionately represented in the military (white, male, southern) have sorted themselves into the Republican Party. The consequence is both an increase in voting *and* partisanship—particularly Republican partisanship, which is more robust among military officers than in the population at large, even controlling for demographic factors.[43] As one West Point cadet said, "Only Republicans support the military, so we have no reservations about showing support for Republicans."[44]

Still, on the margins the old nonpartisan ideal continues to inform the ideal of what it is to be a military officer. Service members of all ranks are exhorted to keep their "politics private."[45] The rules for political activity, however, recede when service members retire—and retired generals have been courted assiduously by the political parties in recent years. Retired admiral William Crowe's endorsement of Bill Clinton in 1992 helped neutralize the charge that Clinton was a draft dodger. In 2004, twelve retired generals endorsed John Kerry in 2004 while incumbent president George W. Bush attracted over 100 endorsements, including that of the just-retired general Tommy Franks (who had led the attack in Afghanistan in 2001 and the invasion of Iraq in 2003). General Franks also spoke at the Republican National Convention.[46]

The generals' authority as political advocates and the reason candidates seek their endorsements relates to their nonpartisan stature. Franks, for instance, in his speech at the Republican convention, insisted, "I'm not a Republican. I'm not a Democrat . . . after four decades as a soldier I've been Independent. But, here I stand tonight, endorsing George W. Bush."[47] Echoing him—but at the 2004 Democratic convention—retired general John Shalikashvili said, "I do not stand here as a political figure. Rather, I stand as an old soldier."[48] It is one thing for retired generals to endorse a party or candidate; it is another for them to insist they are exercising their nonpartisan judgment, akin to the nonpartisan judgment they exercised in war and for which they were admired. By insisting they were impartial, the generals invaded a principle the military had accrued over centuries during which many hundreds of officers built an ideal of a professional military and, among other things, refused to contaminate their military authority by confessing to any partisan loyalties.

The retired generals also betray a profound misunderstanding of the source of their nonpartisan authority. One might situate military authority alongside the authority of all professions and crafts in that it rests on the possession of nonpolitical expertise. As Petraeus said, explaining his principled refusal to vote, "I think a huge principle of civil-military relations is that there is civil control of the military and that the military's job is to accomplish the mission given to it and to provide the best military advice with respect to that mission." The view presupposes a separation in kind between military expertise and political judgment. And many questions may indeed require purely military nonpolitical knowledge: how many divisions were required to take Trier in 1944 was solely a military question (one that General Patton got right and his superiors got wrong). To take another example, whether to bomb Syria after its use of chemical weapons was a political question, and answering it depends on the answers to a number of purely military questions—how to bomb, what and how many weapons to use, which targets to select.

But often the political and the military sides of a question cannot be fully disentangled. The most effective method (the military question) depends on the goal (the political decision), which in turn will depend on what various effective measures might promise to accomplish (the military question). Moreover, the military is often responsible not only for combat operations, but for a range of postcombat activities that are essentially political (peacekeeping, brokering among rival factions, dispensing basic services to civilians, assisting parties who seek to rule, and assisting with the construction of new constitutions). For example, in 2008 the question of when to draw down troops from Iraq was both a military and a political question, and it is not clear that the military side of the question could be addressed without also engaging political judgment about what kind of withdrawal was desirable.

Generals need to assess the probability that they will succeed not only at tasks directly connected to fighting, but also at securing political goals. As a result, generals will engage their own experience and knowledge—their expertise—with respect to evaluating the political goals of a given action. In many ways, the president as commander-in-chief does not exercise a type of judgment that is different in kind from that of the generals who "advise" him. The difference is that the president's judgment has more authority. Military officers do not simply possess a separate and nonoverlapping competence from that possessed by civilian authorities, and at the highest levels their technical military judgment can never be fully separated from political judgment. On any given occasion, they may be better judges of the questions civilian authorities decide. Military officers need to accept this possibility and "tolerate poor policy outcomes in order to preserve the more fundamental, long-term interest of upholding the democratic character of the state."[49] Senior officers should be apolitical because their jobs are political; a general's expertise is political, which is why it poses a threat.

The dangers of being political in the wrong way are extreme: civilian officials could lose their trust in military advisers, just as military officers could lose their respect for civilian superiors. A breakdown in the chain of command invites the more extreme scenario where generals cease obeying lawful orders and substitute the political judgment of elected leaders with their own judgment. If this seems unlikely, one only needs to consider the difficulty President Truman had controlling the heroic General MacArthur in the years immediately following World War II. The specter of a military coup seems fantastic only because the nonpartisan posture of military officers has made it so unthinkable. This professional norm is the principle that retired generals invade when they endorse political candidates.

The constitutional fealty so ingrained in military officers makes something that would ordinarily be an indication of bad citizenship—nonvoting—into something more commendable.

The unacknowledged logic of General Petraeus's apolitical stance is this: because senior military officers *are* political, because their military judgment will often implicate them in political judgments, they need to take special care not to be political in the wrong way. This means adopting a posture of political modesty that refuses to suggest, however slightly, that their judgment contradicts the judgment of their civilian superiors in the chain of command. "Principled officership," Marybeth Ulrich argues, "requires adherence to an ethic of nonpartisanship."[50]

But nonpartisanship should not entail nonvoting. Attuning West Point cadets or officers generally to an ethic of nonvoting runs directly counter to the more general aim of civic education that imparts a sense of duty about voting. The tension between the duty of ordinary citizens to vote and a duty for military officers *not* to vote, if indeed it could be sustained in practice, might exacerbate the gap between military culture and democratic culture. To the extent the ethic of nonvoting took hold, as it would if it were viewed as a soft requirement for all officers, it would invite military officers to go beyond an apolitical stance to an "antipolitical" stance.[51] The antipolitical posture situates one not only apart from partisan politics, but superior to it. A disdain for democratic politics—common enough given democracy's characteristic inefficiency, undiscipline, and inability to impose sacrifice—is an ever-present occupational hazard of military officership. An ethic of nonvoting could fuel and amplify this disdain, producing something stronger and more threatening: disgust.

It would be less corrosive for military officers to vote, even if nearly all of them voted for one party. Even if it means voting against their commander-in-chief, military officers should be able to express their duty to vote just as ordinary citizens do. In contemporary democracy, voting is a private and temperate act—with the secret ballot, no one needs to know how one voted, nor should the mere act of casting a ballot inflame one's party spirit to the point where one loses respect for officials one votes against.

Officers should cultivate political modesty: they should be reticent about how they vote. Where state laws permit it, they should register as independents. And they should refrain from public partisan commentary—even after they retire.[52] A retired general is still, in the public's eye, a general—which is why their endorsements in partisan politics carry force. The privacy that shrouds officers' votes should extend to retired officers: their partisan identity should be something they keep to themselves, not because it corrupts their nonpartisan expertise but because, on the contrary, their position may invest them with exercising political judgments. If their roles were less political, they could afford to be more partisan.

The Ideal of Nonpartisan Enforcement: The Defense of Marriage Act

Low partisan motives, which are necessary to give high partisan goals force, also corrupt that force when they become dominant. But even high partisanship can corrupt certain executive powers. Sometimes executives need to be wary of all partisan motives. This need is not extraordinary or occasional: it arises every day, in ordinary political time.

The president, for example, has a constitutional duty to "take care that the laws be faithfully executed," and this duty of care extends even to laws with which the president disagrees.[53] A future Republican president who may be opposed to the Affordable Care Act of 2010, for example, would nonetheless have a constitutional duty to faithfully execute the law. The duty of care creates a presidential responsibility that extends beyond partisanship to the rule of law. The ideal of "presidents above party" is not merely a rhetorical strategy presidents invoke to amplify their authority. It is a daily presidential duty.

This duty comes into focus in the Office of the Solicitor General. The soliticor general decides when to appeal to the Supreme Court those cases the government loses in lower federal courts. As a rule, the solicitor general defends the constitutionality of federal laws in the Supreme Court. The exceptions to the rule mainly concern laws that in the view of the Justice Department unconstitutionally encroach on presidential power or laws for which no reasonable argument can be adduced in support of their constitutionality. The solicitor general is a partisan or political appointment and serves at the pleasure of the president. Although some have claimed that the solicitor general should be "a foremost promoter of the policies of the president before the Court," a longer custom establishes an independence of the solicitor general from the presidential administration.[54] In defending the constitutionality of duly passed laws, even those with which the president disagrees, the solicitor general also represents Congress—not only the present Congress, but Congress as a constitutional institution. Because of its tradition of scrupulous legal craftsmanship and full disclosure of bad facts, even the Supreme Court has come to rely on the expertise of the Office of the Solicitor General. In the largest sense, the solicitor general's client includes the presidential administration, Congress, and the Court: the Solicitor General's client encompasses, in a sense, "the interests of the United States."[55]

Until 2012, consistent with its customary role, the Office of the Solicitor General defended the constitutionality of the Defense of Marriage Act (DOMA). This law, which prevented the federal government from recognizing same-sex marriages conferred by the states (and which allowed some states to refuse to recognize same-sex marriages granted in other states), was passed by veto-proof bipartisan majorities in the House and the Senate and was signed by President Clinton in 1996. Yet an odd scene presented itself seventeen years later, when the Supreme Court entertained a constitutional challenge to DOMA, *United States v. Windsor.* Rather than defend the constitutionality of the law, the solicitor general sided with the plaintiff in holding that the law was unconstitutional. In the absence of any party to defend the law, the House of Representatives hired its own lawyers to defend it. And because it was not clear that there was an actual legal controversy (with the government and the plaintiff on the same side), the Supreme Court appointed yet a fourth counsel to make the case that the Court lacked jurisdiction.[56]

The dizzying assembly of advocates at the Supreme Court's oral argument on the case came about because of President Obama's 2011 decision to direct the attorney general (and thus the solicitor general) *not* to defend the constitutionality of the law. If DOMA were like most laws, the administration argued, one could adduce a rational basis for it, and the customary duty to defend its constitutionality would apply. But because, in Obama's view, DOMA singled out a group that has historically suffered discrimination (homosexuals), it should be subjected to a more demanding standard of "heightened scrutiny" that the Court applies to laws, for instance, that make racial distinctions. On this more demanding standard, Obama argued, no reasonable argument can be adduced for the constitutionality of the law.

To some observers, Obama's decision violated the presidential duty of care. The duty of care requires the president to defend the constitutionality of all duly passed laws so long as a reasonable case could be made for the laws' constitutionality. The position of the Obama administration itself for two years was that a reasonable case could be made on behalf of DOMA, and for two years Obama's Justice Department defended the law. While Obama himself in the 2008 campaign expressed his belief that the law was unconstitutional, the customary understanding of the duty of care requires the president to defend all laws for which any reasonable argument can be adduced in support of their constitutionality, even if the president himself disagrees with those arguments. Obama's sudden decision not to defend the law smacked of politics: it was anticipated that the enthusiastic support of gay constituencies would help Obama's reelection chances. To his critics, the president seemed to place his partisan conceptions ahead of his constitutional duties.

The charge overlooks an important subtlety in Obama's decision. While Obama's Justice Department would no longer defend the constitutionality of DOMA, the Obama administration insisted it would nonetheless enforce the law. This put the administration in the odd position of agreeing with the petitioner that DOMA was unconstitutional, but denying the petitioner what she was seeking—an exemption from paying estate tax on property left to her in her wife's estate (an exemption that married heterosexual couples would enjoy). The Obama administration agreed with Edith Windsor, the plaintiff, as a matter of constitutional theory, but in practice refused to pay up—costing Windsor hundreds of thousands of dollars. This inconsistency reflected Obama's commitment to uphold the presidential duty of care. The duty of care, Obama's example suggests, may not extend to defending every law the president believes is unconstitutional, but it does extend to enforcing laws, even ones the president thinks are unconstitutional. At its core, the duty of care, in this view, is rather a basic duty to enforce laws until those laws are repealed by the legislature or overturned by the Court.

Yet for some, Obama's carefully considered inconsistency—enforce, but do not defend—stemmed less from constitutional commitment than from political calculation. In this view, Obama calculated that the odds of reversing DOMA in the Court were higher than the chances of reversing it in Congress. So he contrived to put the question to the Court and thus to force the Court to settle a partisan question that he was afraid to submit to the legislature. In oral argument, Chief Justice Roberts suggested that Obama's position was cowardly: "I don't see why he doesn't have the courage of his convictions and exe-cute not only the statute, but do it consistent with his view of the constitution, rather than saying, oh we'll wait till the Su-preme Court tells us we have no choice."[57] Roberts argued that the Supreme Court should not entertain the case, since there was no controversy between the plaintiff and the government.[58]

In the end, Roberts was on the losing side of the 5–4 deci-sion. The majority insisted that a genuine controversy existed because the government continued to enforce the law and re-fused to pay up, whatever its theoretical stance on the constitu-tionality of the law. Had Obama refused to enforce DOMA because he thought it unconstitutional, there indeed would have been no controversy for the Supreme Court to litigate. But to suppose that Obama should have both refused to defend the constitutionality of the law *and* to enforce the law would un-dercut the rule of law. If presidents could refuse to enforce laws they considered unconstitutional, they would routinely stretch the understanding of constitutionality to include laws they con-sidered destructive to the general welfare. This would not only render the presidency a profoundly more partisan office; it would make law itself more partisan, and lead to a consequent erosion of the rule of law. This is why Obama insisted on en-forcing DOMA even as he argued that it was unconstitutional: in that insistence, Obama retained the connection between the institutional authority of the presidency and the moral author-ity of the rule of law. That connection limits what a president can do as a partisan—even a high partisan, concerned with large conceptions of justice and the common good. To insist that the government cease defending the constitutionality of DOMA was a partisan act, in the noblest sense of partisanship. To simultaneously insist that the government continue enforcing DOMA was a presidential act, in the nonpartisan sense that situates the presidency above party.

The Partisan Community Revisited

Perhaps Justice Roberts was goading the president in oral argument: what he likely meant to suggest was not that the president should have both declared the act unconstitutional and refused to enforce it (the seemingly courageous thing, according to his line of questioning), but that he should have done neither. If President Obama felt the act was indeed unconstitutional, he should have made that argument and put the weight of his office and the force of his rhetoric behind a bill to repeal the act. Meanwhile, he could direct the Justice Department to follow its traditional role of defending the constitutionality of *all* acts of Congress where reasonable defenses can be offered. Such a course of action would have honored his presidential duty of care; it would have placed the partisan question of marriage equality in the legislature, where it could be debated; and it would have insulated the Court from that same partisan question, preserving the Court's nonpartisan stature—and in the process preserved the idea that the Constitution, and thus the political community it constitutes, have a nonpartisan basis.

It would be desirable in some respects to insulate the Court from all partisan questions. If partisan questions, even high partisan questions involving contested understandings of equality, were cordoned off from the Court, the justices could confine themselves to matters of brute constitutional interpretation.

"Judges are like umpires," Justice Roberts said in the opening statement of his confirmation hearings. "They don't make the rules. They apply them." In his confirmation hearings, Roberts famously said, "I come before the committee with no agenda," and pledged to "remember that it's my job to call balls and strikes, not to pitch or bat."[59] Having "no agenda," justices should be, in Roberts's view, wholly nonpartisan.

Perhaps this is why Justice Roberts accused Obama of lacking courage: Obama refused to entertain a legislative remedy to the Defense of Marriage Act because he knew his cause would lose in the legislature. Thus he put the issue before the Court, where his chances of victory were higher. This in turn thrust the Court into a political and partisan role—exactly the job that Roberts meant to avoid. Justice Roberts's umpiring image invokes a political modesty that is appropriate for the Court. Prudence compels the Court to shy away from questions that excite active and vigorous controversy—the legislature, after all, is the natural home for partisanship. Unlike courts, legislatures are designed to be responsive to popular pressure, and those on the losing side of a law can at every election try to reverse what they oppose. The only response to a "bad" Court decision is a constitutional amendment.

At the same time, Roberts's idea that Supreme Court justices are akin to umpires invokes an absurdly mechanistic ideal of judging. If it were not necessary to interpret the Constitution, we would not need judges. At the highest levels—such as the Supreme Court—interpretation cannot escape understandings of the Constitution and the country that are profoundly partisan. These understandings should not be partisan in the low sense, of course; judges will corrode and ultimately destroy the courts if they decide with a view to election outcomes (this, of course, is why *Bush v. Gore* was so dangerous). The partisanship of judges is sublimated through the Constitution, and takes the form of a "judicial philosophy" that goes deeper and takes a longer view than even the high partisan conceptions that animate elected officials at their best.

Many judicial decisions will have an obvious relationship to more ordinary partisan conceptions, which is why it makes sense to speak of liberal and conservative judges. Judges cannot wholly avoid partisanship. But their partisanship is always troubling, because it shows we are an essentially partisan community. When the Court agrees to decide something that is a partisan controversy where many millions of people disagree and reasonable arguments abound, the decision—whichever side "wins"— acknowledges that the most authoritative interpretation of the Constitution has an inescapably partisan dimension. The issue, in other words, is not merely that the Court is partisan—but that the community itself is.

As we have seen, even the liberal political community is more partisan than it ordinarily can acknowledge. A nonpartisan community is constituted by incontrovertible first principles of political morality. We may accept that there are such first principles—freedom and equality, for instance. But how these principles apply to concrete cases and controversies cannot itself be wholly determined by the argument for the principles themselves. Partisanship about how these principles apply to particular questions may be fueled by a suppressed and inchoate disagreement about the principles themselves. What matters is that the principles at some general level are taken as a given. This, even if it is not enough to render the Court or the political community essentially nonpartisan, is sufficient to maintain the web of beliefs and aspirations that the idea of the nonpartisan community supports.

This web includes the aspiration to the rule of law and the ideal of justice. We need to believe in the *possibility* of a nonpartisan community in order to make sense of these aspirations and ideals. Ideals of the common good, justice, and the rule of law only make sense if we can imagine a nonpartisan basis for the political community. That we may need to believe in the nonpartisan community, of course, does not make it so. Whether there are in fact nonpartisan first principles of political morality is a question left open by philosophy, from Aristotle to Rawls. But the rule of law—and the idea of a just community—does not require that we have a final settled conviction about first principles of political morality and how they apply to all relevant questions. All they require is the acceptance that there might be such principles, that we might know what they are and might have an opinion about how they should be applied. The modern conceit—that having discovered basic first principles of political morality, we have escaped the partisan predicament of traditional politics—is overdrawn.

Applying the first principles of political morality to any concrete question is a matter of judgment: freedom and equality offer an occasion to disagree, not an end to disagreement. What binds the partisan community together is not a settled conviction that we possess first principles of political morality and agree about precisely how they are to be applied—that our reason has settled what for so long has divided us. It is rather that we agree to argue in terms of these principles. They provide not the substance but the form for contestation.

The agreement to argue in these terms is not trivial. In agreeing to the form, we agree to the possibility of first principles of political morality, to accept the possibility that these first principles might be true, and therefore also to the possibility that the rule of law is not entirely a veil that makes the power some exercise over others palatable. The agreement is not deep or extensive enough to displace partisanship or render it something superficial: it is not a final settlement, only a settlement about the form of argument. But it is sufficient to legitimate the idea of justice. It is enough to create a responsibility that extends to all the officials who are directly connected to law in its most coercive aspect—its execution—to maintain a fealty to nonpartisan forms of enforcement. Judges, prosecutors, and even presidents cannot avoid being partisan all the way down. But neither can they escape the nonpartisan obligations that make the rule of law something real.

CAN THE GOVERNMENT GOVERN?

Amid the extreme partisanship of the moment, it is tempting to idealize the age of bipartisan bargaining that extended from roughly the New Deal to the 1964 Civil Rights Act. In what Ronald Brownstein calls the "golden age of statesmanship and cooperation in Congress,"[1] each party was ideologically diverse. The Republican Party had liberals from the Northeast, and the Democratic Party contained conservatives from the South. Presidents were often frustrated by their own party in Congress, and almost all important legislation required constructing a temporary bipartisan alliance. The "great virtue" of the system, in Brownstein's account, was seen in the way it "compelled political leaders who held contrasting views and represented different constituencies to talk and listen to each other."[2] In Brownstein's view, this is the virtue American politics needs today, since on nearly every major issue America "requires comprehensive solutions that marry ideas favored by one party and opposed by the other."[3]

But the age of bipartisan accommodation was marred by a signal defect. While the less ideological party system of the golden age was more fluid, it was also dominated by an alliance of conservative Democrats (mostly from the South) and conservative Republicans centered in the Midwest. On domestic policy, this coalition disempowered liberals in the Democratic Party and moderates in the Republican Party for over three decades. The alliance defended racial segregation, which was among the notable consequences of twentieth-century bipartisanship. For his part, Brownstein recognizes this defect. As he says, "The greatest shame of the [mid-twentieth-century party system] is that it . . . safeguarded a regime of brutal state-sponsored segregation that denied the rights of millions of black Americans."[4] If anything, Brownstein understates the connection between twentieth-century bipartisanship and racial apartheid in the United States. The Democratic Party was ideologically indistinct *because* of race: southern Democrats could not bring themselves to join the party of Lincoln. Southern Democrats had enormous power both within the Democratic Party and within the country because of racial apartheid. The systematic disenfranchisement of southern blacks via poll taxes, literacy tests (that somehow illiterate whites could pass), and citizenship tests (that somehow only blacks could fail) made the South a one-party region, and this in turn made it easy for southern whites elected to Congress to keep getting reelected, and to eventually rise up through the ranks and occupy the chairmanships of the most important committees.[5] Racial segregation was not a sorry by-product of the system of bipartisan accommodation—it was the cause and the purpose of the system.

In response, liberal reformers imagined a more national party system, where the parties were differentiated enough at a national level to offer voters a "true choice"—this was the spirit that informed E. E. Schattschneider and APSA's 1950 report on the parties.[6] The seniority system in Congress was the target of particular ire because it elevated southern conservatives in the Democratic Party to positions of immense power and equipped them to veto not only all civil rights legislation but also progressive legislation on housing, education, and health care. In the 1970s, the Democratic Party finally weakened the rule of seniority in the selection of committee chairs.[7] Reforming seniority allowed for parties that could be both responsible and ideological; committee chairs who stood in the way of enacting a party program could be removed (or prevented from becoming chair in the first place).

But this reform, in Brownstein's telling, backfired on liberals in the 1990s, when an ascendant Republican majority led by Newt Gingrich concentrated power in the Speaker of the House and disempowered moderate Republicans and the Democratic minority. Congressional Republicans of the 1990s and the early years of the twenty-first century made the Republican Party into the kind of programmatic and responsible party that liberal reformers of the twentieth century had wanted. If only the mid-twentieth-century liberals had left well enough alone, this argument suggests, we might still have a Congress capable of bipartisan accommodation, and might have some hope of solving the major issues of our time in a comprehensive way.

The deeper causes of the destruction of the system of bipartisan accommodation were the 1964 Civil Rights Act and the 1965 Voting Rights Act. By virtue of these acts, especially the latter (which placed federal marshals in southern counties to directly enforce the rights of black citizens to the vote), the Democratic Party decisively abandoned its white southern constituency.[8] That constituency gradually found its way to the Republican Party. The realignment of conservative southern whites away from their habitual attachment to the Democratic Party and toward the Republican Party is what allowed the parties to become more ideologically distinct. No longer would northern liberals and southern conservatives in the Democratic Party have to endure a marriage to each other. As the Republican Party became more conservative, social liberals in the Republican Party found themselves increasingly marginalized, and gravitated toward the Democrats. The decision by leaders in the

Democratic Party under LBJ that racial segregation could no longer be protected is what destroyed the system of bipartisan accommodation and created the system of more ideological partisanship we have today.

The problem with the system of bipartisan accommodation was not simply that there was "too much" consensus. The problem was the nature of the consensus. The price that bipartisan accommodation exacted was maintaining a web of violent and discriminatory practices. We got bipartisan consensus, but only because the country was willing to tolerate educational discrimination, job discrimination, systematic disenfranchisement of millions, entrenched poverty, lynching—in short, racial oppression. The system had its achievements and virtues, to be sure— especially in foreign policy. But its defects were not marginal, nor were they ancillary qualities that might somehow be peeled away. The defects were what made bipartisan accommodation possible.

There is nothing sacred about bipartisanship, though some are fond of it simply because they believe the right answer in politics is always found in the middle. Brownstein seems to think this, at least with respect to "comprehensive solutions" that require mixing ideas from each party. This principled commitment to the middle reflects the Millian idea we encountered in Chapter 4, that "truth, in the great practical concerns of life is . . . a question of reconciling and combining of opposites."[9] The centrist instinct may be appropriate when the extremes are truly ideological and reflect a principled but narrow approach to politics. In these conditions, picking the best from each side may be the most appropriate response to social complexity. But when centrism becomes its own principle ("the middle is always best"), it loses its coherence. No law of nature places the optimal policy between the ideally preferred points of liberals and conservatives. On fiscal policy, health care, foreign policy—on any policy, the best approach might well be the position advocated for by one party.

Centrism makes sense when there is a range of broadly popular policies and programs, but where party loyalty prevents the coalition that could enact them from forming. This happens, as we saw in Chapter 7, when there is a latent majority that combines members of the two parties. Perhaps a minority of Republicans and a minority of Democrats would support a particular policy or reform (for example, reform of the tax code). This latent majority cannot become empowered because each side is defeated within its own party, and each side refuses to cooperate with—or is prevented by legislative rules from cooperating with—partisans of the other side. There may well be a number of important issues that have this character—their support comes from a blend of opposing partisans whose party loyalty prevents them from coming together.

When cases like this arise occasionally, it is reasonable to expect that partisans should relax their loyalty and find a way of coming together—a Speaker of the *whole* House, as we saw in Chapter 7, might allow for issues that combine coalitions from both parties to get a hearing. A small Centrist Party that prevents either of the great parties from constituting a majority in the legislature would also empower the latent bipartisan majority. What is crucial to see, however, is that such a Centrist Party would need to stand for something besides mere centrism. It would need to develop distinct positions across a range of issues. It would need to speak to broad goals and principles in order to be a force that endures across a series of election cycles. And it would need to inspire loyalty in both voters and officials. It would need to be a party, not a position on a line segment. The path to moderating American politics runs through partisanship, not around it. A Centrist Party, if it were a real *party,* might be a powerful force for moderation. Multimember electoral districts for congressional races, combined with proportional representation, might have a similar effect. In both cases, coalitions would need to form in the legislature that might move the center of gravity from the extremes to the center. A constitutional amendment that overturns *Citizens United* and allows governments to regulate the flow of money in campaigns might facilitate parties that are responsible to the electorate rather than to a handful of donors.[10] These innovations attempt to reform partisanship, not abandon it in favor of the bipartisan ideal. They amplify disagreement even as they attempt to strengthen the forces of moderation in American politics.

The problem with partisans of the moment is not that their ideal preferences are too extreme, but rather that they hold to these preferences with uncompromising certitude. It is not their principles but their tactics that give today's partisans the look of fanatics devoted to the whole truth. Today's partisans too often lack any "negative capacity": they cannot turn against their own goals and values even intellectually and experimentally, to see how they might be incomplete or lacking. In their insistence that they possess the whole truth, partisans see every compromise as an existential defeat. The tendency to equate the survival of the party itself with winning on every measure—and thus never compromising—in turn reflects the way low or petty partisanship has come to define all partisanship.

The refusal to compromise reflects a parliamentary style of partisanship that can immobilize a separation-of-powers system (which requires compromise when parties split control of the executive and the legislature, or the two houses of the legislature).[11] When Sam Beer characterized British MPs as manifesting "Prussian discipline," the contrast with members of the U.S. Congress was obvious: fewer than half the votes in Congress were "party votes" (where a majority of one party votes against a majority of the other). The low point came in 1970, when only 32 percent were party votes. Since the Republican Party won control of the House of Representatives in 1994, party votes have always been above 50 percent, and set a new record of 75.8 percent in 2011.[12] When the parties split control of the legislature and the presidency—as in the 2010–2014 period, when the Republicans controlled the House and the Democrats the Senate and the presidency—parliamentary partisanship makes it nearly impossible for the government to govern.

The most obvious manifestation of this was seen in the sheer lack of productivity of Congress. The 112th Congress, which concluded in 2012, passed the fewest laws of any modern Congress (although the Republican majority did manage to vote thirty-three times to repeal Obama's health care act). But nothing illustrated the inability of the government to govern like the unending debt limit debacle that began in 2011. The debt ceiling restricts the Treasury Department's ability to borrow to pay for implementing laws already enacted by Congress. Prior to World War I, the Treasury would request congressional approval every time it needed to borrow, but the expenses of the war made this impractical, and Congress instead approved a general debt limit, below which the Treasury could borrow as it needed. Ever since, Congress has needed from time to time to raise the debt limit. These routine but uncomfortable votes force Congress to squarely face the cumulative effect of budget deficits. In the past, Congress raised the debt limit without undue drama. But what was once routine now illustrates a government that cannot get out of its own way.

Contemplating a Republican takeover of the House in 2010, Alan Simpson (the former Republican senator from Wyoming) said, "I can't wait for the bloodbath in April. When the debt limit time comes, they're going to look around and say, 'What the hell do we do now?' And boy, the blood bath will be extraordinary."[13] From his tone, one might have wondered whether Simpson secretly relished the prospect. What followed was not merely a pointed clash, but a long and reiterated series of failures that together point to a slow-motion constitutional crisis. There is no reason to think the cycle of threats, counterthreats, and repeated failures to broker differences will end any time soon. Amid the repeated failure to broker differences, the repeated near misses where Congress barely avoids catastrophes of its own making, the posturing and obstruction and blaming, one cannot avoid the sense that the government has become incapable of governing. In response to this constitutional crisis, what we need, many say, is less partisanship. In fact, partisanship of a certain sort is part of the solution to the crisis. What we need is less low partisanship.

Low Partisanship

All effective bargaining requires duplicity. Good legislators have to say they will not accept things they will in fact accept, that an offer is insulting when it is actually agreeable, that their followers will not go along when actually they probably will. This is part of the game of legislation, and there is no escaping it. The machinations that are inevitably part of legislative advocacy make politics ethically unsightly, and anyone who follows it should be prepared to see commonsense notions of friendship, loyalty, and patriotism distorted and abused. It is not a game for naïfs, and one might well wonder if a good person can also be a political person. It should not be surprising or disturbing if ordinary people are put off by politics—they should be.

Nonetheless, even accommodating for the normal machinations of politics, there are limits to what partisans should do. The obvious limit is advocating for policies that would be collectively disastrous. "Paint this house the color I want or I will

burn it down (with us all in it)" is the sort of bargaining posture that breaks faith. For that sort of position to have force,
one has to actually be willing to burn the house down, and
anyone who is willing to do that obviously has no concern for
the common good. This was, in effect, the Republican Party's
position on the debt limit: balance the budget our way (by
cutting spending—no new taxes!) or we will take down the
national—and global—economy. We might excuse some (if it is
an excuse) by supposing that they thought failing to raise the
debt ceiling would not provoke default. Or they may have thought
that default would not be so terrible, or would be somewhat less
terrible than not getting their way on fiscal policy. Such a stand
might have been reckless in its disregard for catastrophic economic risk, but it was at least authentic: some people thought
default would be okay. But others knew that failing to raise the
debt ceiling would inject chaos into the financial markets and
would be destructive of the economy. For them, the debt ceiling was simply a point of "leverage" in negotiating for spending cuts.

For instance, Republican senator John Cornyn of Texas long
held that Republicans should hold off on raising the debt ceiling in order to force Democrats to pass cuts to entitlement programs. Then, in the winter of 2013, he suddenly changed his
position, insisting that the Republican Party should not contemplate default. When asked about the change, he said, "You
sometimes try to inject a little doubt in your negotiating partner about where you're going to go, but I would tell you un-
equivocally that we're not going to default."[14] Injecting doubt in
your negotiating partner about whether you are willing to burn
the house down may be effective, but it corrodes public trust.
To disagree about what counts as the common good is one
thing, and makes partisanship both inevitable and interesting;
intentionally threatening to destroy the common good is some-

thing else. The connection to the common good is what makes partisanship legitimate—and admirable. When this connection is broken, partisanship can only reflect political ambition.

The "common good" is so general and elusive that one might think the concept fatuous, of no practical use. Specified in a way that commands general assent—union, justice, common defense, the general welfare, and liberty—it elides any concrete policies. As soon as any concrete way of securing the common good comes into view, agreement dissolves. A shared commitment to the common good does not take us very far in politics. Yet the idea of the common good is essential to healthy partisanship—perhaps nothing is more important. Partisans need to believe that their opponents are genuinely motivated by a desire to serve the common good. This is the basis of good faith and civic respect; it is what makes the permanent and peaceful disagreement of rival partisans possible.[15] Good faith makes compromise palatable for rival partisans—a good faith devotion to the common good is what drives partisans to accept something over nothing, even when the "something" is intensely disappointing. Low partisan calculations that make it thinkable to threaten the common good for the sake of leverage or advantaging one's side not only give partisanship a bad name—they sever partisanship from the people, corrupt the political culture, and ultimately make it impossible for us to cooperate for the sake of the common good.

Republicans are not the only ones who have indulged in low partisanship, especially on the debt limit. President Obama too opposed raising the debt limit in 2006—when he was a Democratic senator and George W. Bush was in the White House. It was, Obama said later, a "political vote."[16] This is the usual pattern: Democrats vote against raising the debt limit when there are Republican presidents, as Republicans do when there are Democratic presidents.[17] This is what is meant by the phrase "playing politics." Individual legislators may have a deep conviction that the public debt is evil. But they indulge that conviction in ways that are either meaningless (because the debt limit increase will pass anyway) or catastrophic (because it might not pass). In either case, their stand is not serious—they do not seriously intend that the nation default on its debts. Like Obama or Cornyn, they reverse themselves when things get serious, as if taking false stands for self-serving reasons is what partisanship is about.

When partisanship amounts to nothing more than "whatever they're for, I oppose," it loses its connection to the common good. To crystallize their case that partisanship in Congress today is "even worse than it looks," Thomas Mann and Norman Ornstein open their argument with an account of the Senate vote on January 26, 2010, that left the Conrad-Gregg Bipartisan Task Force for Responsible Fiscal Action seven votes short of defeating a Republican filibuster. Seven Republicans who had originally cosponsored the bill actually voted against it. Senate Minority Leader Mitch McConnell, who had supported the bill, voted against it.[18] "Why did they do so?" Mann and Ornstein ask. "Because President Barack Obama was for it, and its passage might gain him political credit."[19]

Switching sides on substantive questions as their calculations of political advantage shift is a normal if unseemly part of politics. The most notorious in recent American politics is Mitt Romney's example of supporting public health insurance as governor of Massachusetts (when it was an electoral advantage to support it) and opposing essentially the same plan drawn on a national scale when he was running for president (when the electoral disadvantages of such a position were abundant). But Mitt Romney was taking on a new role as leader of his party and presidential nominee—some trimming will always be necessary when individual officials step into new roles with new constituencies. This is most stark when people become candidates for the vice presidency and need to trim their previous commitments to fit the positions of the presidential candidate. Trimming of this sort is embarrassing, but there is nothing wrong with it—on the contrary, it reflects a willingness to compromise for the sake of leading a broad and diverse coalition. It is corrosive of public trust in government, however, when the cosponsors of legislation vote against their own bill to avoid being on the same side as a president from the opposite party. This is when low partisanship eclipses any sight of the common good.

The problem with partisanship in contemporary American politics is not that officials are too partisan, or even too ideological. The ideological dimensions of politics today are in themselves hardly troubling, and are far less severe than the ideological contests that roiled nineteenth- and twentieth-century politics. The problem is that low partisanship has crowded out the kind of principles, convictions, and attachments that make partisanship something respectable, even noble. Low partisanship threatens to become the whole of partisanship, leaving it without a soul. It is partisanship without spirit.

No remark in recent years captured the dominance of low partisanship better than a stray comment by Senate Minority Leader Mitch McConnell, who on the cusp of the 2010 midterm elections (when the Democrats would be trounced in Congress, only two years after taking the majority) said that the "single most important" goal of the Republican Party was "for President Obama to be a one term president." In the same interview, McConnell softened that formulation by insisting that he wanted the president to "succeed" (though presumably not so well that he would be reelected) and that it would "not be inappropriate" for Republicans to cooperate with the president if he met them "halfway" on "some of the biggest issues."[20]

Perhaps the comment was merely an infelicitous (or "indelicate," as McConnell later put it) formulation on McConnell's part. But to the extent that he said what he meant, McConnell's formulation reveals what is so corrosive about low partisanship. When the *number one* goal is electoral victory (or, in this case, another candidate's defeat), base power seeking obscures the larger purposes that make seeking power something respectable. It was not necessarily wrong or unreasonable of McConnell to hope that a Republican would defeat Obama. It was wrong to cast this as the *number one* goal of the party, prior to everything else—debt reduction, tax policy, foreign relations, and the other issues that make the party something ordinary citizens might have a reason to care about.

When low partisanship displaces anything higher, the gap between political people (who are marked by their desire for power, or who, as Machiavelli says, "want to oppress") and ordinary people (who just want some immunity from other people's power, or who, as Machiavelli says, "want not to be oppressed") becomes a canyon. Causes, principles, convictions lose their force and their allure, and become just the veil that makes power-seeking behavior presentable. Low politics is power seeking, naked and unembarrassed.

As we saw in Chapter 5, party loyalty at its best expresses itself as a kind of remembrance. Put differently, for partisanship to be worthy of our loyalty, it has to engage in a contest worth remembering. There is nothing about the debt limit scares that partisans will wish to remember. The memory of them will not inspire renewed devotion to the ideals that define the parties, nor will it clarify the principles that define future campaigns. Party loyalty at its best also requires patience—but partisan patience only makes sense in response to long-term projects.

Threatening national default did not constitute a program or a goal—it was neither worth remembering nor waiting for. It was solely an act of low partisanship, and made a mockery of those who are inclined, for one reason or another, to be loyal to their party.

High Partisanship

Low partisanship matters, but only because of its connection to high partisanship; reelection matters only because one wants to advance a conception of the national interest. When low partisanship is severed from larger goals and purposes, partisanship expresses nothing more than the pathetic yet possibly dangerous tool of political ambition. As one scholar of Congress asks, "What . . . makes reelection worth pursuing so single-mindedly? In truth, very little," she says. "There are plenty of other jobs that pay more money, are less demanding, and even feed one's ego more generously than those of U.S. representative or senator."[21] When it is subservient to higher partisan goals, low partisanship, however unseemly, is tolerable and, in any case, necessary. In order to serve public purposes, however controversial, one needs to get elected—and reelected. The calculations of low partisanship cannot be neglected. But the petty aspect of partisanship is made legitimate by the broader purposes it serves—by its connection to the common good.

This connection has been weakened in recent years, leaving only base and self-serving partisanship. It is no wonder many thoughtful observers are nostalgic for the golden age of bipartisanship. But to suppose that we would be better off without partisanship is a profound mistake. The delusions of post-partisanship (as if any conception of the common good could avoid controversy) and the fantasy of bipartisan consensus (as if bipartisanship could stand for something substantive) distract us from what we need: not less partisanship, but better partisanship. What vital democratic politics needs is not nonpartisan centrism, or the erasure of disagreement and contestation from politics, but a deeper clarity about the public choices that cannot be avoided. Underlying the dispiriting debates of recent years are real and critical questions about how to understand the national interest. Serious disagreements about the common good are what make bipartisan compromise so wrenching and elusive.

In American politics today, these disagreements are not illusory, nor are they entirely the impositions of a self-serving political class. They reflect real differences about the direction the country should take and about the nature of justice. The Republican Party, in general, wants to vest responsibility in each person for dealing with his or her bad decisions and bad luck, as it wants to allow individuals to fully enjoy the consequences of their good decisions and good luck. The Democratic Party, by contrast, upholds the ideal of standing together to insure each other against the worst consequences of bad luck, as it believes in collectively providing opportunities for children in spite of their parents' bad decisions (or bad luck). These rival conceptions of the common good emphasize different values: one is more individualistic, the other more communal; one more stern, the other more generous; one more interested in virtue, the other in equality. They point to different positions about the scope of government, and to different policies.

Some would prefer a "middle course" because the country at large is not divided so much as it is ambivalent. Elites—opinion leaders, activists, and, most of all, legislators—are divided. While many citizens have "sorted" themselves politically and have aligned with one party or the other, most ordinary citizens do not have views that neatly align with either a conservative or liberal ideology, or with the Democratic or Republican Party.[22]

Most people are simultaneously pulled this way and that.[23] Ordinary voters, Morris Fiorina argues, are not simply more pragmatic and less ideological than party activists and legislators; they "are more *uncertain* about their political views and how they should translate them into voting than members of the political class."[24] Or, as E. J. Dionne argues, we do not face a series of fundamental choices where values "face off against each other. There is not a party of 'individualism' competing at election time against a party of 'community.' Rather, *both* of these values animate the consciousness and consciences of nearly all Americans." We face, he says, not a choice, "but a quest for balance." And "we are not very skilled at balance anymore."[25] The problem in this view is that partisan elites present voters with a choice that voters do not want to make.

Indeed, Americans over the last thirty years have been ambivalent about the scope of government. On one hand, they want smaller government and lower taxes. On the other, they want to sustain and enhance entitlements like Social Security and Medicare. When this ambivalence is mapped onto public policy—through, for instance, the nearly simultaneous expansion of Medicare to include prescription drugs and a series of tax cuts in the early 2000s—the outcome is a structural fiscal deficit. With spending and taxes, there is a basic and unavoidable choice to make. Parties and partisan legislators ought to clarify that choice and to present it to the public, even if members of the public would prefer not to face up to it. This will mean that partisan legislators will take more "extreme" stands than ordinary citizens, who want to have it both ways. There will be an inevitable disconnect between the political class, which sees the choice for what it is, and everyday citizens who want services and entitlements, but who do not want higher taxes.

If many citizens feel they should not have to make this choice, it is partly because party elites have led people to believe they do not have to. Consider, for instance, the popular ambivalence about the scope of the national government. Republican leaders from the 1950s through the 1970s made their peace with the basic orientation toward government at the heart of the New Deal. Eisenhower accepted Social Security, the signal achievement of the New Deal.[26] Nixon signed into law cost of living increases in Social Security, the Clean Water Act, and the Clean Air Act (Democrats joke that he was the last liberal president).[27] It was Reagan who announced a new and more radical posture toward the scope of the national government. This stance was crystallized in the famously forthright statement of his first inaugural address (which might serve as the Republican Party's slogan today): "Government is not the solution to our problem," Reagan said. "Government is the problem."[28]

For his part, Reagan's own public philosophy was highly nuanced. Even in his first inaugural address, Reagan qualified his grand statement by noting that *"in this present crisis"* of inflation and government deficits, "government is not the solution to our problem." Reagan also was careful to say that he did not in fact oppose the muscular national powers created during the New Deal. He praised both Franklin Roosevelt and the spirit of the New Deal, which he thought had harnessed the optimistic power of the American people to conquer domestic and international problems. Reagan had been a Democratic New Dealer in his youth and in some sense never deviated from that conviction. As he said in 1964, "I didn't leave the Democratic Party. It left me."[29] What Reagan opposed was not New Deal liberalism, but what he saw as the excesses of liberalism in the 1960s. As Reagan wrote in his diary (on the day that he visited the FDR exhibit at the Smithsonian and entertained members of the Roosevelt family at the White House): "The press is dying to paint me as trying to undo the New Deal. I remind them I voted for FDR four times. I'm trying to undo the Great Society."[30]

The Reagan Revolution left an ambivalent legacy to the Republican Party. On one hand, it interrupted the trajectory of the New Deal's public philosophy, which aimed ultimately to achieve "freedom from want."[31] On the other hand, it embraced the entitlements, like Social Security, at the heart of the New Deal's achievements. Reagan's ambivalence today marks the Republican Party: Is it a radical party that intends to unwind the regulatory and welfarist functions that go back to the New Deal; or is it a moderately conservative party that aims to correct what it identifies as the excesses of liberalism? President George W. Bush's "compassionate conservatism" was true to the ambivalent spirit of the Reagan Revolution. One consequence of that is large structural budget deficits. Subsequent to President Barack Obama's election in 2008, the Republican Party (through the Tea Party insurgency) has clarified its purpose, and has prioritized tax cuts over entitlements and perhaps even the military. Since 2010, neither party has been able to command a governing majority; the split between the Republicans' control of Congress and the Democrats' control of the presidency and the Senate has rendered the government barely able to govern.

The solution to this crisis is not to pretend that we have nothing to disagree about or no important choices to make. The choice about the responsibilities with which we want to invest the national government is not an easy one, and ambivalence about it is sensible. But it is increasingly an unavoidable choice. Making choices like this is a matter of political judgment and interpretation. Reasons can be adduced to support one or the other (or some conception unlike either). Reasons can persuade, but no reasons can be dispositive. For citizens to reflect on and deliberate over the rival conceptions of the common good that each party stands for, legislators in each party need to speak—explicitly and repeatedly—about the goals that define it.

For the first time in over a century, our national party politics is informed by intense contestation about a conception of the national interest. Through most of the twentieth century, parties were inescapably local affairs, dominated by local powers and local interests. Bipartisanship displaced essential and controversial national questions—principally concerning civil rights—from politics. Nostalgia for such a politics is morally questionable and politically undesirable. We do disagree—not about everything and not all the time, but about enough. Our politics should reflect that disagreement—not silence it.

The Fate of Party Government

Yet disagreement can immobilize the capacity to govern. The way to combine a politics that reflects disagreement with a government that can govern is *party government,* which occurs in the U.S. system only when one party controls the presidency and both houses of the legislature. The aspiration to party government was the soul of the 1950 American Political Science Association report that put "responsible parties" at the heart of political reform, and before that was at the center of Woodrow Wilson's analysis of the defects of American politics. In Wilson's view, American government was a "Whig invention" designed to "curb and regulate the power of the crown."[32] According to Wilson, the U.S. Constitution constrained the nationalization of American politics. Having convinced himself that thorough constitutional change (in order to create cabinet government along the British model) was impractical, Wilson searched for a way to reform American politics within the confines of its constitution.

Wilson's reformist hopes landed on parties. Of course, the parties of Wilson's day—animated by the power of local bosses, sustained by patronage—made them unlikely agents of reform, but Wilson saw in parties the possibility of making the Constitution work for the twentieth century. The trick would be to somehow transform the parties from the amalgamations of local power they were into national institutions that would give a vector and force to national politics. For Wilson, pulling off this trick would mean transforming the president into the national leader of his party, capable of creating a popular coalition that in turn would elect majorities in the legislature. By leading the people in a party, the president could combine what the Whig invention separated, and make the government work in spite of itself.

In the aim to overcome the separation of powers, Wilson's ideal of party government might be cast in opposition to the spirit of the Constitution: Wilson was trying to make the government work in spite of the Constitution.[33] Where the constitutional separation of powers blocked and impeded, Wilson wanted a government that was decisive, energetic, and capable. He wanted to make the Constitution function like what it was not—a parliamentary democracy where the executive and legislative powers were fused. Institutional jealousy is embedded in the Constitution: ambition must counteract ambition, Madison wrote, expecting that the senators would stand for the prerogatives of the Senate and would be naturally skeptical of the passions and assertions of the House. In this light, one might hold that only when parties divide control of the presidency and the legislature does partisanship align with constitutional intentions (also when they divide control of the two houses of the legislature).[34] Under divided party control, partisan aims fuel an oppositional spirit that makes a separation of powers serve as a "check." The partisan interest of a Democratic Senate, for example, is aligned with the institutional interest of the Senate in defending its prerogatives with respect to a Republican president. But when parties unite the executive and the legislature, the partisan motive is in tension with the institutional incentives established by a separation of powers. So much the better, in the Wilsonian view: Wilson's aim was not for partisanship to accentuate the separation of powers, but to relax its force. When one party controls both the legislature and the presidency, for example, the legislature will be less inclined to question presidential initiatives, defend legislative prerogatives against executive encroachments, and investigate executive abuses. One might argue, for instance, that this was the problem in 2002, when a Republican legislature too readily acceded to presidential plans to invade Iraq.[35]

For Wilson, parties were a way of making the eighteenth-century Constitution work in spite of itself. Yet we might see Wilson's aims as profoundly aligned with the Constitution. After all, he saw *in the Constitution* the possibility for party government. Party government might diminish the impediments created by a separation of powers, but by resting both the executive and the legislature on a popular basis, the Constitution invites the people to see the government as something they ultimately control. This control requires "the people" to formulate a purpose sufficiently broad and lasting to constitute a constitutional majority. A constitutional majority requires that both the legislature and the executive have a common, broad, and enduring base in the population. Constructing this base and connecting it to constitutional offices—the president and Congress—are the aims of party government. Wilson's ideal of party government is not disrespectful of constitutional intention. It is a possibility invited by the Constitution.

For this possibility to be realized, parties need to have a certain character. A constitutional majority—a majority of representatives from 435 equally populated districts, *plus* a majority of representatives from fifty geographically dispersed states, plus a combination that reflects both population and states (via the electoral college) sufficiently large to elect a president, *plus* a majority sufficiently durable to control at least five Supreme Court judges—is spatially dispersed and temporally enduring. Any such large and durable majority will not have the singular focus of a movement, the programmatic purity of an ideology, or the intellectual coherence of a philosophic theory. It will inevitably need to be composed of a patchwork of groups and interests bound together by, at best, a loose conception of the common good that invariably must contain commitments in tension with one another. When parties are united by large and general purposes, when they contain a coalition of diverse interests, party government is wholly consistent with the Constitution.[36]

When people look back today at earlier reformers who wanted party government, they tend to say, "Be careful what you wish for."[37] In the midst of a constitutional crisis driven by excessive partisanship, who could wish for a *more* partisan government? Yet the ideal of party government remains an important part of the solution to the current pathology of American politics. When the differences between parties are significant, when partisans have a degree of loyalty, and when parties are of roughly equal size, it is very difficult to imagine how they might successfully share power—which is what they do when they split control of the executive and the legislature (or of the two houses of the legislature). Such parties are congenial to the ideal of party government, since they are necessary to give voters a real choice at election time. The problem remains, as it was in Wilson's day, that the separation-of-powers constitution becomes unworkable with such parties.

Constitutional change to facilitate party government is always extremely unlikely. The eradication of the Senate filibuster—a development now in process—will remove one crucial veto point. In the long run, it would not be entirely surprising to see the Senate as a whole come under pressure—after all, the same

Can the Government Govern?

minority principle that made the filibuster illegitimate also defines the Senate, where Wyoming and California have the same representation. The rise of a small but viable Centrist Party might move the decision point in the legislature closer to the center, which would perhaps better align the legislature's national constituency with the president's.

But ultimately, party government will depend on one of the parties forming a governing coalition of sufficient scope and durability that it constitutes a long-term constitutional majority. The parties, in other words, have to persuade the people to entrust them with responsibility for governance. This, in turn, will require that one party or the other persuade people of their stand on the great debate of contemporary American politics concerning the scope of the national government. That will not happen until partisanship reads as something connected to the common good. It will require a new—a loftier and more noble—spirit of partisanship.

NOTES

ACKNOWLEDGMENTS

INDEX

NOTES

1. THE PARTY PROBLEM

1. Sean Wilentz, "The Mirage: The Long and Tragic History of Post-partisanship from Washington to Obama," *New Republic,* October 26, 2011, accessed at www.tnr.com/print/article/books/maga zine/96706/post-partisan-obama-progressives-washington.

2. Gary C. Jacobson, *A Divider, Not a Uniter: George W. Bush and the American People* (New York: Pearson Education, 2007), 218; Jeffrey M. Jones, "Measuring the Strength of Opinion on Bush's Job as President," *Gallup Poll Tuesday Briefing, September 30, 2003: 39.* The gap between job approval ratings of Republicans and Democrats—70 percent—is the highest recorded; Ronald Brownstein, *The Second Civil War: How Extreme Partisanship Has Paralyzed Washington and Polarized America* (New York: Penguin, 2007), 16.

3. Jonathan Chait, "Mad about You," *New Republic,* September 29, 2003; Jack Huberman, *The Bush-Hater's Handbook* (New York: Nation Books, 2004).

4. Louis Hartz, *The Liberal Tradition in America,* 2nd ed. (New York: Mariner: 1991); Gabriel A. Almond and Sidney Verba, *The Civic Culture: Political Attitudes and Democracy in Five Nations* (Princeton: Princeton University Press, 1963).

5. David Mayhew, *Divided We Govern: Party Control, Lawmaking, and Investigations, 1946–1990* (New Haven: Yale University Press, 1991), 134.

6. Rachel Weiner and Ed O'Keefe, "Judging the (Un)productivity of the 113th Congress," *Washington Post,* August 2, 2013, accessed at www.washingtonpost.com/blogs/the-fix/wp/2013/08/02/judging -the-unproductivity-of-the-113th-congress/.

7. John H. Evans, "Have Americans' Attitudes Become More Polarized?—An Update," *Social Science Quarterly* 84, no. 1 (March 2003): 71–90; Alan Wolfe, *One Nation, After All: What Middle Class Americans Really Think about God, Country, Family, Racism, Welfare, Immigration, Homosexuality, Work, the Right, the Left, and Each Other* (New York: Penguin, 1999).

8. Alan Abramowitz, *The Disappearing Center* (New Haven: Yale University Press, 2011); Carl Desportes Bowman, "The Myth of a Non-polarized America," *Hedgehog Review* 65 (Fall 2010): 66–68.

9. Wolfe, *One Nation, After All;* Stanley B. Greenberg, *The Two Americas: Our Current Political Deadlock and How to Break It* (New York: St. Martin's, 2004).

10. We can get a sense of the size of the latent majority by considering the vote on Hurricane Sandy aid in January 2013, when 49 Republicans voted with 192 Democrats to approve $50 million in federal aid to New Jersey, New York, and Connecticut. More generally, the membership of the Republican Main Street Partnership, a group of moderate Republicans, suggests the dimensions of the disaffected members of the majority caucus: 51 members of the Republican majority belong.

11. Ezra Klein, "Why Obama Won't Get Specific on Immigration—at Least Not Yet," *Washington Post,* January 29, 2013, accessed at www.washingtonpost.com/blogs/wonkblog/wp/2013/01/29/why-obama-wont-get-specific-on-immigration-at-least-not-yet/; also see Newt Gingrich's comment: "An Obama plan led and driven by Obama in this atmosphere with this level of hostility toward the president . . . I think is very hard to imagine that bill . . . is going to pass the House," at *This Week,* full transcript, ABC News, February 17, 2013, accessed at abcnews.go.com/Politics/week-transcript-rep-paul-ryan-white-house-chief/story?id=18515489&singlePage=true.

12. It is possible to conceive of justice, as some modern thinkers have, not in terms of a rationally defensible conception of the common good, but as a contest of competing conceptions that is regulated by fair procedures. Such understandings of justice would be more friendly to partisanship.

13. The Exclusion Crisis concerned the possibility that James, Duke of York, would succeed his brother Charles II as the monarch of

England, Scotland, and Ireland. Because James was a Catholic, some thought his ascension would lead to a kind of absolutism characteristic of French monarchy. Those who wanted to exclude him from the throne organized to elect members of Parliament, with particular success in 1679; they were known (derisively) as Whigs. Those sympathetic to James's claim were known as Tories. See Tim Harris, *Politics under the Later Stuarts* (London: Longman, 1993), 141; Viscount Bolingbroke, "A Dissertation on Parties," in *Political Writings,* ed. David Armitage (1733; Cambridge: Cambridge University Press, 1997), 61; J. A. W. Gunn, *Factions No More: Attitudes to Party in Government and Opposition in Eighteenth-Century England* (London: Frank Cass, 1971).

14. Bolingbroke, "The Idea of a Patriot King," in Armitage, *Political Writings,* 217–294.

15. Edmund Burke, "Thoughts on the Cause of the Present Discontents," in *Select Works of Edmund Burke,* ed. E. J. Payne (1770; Indianapolis: Liberty Fund, 1999), 1:146.

16. George Washington, "Farewell Address" (1796), accessed at avalon.law.yale.edu/18th_century/washing.asp.

17. Thomas Jefferson to Francis Hopkinson, March 13, 1789, in *The Portable Thomas Jefferson,* ed. Merrill D. Peterson (New York: Penguin, 1997), 435; Lance Banning, *Liberty and Order: The First American Party Struggle* (Indianapolis: Liberty Fund, 2004); for the appearance of partisanship in the first sessions of Congress, see John Aldrich, *Why Parties? The Origins and Transformation of Political Parties in America* (Chicago: University of Chicago Press, 1995), 70–82.

18. Robert V. Remini, *Martin Van Buren and the Making of the Democratic Party* (New York: Columbia University Press, 1959), 192–194; James W. Ceaser, *Presidential Selection: Theory and Development* (Princeton: Princeton University Press, 1979).

19. Frank J. Goodnow, *Politics and Administration: A Study in Government,* intro. John A. Rohr (1900; New Brunswick, NJ: Transaction, 2003), 143–147, 162–166, 255–263, esp. 259; A. Lawrence Lowell, *Public Opinion and Popular Government* (New York: Longmans, Green, 1926), 100–102; Woodrow Wilson, *Congressional Government: A Study in American Politics,* 15th ed., intro. William F. Connelly Jr. (1900; New Brunswick, NJ: Transaction, 2002), 97–102.

20. Austin Ranney, *The Doctrine of Responsible Party Government* (Urbana: University of Illinois Press, 1962); for an exception to the responsible party ideal, see Moisey Ostrogorski, *Democracy and the Organization of Political Parties,* trans. Frederick Clark (1902; New York: Macmillan, 1922), 2:646–658.

21. "Toward a More Responsible Two-Party System: A Report of the Committee on Political Parties," supplement, *American Political Science Review 44,* no. 3, pt. 2 (1950): i–xii, 1–99. There was more debate about the responsible party ideal in the 1870–1900 period than there was by the 1950s; see John Kenneth White, "E. E. Schattschneider and the Responsible Party Model," *PS: Political Science and Politics* 25 (June 1992): 167–171.

22. Woodrow Wilson, "First Inaugural Address," March 4, 1913, accessed at avalon.law.yale.edu/20th_century/wilson1.asp.

23. A summary of the beneficial functions parties serve in democracies can be found in Russell J. Dalton and Martin P. Wattenberg's introduction to *Parties without Partisans: Political Change in Advanced Industrial Democracies* (Oxford: Oxford University Press, 2000), 4–10.

24. E. E. Schattschneider, *Party Government,* intro. Sidney A. Pearson Jr. (1942; New York: Transaction, 2004), 1.

25. Martin P. Wattenberg, *The Decline of American Political Parties, 1952–1994* (Cambridge, MA: Harvard University Press, 1994), 176; and Russell J. Dalton and Martin P. Wattenberg, "The Not So Simple Act of Voting," in *The State of the Discipline,* 2nd ed., ed. Ada Finifter (Washington, DC: American Political Science Association, 1993), 193–218. Of course, in the same year (1992), 61 percent identified with either the Republican or Democratic Party, suggesting that nonpartisanship is complicated and elusive. Even partisans share a suspicion of partisanship; see National Election Studies, "Party Identification 7-Point Scale, 1952–200," *The ANES Guide to Public Opinion and Electoral Behavior,* accessed at electionstudies.org//nesguide /toptable/tab2a_1.htm.

26. "Strength of Partisanship, 1952–2008," National Election Studies, Center for Political Studies, University of Michigan; *NES*

Guide to Public Opinion and Electoral Behavior, accessed at election-studies.org//nesguide/toptable/tab2a_3.htm. Independents in these calculations include "pure independents" and those who say they lean to one party or the other.

27. Lydia Saad, "Independents Rank as Largest U.S. Political Group," Gallup Poll release, April 9, 1999 (Princeton, NJ).

28. Matthew Levendusky, *The Partisan Sort: How Liberals Became Democrats and Conservatives Became Republicans* (Chicago: University of Chicago Press, 2009).

29. Bruce E. Keith, David B. Magleby, Candice J. Nelson, Elizabeth Orr, Mark C. Westlye, and Raymond E. Wolfinger, *The Myth of the Independent Voter* (Berkeley: University of California Press, 1992), 4, 49–59, 65, 73, 179. "Undercover Partisans" are discussed in Angus Campbell, Philip Converse, Warren Miller, and Donald Stokes, *The American Voter* (New York: John Wiley and Sons, 1960), 123–126. The authors estimated that of independents thirty-five years old or older in 1956, only 11 percent were "concealed partisans."

30. Christopher Hare, Nolan McCarty, Keith T. Poole, and Howard Rosenthal, "Polarization Is Real (and Asymmetric)," *Voteview* (blog), May 15, 2012, accessed at http://voteview.com/blog/?p=494.

31. Geoffrey Kabaservice, *Rule and Ruin: The Downfall of Moderation and the Destruction of the Republican Party, from Eisenhower to the Tea Party* (Oxford: Oxford University Press, 2012).

32. Thomas E. Mann and Norman J. Ornstein, *It's Even Worse Than It Looks: How the American Constitutional System Collided with the New Politics of Extremism* (New York: Basic Books, 2012), xvi.

33. Robin Toner, "A Partisan Leaves; Will an Era Follow?," *New York Times,* April 5, 2006, accessed at www.nytimes.com/2006/04/05/us/05assess.html?_r=0.

34. "Rep. Tom DeLay Delivers His Farewell Address," CQ transcripts wire, *Washington Post,* June 8, 2006, available at www.washingtonpost.com/wp-dyn/content/article/2006/06/08/AR2006060801376.html.

35. A more sophisticated account that sees partisanship as a response to modern progress is located in Harvey C. Mansfield's argument

about the connection between Edmund Burke's conservatism and his defense of party in *Statesmanship and Party Government* (Chicago: University of Chicago Press, 1965).

36. See ibid.

37. Alexis de Tocqueville, *Democracy in America,* ed. Harvey C. Mansfield and Delba Winthrop (Chicago: University of Chicago Press, 2000), 1:7: "To wish to stop democracy would then appear to be to struggle against God himself."

38. Robert B. Reich, *Reason: Why Liberals Will Win the Battle for America* (New York: Alfred A. Knopf, 2004); Al Gore, *The Assault on Reason* (New York: Penguin, 2007).

39. Mann and Ornstein, *It's Even Worse Than It Looks.*

40. James Johnson, "Political Parties and Deliberative Democracy?," in *Handbook of Party Politics,* ed. Richard S. Katz and William J. Crotty (London: Sage, 2006); Russell Muirhead, "A Defense of Party Spirit," *Perspectives on Politics* 4, no. 4 (2006): 713–727; Nancy L. Rosenblum, *On the Side of the Angels: An Appreciation of Parties and Partisanship* (Princeton: Princeton University Press, 2008); Michael Seward, "Democratic Theorists and Party Scholars: Why They Don't Talk to Each Other and Why They Should," *Perspectives on Politics* 6, no. 1 (2008): 21–35; Jonathan White and Lea Ypi, "Rethinking the Modern Prince: Partisanship and the Democratic Ethos," *Political Studies* 58 (2010): 809; Dmitris Efthymiou, "When and Why Partisanship Matters: A Moderate Defense of Partisanship" (paper presented at the Fifth European Consortium for Political Research General Conference, Potsdam, September 10–12, 2009); Jonathan White and Lea Ypi, "On Partisan Political Justification," *American Political Science Review* 105, no. 2 (May 2011): 381–396.

41. Rosenblum, *On the Side of the Angels,* 361; Amy Gutmann and Dennis Thompson, *The Spirit of Compromise: Why Governing Demands It and Campaigning Undermines It* (Princeton: Princeton University Press, 2012), 126–127.

42. As Nadia Urbinati says, "A political party translates the many instances and particularities in a language that is general and wants to represent the general. No party claims to represent only the interests

of those who belong to or side with it." See Nadia Urbinati, *Representative Democracy: Principles and Genealogy*, (Chicago: The University of Chicago Press, 2006), 37.

2. THE PARTISAN THREAT

1. Nancy L. Rosenblum, *On the Side of the Angels: An Appreciation of Parties and Partisanship* (Princeton: Princeton University Press, 2008), 107.

2. Ibid., 165–209.

3. Aristotle, *The Politics,* trans. Carnes Lord (Chicago: University of Chicago Press, 1984), bk. IV, chap. 3, p. 121; bk. IV, chap. 4, p. 123; bk. V, chap. 1, p. 148.

4. Ibid., bk. III, chap. 13, p. 105; bk. III, chap. 11, p. 101.

5. The previous two paragraphs expand on the following sections of ibid.: bk. III, chap. 9; bk. III, chap. 13; bk. IV, chap. 4; bk. V, chap. 1; bk. VI, chap. 2. The definitive description of the difference between traditional and modern party is found in Harvey C. Mansfield Jr., *Statesmanship and Party Government* (Chicago: University of Chicago Press, 1965), especially the traditional view of party at 13–16.

6. Aristotle, *The Politics,* bk. III, chap. 9, p. 97.

7. Ibid., bk. III, chap. 9, p. 97.

8. Harvey C. Mansfield, *A Student's Guide to Political Philosophy* (Wilmington, DE: ISI Books, 2001), 4–5.

9. Isaiah Berlin, "Two Concepts of Liberty," in *Four Essays on Liberty* (Oxford: Oxford University Press, 1969), 167–172; John Rawls, *Political Liberalism* (New York: Columbia University Press, 1996), 197.

10. Aristotle, *The Politics,* bk. IV, chaps. 7–9, pp. 129–132; bk. V, chap. 9, pp. 166–167.

11. Ibid., bk. IV, chap. 9, p. 132.

12. Ibid., bk. IV, chap. 11, p. 135.

13. James Madison, "Federalist #10," *The Federalist Papers,* ed. Clinton Rossiter (New York: NAL Penguin, 1961), 77–78.

14. Ibid., 78, 79.

15. Ibid., 80.

16. Ibid., 82.

17. Mansfield, *Statesmanship and Party Government,* 16.

18. Ibid.

19. David Hume, "Of Parties in General," in *Essays, Moral, Political, and Literary,* ed. Eugene F. Miller (1742; Indianapolis: Liberty Fund, 1987), pt. 1, essay 8; Alexis de Tocqueville, *Democracy in America,* ed., trans., intro. Harvey C. Mansfield and Delba Winthrop (Chicago: University of Chicago Press, 2000), vol. 1, pt. 2, chap. 10.

20. Tocqueville, *Democracy in America,* 167.

21. Mansfield, *Statesmanship and Party Government,* 109–111; for Bolingbroke's writings, see Viscount Bolingbroke, "The Idea of a Patriot King" and "A Dissertation upon Parties," in *Political Writings,* ed. David Armitage, (Cambridge: Cambridge University Press, 1997).

22. Mansfield, *Statesmanship and Party Government,* 113.

23. Karl Marx and Frederick Engels, "The Communist Manifesto," in *The Marx-Engels Reader,* ed. Robert C. Tucker (New York: W. W. Norton, 1972), 490–491.

24. Francis Fukuyama, *The End of History and the Last Man* (New York: Avon, 1993).

25. Robert Reich, *Reason: Why Liberals Will Win the Battle for America* (New York: Alfred A. Knopf, 2004); in a similar vein, see Al Gore, *The Assault on Reason* (New York: Penguin, 2007).

26. John Rawls, *A Theory of Justice,* rev. ed. (Cambridge, MA: Harvard University Press, 1999).

27. Ibid., 79.

28. This is not to argue that partisanship has no place in the just utopia that Rawls described, only that traditional partisanship has no place in his ideal. To be sure, Rawls suggests in moments that politics needs competent administration rather than vibrant partisan contestation, but in fact parties and partisanship are quite at home in his theory; see Russell Muirhead and Nancy L. Rosenblum, "Political Liberalism vs. the Great Game of Politics," *Perspectives on Politics* 4, no. 1 (March 2006): 99–108.

29. For a view that primary goods represent a partisan conception, see Eric Nelson, "From Primary Goods to Capabilities: Distributive

Justice and the Problem of Neutrality," *Political Theory* 36, no. 1 (February 2008): 93–122.

30. Anthony Downs, *An Economic Theory of Democracy* (New York: Addison-Wesley, 1957), 28, 96–97; Joseph A. Schumpeter, *Capitalism, Socialism, and Democracy* (New York: Harper and Brothers, 1942), 53–61.

31. John Aldrich, *Why Parties? The Origins and Transformation of Political Parties in America* (Chicago: University of Chicago Press, 1995), 21.

32. Tocqueville, *Democracy in America,* 169.

33. Robert Michels, *Political Parties* (New York: The Free Press, 1962), 50.

34. *Mr. Smith Goes to Washington,* directed by Frank Capra (1939; Sony Pictures Home Entertainment, 2008), DVD.

35. *Wayne Morse: The Record of a Working Senator . . . in Detail* (Portland, OR: Re-elect Wayne Morse Committee, 1968), 7, accessed at http://ir.library.oregonstate.edu/xmlui/bitstream/handle/1957/9750/Compressed_way_mor_the_rec_wor_sen.pdf?sequence=1.

36. Henry David Thoreau, "Resistance to Civil Government," in *Political Writings,* ed. Nancy Rosenblum (Cambridge: Cambridge University Press, 1996), 6.

37. Ibid., 2.

38. Morris P. Fiorina, with Samuel J. Abrams and Jeremy C. Pope, *Culture War? The Myth of a Polarized America* (New York: Pearson Longman, 2005), 94; for Fiorina's description of Wilson's and Wildavsky's accounts, see 94.

39. F. C., *The Unabomber Manifesto: Industrial Society and Its Future* (New York: Jolly Roger Press, 1995).

40. Thomas Hobbes, *Leviathan,* ed. Richard Tuck (Cambridge: Cambridge University Press, 1991), pt. I, chaps. 12, 13.

3. THE PARTISAN COMMUNITY

1. John Jay, *The Federalist #2,* in *The Federalist Papers,* ed. Clinton Rossiter (New York: NAL Penguin, 1961), 37, 38.

2. George Washington, "Farewell Address to the People of the United States," in *The Writings of George Washington,* ed. Worthington Chauncey Ford (New York: G. P. Putnam's Sons, 1892), 13:286, 288.

3. Ibid., 13:295, 299, 298, 299, 303, 304.

4. James Madison, *The Federalist #10,* in Rossiter, *Federalist Papers,* 79.

5. Washington, "Farewell Address," 13:300.

6. Louis Hartz, *The Liberal Tradition in America* (New York: Harcourt, Brace, 1955).

7. Ibid., 3–32, 188–189.

8. Ibid., 177, 7, 175, 205.

9. V. O. Key, *Southern Politics in State and Nation,* (New York: A. A. Knopf, 1949).

10. As a literal creed, the American's Creed was written in 1917 and adopted by the House of Representatives in 1918. It states, "I believe in the United States of America as a government of the people, by the people, and for the people; whose just powers are derived from the consent of the governed, a democracy in a republic, a sovereign Nation of many sovereign States; a perfect union, one and inseparable; established upon those principles of freedom, equality, justice, and humanity for which American patriots sacrificed their lives and fortunes. I therefore believe it is my duty to my country to love it, to support its Constitution, to obey its laws, to respect its flag, and to defend it against all enemies." See also Gunnar Myrdal, *An American Dilemma: The Negro Problem and Modern Democracy,* with a new introduction by Sissela Bok, (1944; repr., New Brunswick, NJ: Transaction Publishers, 1996), 1–13.

11. For the definitive rejection of Myrdal, Hartz, and the general view that a belief in equality and democracy constitutes the core of American national identity, see Rogers Smith, *Civic Ideals: Conflicting Visions of Citizenship in U.S. History* (New Haven: Yale University Press, 1997), 14–30 and throughout.

12. Gabriel A. Almond and Sidney Verba, "Patterns of Partisanship," in *The Civic Culture: Political Attitudes and Democracy in Five*

Nations (Princeton: Princeton University Press, 1963), 86–93, 97–102. Still, Americans tend not to take partisanship too personally: most, for instance, do not think political views are a "deal breaker" in romantic relationships; see Heather Mason Kiefer, "Is Love Nonpartisan?," *Gallup Poll Tuesday Briefing*, August 10, 2004, accessed at www.gallup.com/poll/12655/love-nonpartisan.aspx.

13. Almond and Verba, *Civic Culture*, 109.

14. E. E. Schattschneider, *Party Government: American Government in Action*, with a new introduction by Sidney A. Pearson Jr. (1942 repr., New Brunswick, NJ: Transaction, 2004), 88.

15. Angus Campbell, Philip Converse, Warren Miller, and Donald Stokes, *The American Voter* (New York: John Wiley and Sons, 1960.

16. Ibid., 143.

17. "Toward a More Responsible Two-Party System: A Report of the Committee on Political Parties," supplement, *American Political Science Review* 44, no. 3, pt. 2 (1950): 1–2, 18–19 (italics added).

18. Ibid., 25.

19. Anthony Downs, *An Economic Theory of Democracy* (Boston: Addison-Wesley, 1957), 117–122.

20. Ibid., 120. Downs notes that it is "doubtful" whether a radically polarized electorate can "function as a democracy, since internal conflict will be intense no matter which party wins" (127n13).

21. "Toward a More Responsible Two-Party System," 4, 20–21, 22.

22. Gerald M. Pomper and Marc D. Weiner, "Towards a More Responsible Two-Party Voter," and John Kenneth White and Jerome M. Mileur, "In the Spirit of Their Times," in *Responsible Partisanship: The Evolution of American Parties since 1950,* ed. John C. Green and Paul S. Herrnson (Lawrence: University Press of Kansas, 2002), 33, 195; as Pomper and Weiner write, "The Committee on Political Parties saw the development of distinct parties as the elite stimulus of a responsible two-party system. We now have such parties" (195).

23. Chantal Mouffe, *The Democratic Paradox* (New York: Verso, 2000), 102.

24. Thomas Jefferson, "Inaugural Address," in *The Portable Thomas Jefferson,* ed. Merrill Peterson (New York: Viking, 1975), 292.

For a more recent example, consider Karl Rove's statement to Nicolas Lemann, in "Karl Rove Is Working to Get George Bush Re-elected, but He Has Larger Plans," *New Yorker,* May 12, 2003: "'I think we're at a point where the two major parties have sort of exhausted their governing agendas,' Rove told me. 'We had agendas that were originally formed, for the Democrats, in the New Deal, and, for the Republicans, in opposition to the New Deal—modified by the Cold War and further modified by the changes in the sixties, the Great Society and societal and cultural changes. It's sort of like the exhaustion of two boxers fighting it out in the middle of the ring. This periodically happens. This happened in 1896, where the Civil War party system was in decline and the parties were in rough parity and somebody came along and figured it out and helped create a governing coalition that really lasted for the next some-odd years. Similarly, somebody will come along and figure out a new governing scheme through which people could view things and could, conceivably, enjoy a similar period of dominance.'"

25. Harry V. Jaffa, "The Nature and Origin of the American Party System," in *Political Parties, USA,* ed. Robert Goldwin (Chicago: Rand McNally, 1961), 63.

26. Sidney Milkis, *Political Parties and Constitutional Government: Remaking American Democracy* (Baltimore: Johns Hopkins University Press, 1999), 72–136; this work shows how the ever-present desire of partisans to place their accomplishments beyond the touch of future contestation stands among the most powerful forces that sap party spirit of its vitality.

27. Peter Mair, "Political Opposition and the European Union," *Government and Opposition* 42, no. 1 (2007): 1–17.

28. Harvey C. Mansfield, "Ronald Wilson Reagan," in *Presidential Leadership,* ed. James Taranto and Leonard Leo (New York: Wall Street Journal Books, 2004), 193.

29. Harvey Mansfield, *Statesmanship and Party Government* (Chicago: University of Chicago Press, 1965), 109–111; see chap. 2, note 21.

30. David Hume, "Of Parties in General," in *Essays Moral, Political, and Literary,* ed. Eugene F. Miller (Indianapolis: Liberty Fund, 1985), 63.

31. John Rawls singles out the latter two of these agreements, the rejection of religious intolerance and the rejection of slavery, as central to the public culture that sustains political liberalism. He does not give so much attention to the rejection of kingly rule, though this is part of the circumstances of justice: we need to work out what justice means for ourselves because we reject that any earthly authority can be trusted to rightly work it out for us. See Rawls, *Political Liberalism*, expanded ed. (New York: Columbia University Press, 1998), introduction.

32. See Chapter 5 in this book.

33. Insofar as global warming calls into question the basic consumption habits and productive technologies of commercial society, I take it to be a "fundamental controversy."

34. Smith, *Civic Ideals*, 489–503.

35. Ibid., 497.

36. Ibid., 491.

37. Ibid., 502.

38. Benjamin Franklin, *Autobiography*, intro. Dixon Wecter (New York: Holt, Rinehart and Winston, 1948), 32.

39. Gary Jacobson, "Partisan Polarization in Presidential Support: The Electoral Connection" (paper delivered at the 2002 annual meeting of the American Political Science Association, Boston, MA), 14.

4. Reasonable Partisans

1. Diana C. Mutz, *Hearing the Other Side: Deliberative versus Participatory Democracy* (Cambridge: Cambridge University Press, 2006); Lawrence R. Jacobs, Fay Lomax Cook, and Michael X. Delli Carpini, *Talking Together: Public Deliberation and Political Participation in America* (Chicago: University of Chicago Press, 2009).

2. Amy Gutmann and Dennis Thompson, *Why Deliberative Democracy?* (Princeton: Princeton University Press, 2004), 3.

3. Joshua Cohen, "Democracy and Liberty," in *Deliberative Democracy*, ed. Jon Elster (Cambridge: Cambridge University Press, 1998), 194.

4. John Rawls, "The Idea of Public Reason Revisited," in *Collected Papers,* ed. Samuel Freeman (Cambridge: Harvard University Press, 1999), 578.

5. Ibid., 579.

6. Ibid., 581.

7. "Deliberative democrats do not expect deliberation always or even usually to yield agreement"; Gutmann and Thompson, *Why Deliberative Democracy?,* 7.

8. In contrast to the relative absence of parties in deliberative democratic theory, notice the explicit attention they command in the archetype of aggregative democratic theories. Anthony Downs, *An Economic Theory of Democracy* (Boston: Addison-Wesley, 1957), 24–27.

9. Nancy L. Rosenblum, *On the Side of the Angels: An Appreciation of Parties and Partisanship* (Princeton: Princeton University Press, 2008), 286, 306–310.

10. Mutz, *Hearing the Other Side,* 102–105, 116–139.

11. Cass Sunstein, *Going to Extremes: How Like Minds Unite and Divide* (Oxford: Oxford University Press, 2009).

12. The principal contender would be some form of aggregative democracy that relies heavily on the "miracle of aggregation," by which relatively uninformed individuals can, without discussion, produce rational aggregate outcomes. But even this miracle can do nothing to assure that aggregate outcomes are fair or decent, and this defect would push every normative aggregative conception in a deliberative direction.

13. For a convincing attempt to defend the epistemic claim for democracy—though not simple majorities—see Helene Landemore, *Democratic Reason: Politics, Collective Intelligence, and the Rule of the Many* (Princeton: Princeton University Press, 2013).

14. John Stuart Mill attributes this to Jeremy Bentham in chapter 5 of *Utilitarianism* (1861), accessed at www.gutenberg.org/files/11224/11224-h/11224-h.htm#CHAPTER_V.

15. For an assessment of contemporary democracies on this dimension, see Arend Lijphart, *Patterns of Democracy: Government Forms*

and Performance in Thirty-Six Countries (New Haven: Yale University Press, 1999), 289–293.

16. See the conception of the ideal citizen in Rawls, "Public Reason Revisited," 578: "Citizens are reasonable when . . . they are prepared to offer one another fair terms of cooperation according to what they consider the *most reasonable conception of justice*" (italics added).

17. For John Locke's concession to majority rule, see Locke, *Two Treatises of Government* (Cambridge: Cambridge University Press, 1988), 332–333; for a contemporary effort to defend the moral claim of the majority, see Jeremy Waldron, *The Dignity of Legislation,* (Cambridge: Cambridge University Press, 1999), chaps. 5 and 6.

18. Bruce Ackerman and James S. Fishkin, *Deliberation Day* (New Haven: Yale University Press, 2004); and James S. Fishkin and Robert C. Luskin, "Experimenting with a Democratic Ideal: Deliberative Polling and Public Opinion," *Acta Politica* 40 (September 2006): 284–298.

19. Norman J. Ruff, "Electoral Reform and Deliberative Democracy: The British Columbia Citizens' Assembly," in *Steps toward Making Every Vote Count: Electoral System Reform in Canada and Its Provinces,* ed. Henry Milner (Peterborough, Ontario: Broadview Press, 2004), 236–239; and Mark E. Warren, ed., *Designing Deliberative Democracy* (Cambridge: Cambridge University Press, 2008).

20. Bernard Manin, *The Principles of Representative Government* (Cambridge: Cambridge University Press, 1997), 8–79.

21. Consider, in this context, Madison's argument that elections in large districts are meant to "refine and enlarge public views"; Madison, *The Federalist #10,* in *The Federalist Papers,* ed. Clinton Rossiter (New York: NAL Penguin, 1961), 82.

22. I am indebted to Joel Parker of the Department of Government, University of Texas at Austin, for a sympathetic and extensive elaboration of this argument; see his "Randomness and Legitimacy in Selecting Democratic Representatives" (PhD diss., University of Texas at Austin, December 2011).

23. John Rawls, *Justice as Fairness Revisited: A Restatement,* ed. Erin Kelly (Cambridge, MA: Harvard University Press, 2001), 118.

24. Rawls, "Public Reason Revisited," 580–581.

25. For a contrary view, see Ackerman and Fishkin, *Deliberation Day*, 62–65.

26. John Stuart Mill, *Autobiography* (1873; New York: Signet Classics, 1964), 122 (italics added).

27. John Stuart Mill, "Bentham 1838," in *The Collected Works of John Stuart Mill: Essays on Ethics, Religion, and Society*, ed. John M. Robson, intro. F. E. L. Priestley, (Toronto: University of Toronto Press, 1985), 10:107.

28. John Stuart Mill, *On Liberty* (1869; Cambridge: Cambridge University Press, 1989), 48–49.

29. Mill, "Bentham," 94.

30. John Stuart Mill, "Considerations on Representative Government," in *On Liberty and Other Essays*, ed. John Gray (1861; Oxford: Oxford University Press, 1991), 340.

31. Amy Gutmann and Dennis Thompson, *The Spirit of Compromise: Why Governing Demands It and Campaigning Undermines It* (Princeton: Princeton University Press, 2012), 10, 64–69.

32. Mill, "Representative Government," 224.

33. Mill, "Bentham," 91.

34. Ibid., 78.

35. John Stuart Mill, "Coleridge 1840," in *The Collected Works of John Stuart Mill: Essays on Ethics, Religion, and Society*, ed. John M. Robson, intro. F. E. L. Priestley, (Toronto: University of Toronto Press, 1985), 10: 120.

36. Mill, "Coleridge," 120.

37. Mill, "Bentham," 94.

38. Mill, *On Liberty*, 53; for a discussion of this, see Dana Villa, *Socratic Citizenship* (Princeton: Princeton University Press, 2001), 94–95.

39. Mill hoped that impartiality, or resistance to a legislature dominated by "sinister interests," would come from the influence of the educated class and the institution of proportional representation; see "Representative Government," 292–341.

40. Michael Walzer, *Politics and Passion: Toward a More Egalitarian Liberalism* (New Haven: Yale University Press, 2004), 110–130.

41. Mutz, *Hearing the Other Side*, 106.

42. Chantal Mouffe, *On the Political* (New York: Routledge, 2005), 5, 20–21.

43. Alexis de Tocqueville, *Democracy in America*, ed. Harvey C. Mansfield and Delba Winthrop (Chicago: University of Chicago Press, 2000), 170.

44. William Connolly, *The Terms of Political Discourse*, 3rd ed. (Princeton: Princeton University Press, 1993), viii.

5. LOYAL PARTISANS

1. "Specter's Statement on His Decision to Switch Parties," *New York Times*, April 28, 2009, accessed at www.nytimes.com/2009/04 /28/us/politics/28caucus.specter.html.

2. The full quote, with the excised part in italics, is "My change in party will enable me to get reelected *and I have heard that again and again and again on the street: 'Senator, we're glad you'll be able to stay in the Senate and help the state and nation.'*" From "Specter: Killer Ad out of Context," *Philadelphia Inquirer*, May 13, 2010, accessed at www.philly.com/philly/blogs/harrisburg_politics/Specter_Killer_ad _out_of_context.html?viewAll=Y&text=.

3. Quoted in Marc Levy, "Specter Defeated by Sestak in Bid for 6th Term," *Times-Tribune*, May 19, 2010, accessed at http://thetimes -tribune.com/news/u-s-senate-specter-defeated-by-sestak-in-bid-for -6th-term-1.794984#axzz1DZVOhLa4.

4. Albert O. Hirschman, *Exit, Voice, and Loyalty: Responses to Decline in Firms, Organizations, and States* (Cambridge, MA: Harvard University Press, 1970).

5. Angus Campbell, Philip E. Converse, Warren E. Miller, and Donald E. Stokes, *The American Voter* (Chicago: University of Chicago Press, 1960), 133.

6. George P. Fletcher, *Loyalty: An Essay on the Morality of Relationships* (Oxford: Oxford University Press, 1993), 61.

7. Alasdair MacIntyre, *Is Patriotism a Virtue?* (Lawrence: University Press of Kansas, 1984), quoted in Fletcher, *Loyalty*, 34.

8. Sarah Stroud, "Epistemic Partiality in Friendship," *Ethics* 116 (April 2006): 498–524; quotation from p. 502.

9. Ibid., 505.

10. Ronald Brownstein, *The Second Civil War: How Extreme Partisanship Has Paralyzed Washington and Polarized America* (New York: Penguin, 2007), 16; Jeffrey M. Jones, "Views of Bush Reach New Heights of Polarization," *Gallup News Service,* October 21, 2004, accessed at www.gallup.com/poll/13735/views-bush-reach-new-heights-polarization.aspx.

11. Stroud, "Epistemic Partiality," 511.

12. Geoffrey Cohen, "Party over Policy: The Dominating Impact of Group Influence on Political Beliefs," *Journal of Personality and Social Psychology* 85, no. 5 (2003): 811.

13. Became Speaker of the House in 2011; Republican representative from the Eighth Congressional District of Ohio since 1991.

14. Stroud, "Epistemic Partiality," 507.

15. Ibid., 508.

16. Larry Bartels, "Beyond the Running Tally: Partisan Bias in Political Perceptions," *Political Behavior* 24, no. 2 (2002): 134.

17. "58% of GOP Not Sure/Doubt Obama Born in US," *Politico,* July 31, 2009, accessed at www.politico.com/blogs/glennthrush/0709/58_of_GOP_not_suredont_beleive_Obama_born_in_US.html. Seventy-seven percent of Americans overall thought he was a citizen, and 93 percent of Democrats. In a later poll, 51 percent of GOP primary voters thought Obama was not born in the United States (another 26 percent were "not sure"); see "Public Policy Polling Survey of February 11–13, 2011," accessed at www.publicpolicypolling.com/pdf/PPP_Release_US_0215.pdf.

18. For instance, some "citizen grand juries" have attempted to charge Obama with treason, though they were immediately dismissed by the U.S. District Court for the District of Columbia; see "Judge Dismisses Obama 'Indictment,'" *The BLT: The Blog of LegalTimes,* accessed at http://legaltimes.typepad.com/blt/2009/07/super-american-grand-jury-indicts-obama-.html.

19. Mitt Romney, speech at the Conservative Political Action Conference, February 12–13, 2011, accessed at http://factcheck.org/2011/02/factchecking-republicans-at-cpac/.

20. William G. Gale, "Five Myths about the Bush Tax Cuts," *Washington Post*, August 2, 2010, accessed at www.washingtonpost.com/wp-dyn/content/article/2010/07/30/AR2010073002671.html.

21. Stuart Hampshire, *Justice Is Conflict* (Princeton: Princeton University Press, 2001), ix, xiii.

22. Brownstein, *Second Civil War;* Morris Fiorina, with Samuel J. Abrams and Jeremy C. Pope, *Culture War? The Myth of a Polarized America* (New York: Pearson Longman, 2005).

23. Omnibus Budget Reconciliation Act of 1993.

24. Bruce Bartlett, "Starve the Beast: The Origin and Development of a Budgetary Metaphor," *Independent Review: A Journal of Political Economy* 12, no. 7 (Summer 2007): 5–26.

25. Sebastian Mallaby, "Don't Feed the Beast," *Washington Post*, May 8, 2006, accessed at www.washingtonpost.com/wp-dyn/content/article/2006/05/07/AR2006050700924.html.

26. Morris P. Fiorina, *Retrospective Voting in American National Elections* (New Haven: Yale University Press, 1981).

27. Peter Coy, "The Wisdom and Folly of the Bush Tax Cuts," *Bloomberg Businessweek*, August 5, 2010, accessed atwww.businessweek.com/magazine/content/10_33/b4191056654282.html.

28. Federal News Service, "There Is No Justice without Freedom," *Washington Post*, January 21, 2005, accessed at www.washingtonpost.com/wp-dyn/articles/A23747-2005Jan20.html.

29. Anne Gearan, "Gates Says History Will Judge Worth of Iraq War," *The Guardian*, September 1, 2010, accessed at www.guardian.co.uk/world/feedarticle/9245750.

30. Catriona Davies, "What Will History Make of the U.S. Mission in Iraq?," *CNN Opinion*, August 19, 2010, accessed at www.cnn.com/2010/OPINION/08/19/iraq.historians.comment/.

31. Alexander Hamilton, "The Federalist #72," in *The Federalist Papers*, ed. Clinton Rossiter, intro. Charles R. Kesler (New York: NAL Penguin, 1961), 437.

32. James Fearon, "Iraq's Civil War," *Foreign Affairs,* March/April 2007.

33. "Rumsfeld Foresees Swift Iraq War," *BBC News,* February 7, 2003, accessed at http://news.bbc.co.uk/2/hi/middle_east/2738089.stm.

34. Thom Shanker, "New Strategy Vindicates Ex-Army Chief Shinseki," *New York Times,* January 12, 2007, accessed at www.nytimes.com/2007/01/12/washington/12shinseki.html.

35. Mitt Romney, "As First Act, out with ObamaCare," *USA Today,* May 11, 2011, accessed at www.usatoday.com/news/opinion/forum/2011-05-11-Romney-on-fixing-health-care_n.htm.

36. Peter Grier, "Health Care Reform Bill 101: Who Gets Subsidized Insurance?," *Christian Science Monitor,* March 20, 2010, accessed at www.csmonitor.com/USA/Politics/2010/0320/Health-care-reform-bill-101-Who-gets-subsidized-insurance. Timelines that detail when each provision in the Affordable Care Act is implemented accessed at http://healthreform.kff.org/Timeline.aspx and www.healthcare.gov/law/timeline/index.html.

37. Andrew Cohen, "Patient Protection and Affordable Care Act—Pilot Programs, Demonstration Programs, and Grants," UMass Medical School Center for Health, Law, and Economics, April 2, 2010, accessed at http://www.umassmed.edu/uploadedFiles/CWM_CHLE/Landing_Pages/Pilot%20Programs%20Demonstration%20Projects%20and%20Grants%20in%20PPACA%204-26-10%20Final.pdf.

38. Austin Ranney, "Toward a More Responsible Two-Party System: A Commentary," *American Political Science Review* 45, no. 2 (1951): 499; Evron M. Kirkpatrick, "Toward a More Responsible Two-Party System: Party Systems, Policy-Science, or Pseudo-Science?" *American Political Science Review* 65, no. 4 (December 1971): 969–970.

39. Charles E. Lindblom, "The Science of 'Muddling Through,'" *Public Administration Review* 19, no. 2 (Spring 1959): 79–88; Rune Premfors, "Review Article: Charles Lindblom and Aaron Wildavsky," *British Journal of Political* Science 11, no. 2 (April, 1981): 205–206.

40. Lindblom, "Muddling Through," 81.

41. Ibid., 86.

42. Ibid.

43. Ibid., 84.

44. John Kenneth White and Jerome Mileur, "In the Spirit of Their Times," in *Responsible Partisanship: The Evolution of American Political Parties since 1950,* ed. John C. Green and Paul S. Herrnson (Lawrence: University Press of Kansas, 2002), 16.

45. Wilson, *Constitutional Government* (New York: Columbia University Press, 1908), 217, as quoted in White and Mileur, "In the Spirit of Their Times," 19.

6. THE PRIMARY PROBLEM

1. Author's interview with poll worker in Travis County, Texas, March 4, 2008.

2. Alan Ware, *The American Direct Primary: Party Institutionalization and Transformation in the North* (Cambridge: Cambridge University Press, 2002), 15.

3. This is chronicled in Austin Ranney, *Curing the Mischiefs of Faction* (Berkeley: University of California Press, 1975); Ranney was a member of the Democratic Party's Commission on Party Structure and Delegate Selection (the McGovern-Frasier Commission), which composed and recommended the reforms after the 1968 convention.

4. John F. Reynolds, *The Demise of the American Convention System, 1880–1911* (Cambridge: Cambridge University Press, 2006), 184.

5. Quoted in Ranney, *Curing the Mischiefs,* 25–26.

6. Ware, *American Direct Primary,* 160, 200.

7. Ranney, *Curing the Mischiefs,* 121.

8. Two center-left parties in Italy have used primaries (mainly for regional elections) since 2004, as have fifteen Latin American countries in elections from 1978 to the present; some South Korean parties have used primaries for presidential nominations since 2002; and the Armenian Revolutionary Federation nominated its presidential candidate in 2008 by means of an open primary. No country that I can locate outside of Uruguay (itself, only since 1999) uses primaries

for all or nearly all offices; in general, the primary is an option that particular parties might choose as they see fit for particular offices. See, for instance, John M. Carey and John Polga-Hecimovich, "Primary Elections and Candidate Strength in Latin America," *Journal of Politics* 68, no. 3 (August 2006): 536. The absence of primary elections in most democracies may be partly due to the prevalence of multimember proportional representation electoral systems. In a multimember district, voters generally vote for a party slate and focus more on the party than on the individual candidates. Only in single-member districts does it matter intensely which single individual is chosen to represent the party in the general election.

9. Ware reports that in the first instance where primary nominations were attempted for a large population—Cleveland in the 1890s—even nonpartisan reformers found it unsatisfactory; Ware, *American Direct Primary*, 26.

10. Ibid., 112.

11. Reynolds, *Demise*, 194.

12. *Ballot Access News*, 29, no. 4 (September 2013), accessed at www.ballot-access.org/2013/09/september-2013-ballot-access-news -print-edition.

13. Ware, *American Direct Primary*, 127–128.

14. Ranney, *Curing the Mischiefs*, 85.

15. Ware, *American Direct Primary*, 215–216. Italics in the *Outlook* statement (as quoted in ibid., 216) are mine.

16. M. J. Lee, "Mitt Romney Rips Rick Santorum's 'Dirty Trick' Robocalls," accessed at www.politico.com/news/stories/0212/73367 .html.

17. Roberto Suro, "Bush Denounces Duke as Racist and Charlatan," *New York Times*, November 7, 1991, accessed at www.nytimes .com/1991/11/07/us/the-1991-election-louisiana-bush-denounces -duke-as-racist-and-charlatan.html?pagewanted=all&src=pm.

18. *California Democratic Party v. Jones*, 530 U.S. 11 (2000).

19. *California Democratic Party v. Jones*, 530 U.S. 6 (2000).

20. As of May 2012, in presidential primaries, in the Democratic Party twenty-two states have open primaries, twenty-one have semi-

closed primaries, and eight have closed primaries; in the Republican Party, seventeen states have open primaries twenty-seven have closed primaries and seven have semi-closed primaries (tabulated from "Primaries: Open and Closed)," accessed at http://www.fairvote.org/research-and-analysis/presidential-elections/congressional-and-presidential-primaries-open-closed-semi-closed-and-top-two/.

21. "Presidential Primary Turnout Report," Center for the Study of the American Electorate, American University, October 1, 2008, accessed at www1.american.edu/ia/cdem/csae/index.cfm. Thirty-nine states held Republican primaries, and thirty-seven held Democratic primaries; thirty-six states held both Republican and Democratic primaries.

22. Ibid., table 2, "Relationship between Presidential Primary Turnout and General Election Turnout 1968–2008." I looked only at presidential primaries since the McGovern-Frasier Commission, which vastly expanded the system of primary elections.

23. Ibid., table 4, "Overall Turnout Trend Statewide Primaries for Governor and U.S. Senate." Average turnout for statewide primaries in presidential election years for states that have statewide primaries at a different time than the presidential primaries is 20.4 percent since 1972.

24. "2004 Primary Turnout Report," Center for the Study of the American Electorate, American University, March 9, 2004, 2.

25. Barry C. Burden and Marni Ezra, "Calculating Voter Turnout in U.S. House Primary Elections," *Electoral Studies* 18 (1999): 96, table 4; Burden notes that "voter turnout in congressional primaries remains virtually unexplored" (90).

26. Morris P. Fiorina, with Samuel J. Abrams, *Disconnect: The Breakdown of Representation in American Politics* (Norman: University of Oklahoma Press, 2009), 163–168. While Fiorina believes that low turnout in primaries may be partly responsible for polarization, he remains "dubious that primary reform would have a major impact on polarization" (167).

27. See Ware, *American Direct Primary,* 115, on the Doc Ames scandal that plagued the first mayoral primary in Minneapolis. For

more recent evidence, see Ranney, *Curing the Mischiefs*, 144–150; William Crotty and John S. Jackson III, *Presidential Primaries and Nominations* (Washington, DC: Congressional Quarterly Press, 1985); and Nelson Polsby, *Consequences of Party Reform* (Oxford: Oxford University Press, 1983).

28. This contrast is found in Nelson W. Polsby and Aaron B. Wildavsky, *Presidential Elections: Strategies of American Electoral Politics* (New York: Charles Scribner's Sons, 1968), 230, 275; James Q. Wilson calls the purists "amateurs" in *The Amateur Democrat* (Chicago: University of Chicago Press, 1962), 3–4.

29. David C. King, "Congress, Polarization, and Fidelity to the Median Voter," 7, accessed at www.hks.harvard.edu/fs/dking/Extreme _Politics.pdf.

30. Morris P. Fiorina, with Samuel J. Abrams and Jeremy C. Pope, *Culture War? The Myth of a Polarized America* (New York: Pearson Longman, 2005), 5.

31. Alan Abramowitz, "Don't Blame Primary Voters for Polarization," *The Forum* 5, no. 4 (2008); John Sides and Lynn Vavreck, "On the Representativeness of Primary Electorates" (paper prepared for the conference "Political Representation: Fifty Years after Miller and Stokes," Vanderbilt University, March 1–2, 2013), preliminary draft v. 1.0, accessed at www.vanderbuild.edu/csdi/miller-stokes/07_Miller Stokes_SidesVavreck.pdf.

32. *California Democratic Party v. Jones*, 530 U.S. 567 (2000).

33. *Washington State Grange v. Washington State Republican Party*, 552 U.S. 442 (2008).

34. Eric McGhee, Seth Masket, Boris Shor, Steven Rogers, and Nolan McCarty, "A Primary Cause of Partisanship? Nomination Systems and Legislator Ideology," *American Journal of Political Science* 58, no. 2, (April 2014): 337–351; Douglas J. Ahler, Jack Citrin, and Gabriel S. Lenz, "Can California's New Primary Reduce Polarization? Maybe Not," *Monkey Cage*, March 27, 2013, accessed at http://themonkeycage.org/2013 /03/27/can-californias-new-primary-reduce-polarization-maybe-not/.

35. McGhee et al., "Primary Cause," 12.

36. Ahler, Citrin, and Lenz, "Can California's New Primary Reduce Polarization?"

7. Partisanship at Home

1. Jonathan Riskind, "Senate's 'I's: King Will Have to Choose," *Portland Press Herald*, March 8, 2014, accessed at http://www.press herald.com/news/senates-is-king-will-have-to-choose-_2012-03-18 .html?pagenum=full.

2. John M. Carey, *Legislative Voting and Accountability* (Cambridge: Cambridge University Press, 2009), 20.

3. Arend Lijphart, *Patterns of Democracy: Government Forms and Performance in Thirty-Six Countries*, 2nd ed. (New Haven: Yale University Press, 2012), 133–134 (note that one of the eighteen countries, France, only used this system for a single year).

4. See Carey's observations about a different set of countries in South America; *Legislative Voting*, 26.

5. Samuel H. Beer, *Modern British Politics* (New York: W. W. Norton, 1982), 350–351.

6. Christopher J. Kam, *Party Discipline and Parliamentary Politics* (Cambridge: Cambridge University Press, 2009), 3.

7. Jeremy Waldron, *The Dignity of Legislation* (Cambridge: Cambridge University Press, 1999), 2.

8. Peter Mair, "Democracy without Parties," Center for the Study of Democracy, University of California, Irvine, paper 05–06, pp. 8–17, accessed at http://repositories.cdlib.org/csd/05–06.

9. Countries that have adopted "mixed" systems in the past twenty years include Bolivia, Guatemala, Panama, Venezuela, Mexico, Italy, Japan, New Zealand, the Philippines, Russia, and Ukraine. See Carey, *Legislative Voting*, 31–32.

10. Suzanne Dovi, *The Good Representative* (Oxford: Blackwell, 2007), 3.

11. Ibid., 5.

12. Ibid., 6.

13. This is understandable, since Dovi wants to address representation in the general sense, not only the representation undertaken by elected legislators.

14. Also see Alex Tuckness, *Locke and the Legislative Point of View* (Princeton: Princeton University Press, 2002), in which the point of view of the "reasonable legislator" is not distinctively partisan.

15. Carey, *Legislative Voting,* 8.

16. Ibid.

17. Charlyne Berens, *One House: The Unicameral's Progressive Vision for Nebraska* (Lincoln: University of Nebraska Press, 2005), 36–40.

18. Ibid., 15; details of the Nebraska case also rely on the following: John P. Senning, *The One-House Legislature,* foreword by Senator George W. Norris (New York: McGraw-Hill, 1937); Susan Welch and Eric H. Carleson, "The Impact of Party on Voting Behavior in a Nonpartisan Legislature," *American Political Science Review* 67, no. 3 (September 1973): 854–867; John C. Comer, "The Nebraska Nonpartisan Legislature: An Evaluation," *State and Local Government Review* 12, no. 3 (September 1980): 98–102; Brian F. Schaffner, Matthew Streb, and Gerald Wright, "Teams without Uniforms: The Nonpartisan Ballot in State and Local Elections," *Political Research Quarterly* 54, no. 1 (March 2001): 7–30; and Richard Wright and Brian F. Schaffner, "The Influence of Party: Evidence from the State Legislatures," *American Political Science Review* 96, no. 2 (June 2002): 367–379.

19. Berens, *One House,* 186, tables 24 and 25.

20. Schaffner and Wright, "Teams without Uniforms," 374, 376.

21. Berens, *One House,* 102–103.

22. Senning, *One-House Legislature,* 66; also see Schaffner and Wright, "Teams without Uniforms," 377.

23. Schaffner and Wright, "Teams without Uniforms," 377.

24. Nancy L. Rosenblum, *On the Side of the Angels: An Appreciation of Parties and Partisanship* (Princeton: Princeton University Press, 2008), 11, 25–59.

25. Nadia Urbinati, *Representative Democracy: Principles and Genealogy* (Chicago: The University of Chicago Press, 2008), 39.

26. Thomas Brackett Reed was Speaker of the House from 1889 to 1891 and from 1895 to 1899; in 1890 he passed a series of rules that successfully curtailed the power of the minority to obstruct legislation; see Gary W. Cox and Mathew D. McCubbins, *Setting the Agenda: Responsible Party Government in the U.S. House of Representatives* (Cambridge: Cambridge University Press, 2005), 56–57.

27. Michael Grunwald and Jim VandeHei, "Hastert's Team Mentality to Be Tested as Foley Scandal Unfolds," *Washington Post,* October 16, 2006, accessed at www.washingtonpost.com/wp-dyn/content/article/2006/10/15/AR2006101501096_pf.html.

28. Congressional Budget Office, "Economic Effects of Policies Contributing to Fiscal Tightening in 2013," November 8, 2012, accessed at http://cbo.gov/publication/43694.

29. Derek Willis, "Tracking Hastert Rule Violations in the House," *New York Times,* April 11, 2013, accessed at http://thecaucus.blogs.nytimes.com/2013/04/11/tracking-hastert-rule-violations-in-the-hous/.

30. Russell Muirhead, "A Bipartisan Speaker of the House?," *Balkinization,* December 26, 2012, accessed at http://balkin.blogspot.com/2012/12/a-bipartisan-speaker-of-house.html.

31. Jennifer Steinhauer, "Divided House Passes Tax Deal in End to Latest Fiscal Standoff," *New York Times,* January 1, 2013, accessed at www.nytimes.com/2013/01/02/us/politics/house-takes-on-fiscal-cliff.html. It might be argued that the Republican majority did not *really* object, since it acceded to the procedural votes by which the bill was brought to the floor; see David Karol, "The House GOP and the Fiscal Cliff: Position-Taking vs. Policy-Making," *Monkey Cage,* January 3, 2013, accessed at http://themonkeycage.org/2013/01/03/the-house-gop-and-the-fiscal-cliff-position-taking-vs-policy-making/.

32. Data accessed at http://politics.nytimes.com/congress/votes/house/hastert-rule; and Susan Davis and Gregory Korte, "Boehner, Like Past Speakers, Sometimes Needs Democrats," *USA Today,* April 1, 2013, accessed at www.usatoday.com/story/news/politics/2013/04/01/hastert-rule-boehner-majority-gop/2041857/.

33. Charles Wheelan, *The Centrist Manifesto* (New York: W. W. Norton, 2013).

34. John P. Avalon, *Independent Nation* (New York: Three Rivers Press, 2004), 1.

35. Ted Halsted and Michael Lind, *The Radical Center: The Future of American Politics* (New York: Random House, 2001), 2, 11.

36. Morris P. Fiorina, with Samuel J. Abrams, *Disconnect: The Breakdown of Representation in American Politics* (Norman: University of Oklahoma Press, 2009).

37. Ibid., 35.

38. Alasdair MacIntyre, *After Virtue: A Study in Moral Theory,* 3rd ed. (South Bend: University of Notre Dame Press, 2007), 253.

39. David Mayhew, *Divided We Govern: Party Control, Lawmaking, and Investigations, 1946–1990* (New Haven: Yale University Press, 1991).

8. Partisanship beyond the Legislature

1. James Madison, "Virginia Plan," resolution number 9 (1787), accessed at www.ourdocuments.gov/doc.php?doc=7&page=transcript.

2. Ralph Kethcham, *Presidents above Party: The First American Presidency, 1789–1829* (Chapel Hill: University of North Carolina Press, 1984).

3. The restorative interpretation of the Obama presidency comes from Professor Jeffrey Tulis, University of Texas at Austin.

4. James W. Ceaser, *Presidential Selection: Theory and Development* (Princeton: Princeton University Press, 1979), 123–169.

5. "The president is at liberty, in both law and conscience, to be as big a man as he can"; Woodrow Wilson, *Constitutional Government in the United States* (New York: Columbia University Press, 1908), 70.

6. Sidney M. Milkis, "E. E. Schattschneider, the New Deal, and the Rejection of the Responsible Party Doctrine," *PS: Political Science and Politics* 25, no. 2 (June, 1992): 181, 183.

7. Michael D. Shear, "N.Y. Mayor Bloomberg Leaves GOP," *Washington Post,* June 20, 2007, accessed at www.washingtonpost

.com/wp-dyn/content/article/2007/06/19/AR2007061901769 .html.

8. Barack Obama, *The Audacity of Hope: Thoughts on Reclaiming the American Dream* (New York: Crown, 2006), 39.

9. Ibid., 38.

10. Ibid.

11. Ibid., 62.

12. "Remarks by the President on Reforming the Health Care System to Reduce Costs," May 11, 2009, White House Office of the Press Secretary, accessed at www.whitehouse.gov/the_press_office /Remarks-by-the-President-on-Reforming-the-Health-Care-System -to-Reduce-Costs/.

13. "Obama's Health Care Speech to Congress," September 9, 2009, *New York Times,* accessed at www.nytimes.com/2009/09/10/us /politics/10obama.text.html.

14. Ibid.

15. "Remarks by the President and Vice President at Signing of the Health Insurance Reform Bill," Office of the Press Secretary, the White House, March 23, 2013, accessed at www.whitehouse.gov/the -press-office/remarks-president-and-vice-president-signing-health -insurance-reform-bill.

16. "Obama's Health Care Speech to Congress."

17. Thanks to my colleague Bernie Avishai for this insight, and for rendering it so memorably.

18. "An Investigation into the Removal of Nine U.S. Attorneys in 2006," United States Department of Justice, Office of the Inspector General and the Office of Professional Responsibility, September 2008, accessed at www.justice.gov/oig/special/s0809a/final.pdf.

19. Ibid., 115–147.

20. Ibid., 166.

21. Justin Levitt, "The Truth about Voter Fraud," Brennan Center for Justice at New York University Law School, 2007, accessed at http://brennan.3cdn.net/c176576c0065a7eb84_gxm6ib0hl.pdf; John S. Ahlquist, Kenneth R. Mayer, and Simon Jackman, "Fraudulent Votes, Voter Identification, and the 2012 General Election," preliminary draft,

April 23, 2013, accessed at http://users.polisci.wisc.edu/behavior/Papers/AhlquistMayerJackman2013.pdf.

22. Some studies suggest that voter ID laws have no impact on turnout (and therefore also on fraud); see Stephen Ansolabehere, "Effects of Identification Requirements on Voting: Evidence from the Experience of Voters on Election Day," *PS: Political Science and Politics* 42, no. 1 (January 2009): 127–130. However, looking over a variety of studies, Nate Silver estimates that strict voter ID laws (requiring a photo) reduce turnout by 2–3 percent; see Nate Silver, "Measuring the Effects of Voter Identification Laws," *fivethirtyeight.com,* July 15, 2012, accessed at http://fivethirtyeight.blogs.nytimes.com/2012/07/15/measuring-the-effects-of-voter-identification-laws/.

23. "Investigation into the Removal of Nine U.S. Attorneys," 160.

24. Ibid., 149.

25. Ibid., 159–160.

26. Ibid., 165.

27. Ibid., 191.

28. Ibid., 179.

29. Ibid., 192.

30. Ibid., 188.

31. Ibid., 327, 331.

32. Ibid., 193.

33. Ibid., 194.

34. Nicholas Lemann, "The Controller: Karl Rove Is Working to Get George Bush Reelected, but He Has Bigger Plans," *New Yorker,* May 12, 2003, accessed at www.newyorker.com/archive/2003/05/12/030512fa_fact_lemann?printable=true&currentPage=all.

35. As quoted by David E. Lewis, *The Politics of Presidential Appointments: Political Control and Bureaucratic Performance* (Princeton: Princeton University Press, 2008), 6.

36. Marc Jacoby, "Cheney Says Obama, Not Holder, Is Chief Law Enforcement Officer," *Main Justice: Politics, Policy, and the Law,* August 30, 2009, accessed at www.mainjustice.com/2009/08/30/cheney-says-obama-not-holder-is-chief-law-enforcement-officer/.

37. "Sizing Up the Executive Branch of the Federal Workforce," United States Office of Personnel Management, January 2013, accessed at www.opm.gov/policy-data-oversight/data-analysis-documentation /federal-employment-reports/reports-publications/sizinguptheexec utivebranch.pdf.

38. "Hatch Act," United States Office of Special Counsel, January 23, 2013, accessed at www.osc.gov/hatchact.htm.

39. I would like to thank Hy Rothstein of the Department of Defense Analysis, Naval Postgraduate School, for bringing this issue to my attention; Charles G. Gels, "The Nonpartisan Military," *Armed Forces Journal,* July 8, 2010, accessed at www.afji.com/2008/08 /3599019/; "General Petraeus Addresses His 'Legacy,'" interview with Alex Chadwick, National Public Radio, March 19, 2008, transcript accessed at www.npr.org/templates/transcript/transcript.php ?storyId=88584830.

40. Jason K. Dempsey, *Our Army: Soldiers, Politics, and American Civil-Military Relations* (Princeton: Princeton University Press, 2010), 10–33; Steve Corbett and Michael J. Davidson, "The Role of the Military in Presidential Politics," *Parameters* 39, no. 4 (Winter 2009–2010): 61.

41. Dempsey, *Our Army,* 29.

42. Corbett and Davidson, "Role of the Military," 63.

43. Lance Betros, "Political Partisanship and the Military Ethic in America," *Armed Forces and Society* 27, no. 4 (Summer 2001): 501–523; Dempsey, *Our Army,* 102.

44. Dempsey, *Our Army,* 174.

45. Corbett and Davidson, "Role of the Military," 63.

46. Marybeth Peterson Ulrich, "Infusing Normative Civil-Military Relations Principles in the Officer Corps," in *The Future of the Army Profession,* ed. Don Snider and Lloyd J. Matthews, 2nd ed. (Boston: McGraw-Hill, 2005), 670–671; Corbett and Davidson, "Role of the Military," 58.

47. Dempsey, *Our Army,* 3.

48. Ibid., 191.

49. Ulrich, "Civil-Military Relations," 659.

50. Ibid., 669.

51. Dempsey, *Our Army,* 187; Betros, "Political Partisanship and the Military Ethic," 515.

52. Dempsey persuasively suggests that generals who engage in partisan advocacy within five years of retirement should no longer be addressed as "General" in official military correspondence. Such a gentle penalty, designed to appeal to their sense of honor more than to establish a false distinction between politics and military expertise, seems perfectly calibrated. See Dempsey, *Our Army,* 191.

53. United States Constitution, Article II, section 3.

54. Lincoln Caplan, *The Tenth Justice: The Solicitor General and the Rule of Law* (New York: Alfred A. Knopf, 1987), 80.

55. Seth Waxman, "The Solicitor General in Historical Context," address to the Supreme Court Historical Society, June 1, 1998, accessed at www.justice.gov/osg/aboutosg/historic-context.html.

56. *United States v. Windsor,* Docket no. 12–307, oral argument, March 27, 2013, p. 9, accessed at http://www.supremecourt.gov/oral _arguments/argument_transcripts/12-307_c18e.pdf.

57. Ibid., 12.

58. *United States v. Windsor,* Docket no. 12–307 slip op. 570 U.S. ____ (2013): Roberts, Scalia (joined by Thomas), and Alito issued three separate dissents, each of which argued that the United States was not a proper petitioner and that the case lacked standing.

59. "Roberts: 'My Job Is to Call Balls and Strikes and Not to Pitch or Bat,'" *CNN.com,* September 12, 2005, accessed at www.cnn.com /2005/POLITICS/09/12/roberts.statement/.

9. CAN THE GOVERNMENT GOVERN?

1. Ronald Brownstein, *The Second Civil War: How Extreme Partisanship Has Polarized Washington and Polarized America* (New York: Penguin, 2007), 58.

2. Ibid., 79.

3. Ibid., 10.

4. Ibid., 79.

5. V. O. Key Jr., *Southern Politics in State and Nation* (New York: A. A. Knopf, 1949).

6. "Toward a More Responsible Two-Party System: A Report of the Committee on Political Parties," supplement, *American Political Science Review* 44, no. 3, pt. 2 (1950): 18.

7. Eric Schickler, "Remaking the House and the Senate: Personal Power, Ideology, and the 1970s Reforms," *Legislative Studies Quarterly* 18, no. 3 (August 2003): 301.

8. As Lyndon Johnson said to Bill Moyers after signing the Civil Rights Act of 1964, "I think we have just delivered the South to the Republican Party for a long time to come." See Bill Moyers, "Second Thoughts: Reflections on the Great Society," *New Perspectives Quarterly* 4, no. 1 (Winter 1987), accessed at www.digitalnpq.org/archive /1987_winter/second.html.

9. John Stuart Mill, *On Liberty* (1869; Cambridge: Cambridge University Press, 1989), 48–49.

10. *Citizens United v Federal Election Commission,* 558 U.S. 310 (2010); for a plan to overturn the case by constitutional amendment, see Jeffrey D. Clements, *Corporations Are Not People: Why They Have More Rights Than You Do and What You Can Do About It* (San Francisco: Berrett-Koehler Publishers, 2012).

11. Thomas E. Mann and Norman J. Ornstein, *It's Even Worse Than It Looks: How the American Constitutional System Collided with the New Politics of Extremism* (New York: Basic Books, 2012), xiii.

12. Ezra Klein, "14 Reasons Why This Is the Worst Congress Ever," *The Washington Post,* July 13, 2012, accessed at http://www .washingtonpost.com/blogs/wonkblog/wp/2012/07/13/13-reasons -why-this-is-the-worst-congress-ever/.

13. Jon Ward, "Debt Commission Co-chair Says Upcoming Debt Limit 'Bloodbath' Will Force Action on Recommendations," *Daily Caller,* November 19, 2010, accessed April 27, 2013, at http://daily caller.com/2010/11/19/debt-commission-co-chair-says-upcoming -debt-limit-bloodbath-will-force-action-on-recommendations/.

14. Joe Holley, "Cornyn on Debt Ceiling: We're Not Going to Default," *Houston Chronicle,* January 17, 2013, accessed at www.chron

.com/news/houston-texas/houston/article/Cornyn-on-debt-ceiling
-We-re-not-going-to-default-4203429.php.

15. This point is inspired by William A. Galston, "The Common Good: Theoretical Content, Practical Unity," *Daedalus* 142, no. 2 (Spring 2013): 9–14.

16. Glenn Kessler, "Annotating Obama's 2006 Speech against Boosting the Debt Limit," The Fact Checker, *Washington Post,* January 15, 2013, accessed at www.washingtonpost.com/blogs/fact-checker/post/annotating-obamas-2006-speech-against-boosting-the-debt-limit/2013/01/14/aa8cf8c4-5e9b-11e2-9940-6fc488f3fecd_blog.html.

17. The minority party in Congress is also more likely to vote against raising the debt limit; see Linda K. Kowalcky and Lance T. LeLoup, "Congress and the Politics of Statutory Debt Limitation," *Public Administration Review* 51, no. 1 (January-February 1993): 14–15.

18. "McConnell Reverses Position on Conrad-Gregg Budget Commission," Politifact, *Tampa Bay Times,* February 1, 2010, accessed May 5, 2012, at www.politifact.com/truth-o-meter/statements/2010/feb/01/mitch-mcconnell/mcconnell-reverses-position-conrad-gregg-budget-co/.

19. Mann and Ornstein, *It's Even Worse Than It Looks,* x.

20. Glenn Kessler, "When Did McConnell Say He Wanted to Make Obama a 'One-Term President'?," *Washington Post,* September 25, 2012, accessed at www.washingtonpost.com/blogs/fact-checker/post/when-did-mcconnell-say-he-wanted-to-make-obama-a-one-term-president/2012/09/24/79fd5cd8-0696-11e2-afff-d6c7f20a83bf_blog.html.

21. Patricia A. Hurley, "David Mayhew's *Congress: The Electoral Connection* after 25 Years," *PS: Political Science and Politics* 34, no. 2 (June 2001): 259.

22. Matthew Levendusky, *The Partisan Sort: How Liberals Became Democrats and Conservatives Became Republicans* (Chicago: University of Chicago Press, 2009).

23. E. J. Dionne Jr., *Why Americans Hate Politics* (1991 repr., New York: Simon and Schuster, 2004), and Dionne, *Our Divided Political Heart: The Battle for the American Idea in an Age of Discontent* (New

York: Bloomsbury, 2012); Alan Wolfe, *One Nation, After All: What Middle Class Americans Really Think about God, Country, Family, Racism, Welfare, Immigration, Homosexuality, Work, the Right, the Left, and Each Other* (New York: Penguin, 1999); Morris P. Fiorina, with Samuel J. Abrams and Jeremy C. Pope, *Culture War? The Myth of a Polarized America,* 3rd ed. (New York: Pearson Longman, 2010); and Morris P. Fiorina, with Samuel J. Abrams, *Disconnect: The Breakdown of Representation in American Politics* (Norman: University of Oklahoma Press, 2009).

24. Fiorina, *Disconnect,* 30.

25. E. J. Dionne Jr., *Our Divided Political Heart* (New York: Bloomsbury, 2012), 4–5.

26. Vincent P. De Santis, "Eisenhower Revisionism," *Review of Politics* 38, no. 2 (April 1976): 190.

27. David R. Mayhew, *Divided We Govern: Party Control, Lawmaking, and Investigations, 1946–1990* (New Haven: Yale University Press, 1991), 61–63, table 4–1.

28. Speech catalogued at http://avalon.law.yale.edu/20th_century/reagan1.asp.

29. Edmund Morris, *Dutch: A Memoir of Ronald Reagan* (1999; repr., New York: Modern Library, 2000), 133.

30. K. Alan Snyder, "Ronald Reagan on Franklin Roosevelt: The Significance of Style," *First Principles: ISI Web Journal,* August 20, 2008, accessed at www.firstprinciplesjournal.com/articles.aspx?article=1082&theme=home&page=2&loc=b&type=ctbf; also Samuel H. Beer, "Ronald Reagan: New Deal Conservative," *Society* 42 (January–February 1983): 40–44.

31. Franklin D. Roosevelt, Annual Message to Congress on the State of the Union, January 6, 1941, accessed May 7, 2013, at www.fdrlibraryree.marist.edu/pdfs/fftext.pdf.

32. Woodrow Wilson, *Constitutional Government in the United States* (New York: Columbia University Press, 1908), 198, and especially chap. 8, "Party Government in the United States."

33. James W. Ceaser, *Presidential Selection: Theory and Development* (Princeton: Princeton University Press, 1979), 170–175.

34. Daryl J. Levinson and Richard H. Pildes, "Separation of Parties, Not Powers," *Harvard Law Review* 119 (2006): 2311–2386.

35. See Authorization for the Use of Military Force against Iraq Resolution of 2002; House bill summary at the Library of Congress, accessed at http://thomas.loc.gov/cgi-bin/bdquery/z?d107:HJ00114 :@@@L&summ2=m&.

36. Paul J. Pollock, "Is the *Federalist* Anti-party?," *Political Science Reviewer* 12 (Fall 1982): 84.

37. Nicol C. Rae, "Be Careful What You Wish For: The Rise of Responsible Parties in American National Politics," *Annual Review of Political Science* 10 (2007): 169–191.

the Radcliffe Institute, the Dartmouth Ethics Institute, and the Bill and Jill Smith Task Force on the Virtues of a Free Society at the Hoover Institution. My deans at Dartmouth, Mike Mastanduno and Nancy Marion, gave me critical support at a critical time. I would also like to thank my editors at various journals and presses for giving me the chance to publish the following pieces in which I worked out some of the ideas that inform this book: "A Defense of Party Spirit," *Perspectives on Politics* 4, no. 4 (December 2006): 713–727; "Respectable Partisanship," in Mary Ann McGrail and Sharon R. Krause, eds., *The Arts of Rule: Essays in Honor of Harvey C. Mansfield* (Boston: Lexington Books, 2008), 377–394; "Can Deliberative Democracy Be Partisan?," *Critical Review* 22, nos. 2–3 (2010): 129–157; and "The Case for Party Loyalty," in Sanford Levinson, Joel Parker, and Paul Woodruff, eds., *Loyalty: Nomos LIV* (New York: NYU Press, 2013), 229–254. Of all my editors, I have a special gratitude for Mike Aronson at Harvard University Press, who cares so deeply for books—and their authors.

And my heartful thanks to Allie and Lila for offering such a perfect distraction.

ACKNOWLEDGMENTS

I am profoundly grateful to Nicole Mellow and Lea Ypi, who read the entire manuscript with care and gave me a wealth of astute suggestions. My efforts all along were sustained and improved by many colleagues, and I am grateful for their friendship and talk, including Bernie Avishai, Sonu Bedi, John Carey, Michelle Clarke, Sandy Levinson, Mike MacDonald, Pratap Mehta, Glyn Morgan, Jim Murphy, Tom Pangle, Anne Sa'adah, Devon Stauffer, Lucas Swaine—and, most crucially, Gary Jacobsohn and Jeffrey Tulis, whose mastery of constitutional democracy so seamlessly combines the empirical and the philosophic. So many others in political theory have been willing to get their minds into this project and share their thoughts, including Peter Berkowitz, David Brady, Yasmin Daewood, Jeffrey Friedman, Brian Garsten, Sally Gibbons, Sharon Krause, Jason Maloy, Shep Melnick, Andrew Rehfeld, Andy Sabl, Daniel Stid, Nadia Urbinati, and Dana Villa. Since I first took up the subject, I benefited from the energetic and expert assistance of Yannis Evrigenis, Isaac Nakimovsky, and Marc Somos. Liz Adams and Barbara Goodhouse gave me essential help with pulling the final manuscript together. My friend and collaborator Nancy Rosenblum has been unstinting in her support and indispensable in sustaining the conviction that political theory should attend to the problem of partisanship. My undergraduate students have been sharp readers, including, most recently, Emily Hyman and Han Suh. And I will always be in debt to those great teachers who set me on this task: Sam Beer, Morris Fiorina, Harvey Mansfield, Michael Sandel, and Shannon Stimson.

Several people and institutions have supported me and this project in ways that made its undertaking possible and pleasurable: notably

INDEX

Bush, George W. *(continued)*
partisanship, 217–224; military
endorsements, 228; mentioned,
251; compassionate conservatism,
259
Bush v. Gore, 77, 238
business, politics as a, 187–188

California, blanket primary in, 147,
161, 163, 165
*California Democratic Party v.
Jones*, 161–163
candidates, ideological, 166, 257
caucus-convention system of
presidential nominations,
148–149
centrism, the latent majority, 4,
194–200, 246, 268n10
The Centrist Manifesto (Wheelan),
195
Centrist Party, 194–200, 245–247,
264
citizen partisanship: hyper-
partisanship, 3, 160; beginnings,
6–7; party identification and, 16;
loyalist vs., 42–44; reasons for
choosing, 109
citizens: claims of, 28; as partisans
vs. loyalists, 42–44; characteristics of, 42; partisanship and
disengagement of, 63, 65–66,
105–106; expectations of good,
111; effective political action,
111; burden of primaries, 166;
modern, 178–179; uncertainty
about ideology, 256–257;
ambivalence toward government,

257–258; educating, 258, 259.
See also voters
*Citizens United v. Federal Election
Commission*, 247
The Civic Culture (Almond &
Verba), 62, 63
civic education, 30, 168–172
Civic Ideals (Smith), 76
civic identity, 76–77
civic virtue, 33–34
Civil Rights Act, 131, 139, 170,
242–245
civil service employees, restrictions
on partisanship, 226
claim to rule, 24–29
Clean Air Act, 258
Clean Water Act, 258
Clinton, William (Bill), 2, 207, 212,
214, 216, 223, 228, 234
Clinton, Hillary, 146
closed list electoral systems, 175
closed list proportional systems,
175, 178, 179–181
closed primary, 147–148, 150–156,
160, 162–163, 167
closet partisans, 10
Colbert, Stephen, 164
cold war, 170
Coleridge, Samuel Taylor, 103, 105
commercial society, 32–34
common good: partisanship and the,
4–5, 9, 16, 18–19, 23–25, 89–90;
ideal of, 21, 178, 190; empowering the, 33–34, 58–59, 198–199;
ambition and the, 45; loyalty in
attaining the, 128–129; patience
in attaining the, 139–140;
muddling through toward the,

democratic legitimacy, 85, 88–90,
187–188
Democratic Party: partisanship, 11;
view of Republican partisanship,
63, 69; identity, elements of, 171,
206–209, 212, 215, 242–245;
liberals move toward the,
243–244; disagreements about
common good, 256
democratic revolution, 104–105
Dionne, E. J., 257
District Attorneys, firing of US,
217–224
diversity, 188
Domenici, Pete, 219, 221
Dovi, Suzanne, 179–180
Downs, Anthony, 66–67
Duke, David, 155
duty of care, presidential, 231–232,
234–237

education, civic, 30, 168–172
Eisenhower, Dwight D., 258
elections, random selection vs.,
94
Electoral College, 205–206
electoral districts, 34
electoral reform, 181
emotive partisanship, 126–127
England, 5
epistemic loyalty, 117–120
equality: foundational agreement
about, 73–79, 101, 105, 179;
political, 88; J. S. Mill's position
on, 101–103
ethical partisans: renunciation of
violence, 55, 77–79, 98, 107–108;

negative capacity, 98–99,
106–107, 111
Europe, partisanship in, 63–64, 71
European Union, 71, 178
Exclusion Crisis, 5
executive power, 201

factions, 5, 31–35, 58, 73
*Federal Election Commission,
Citizens United v.*, 247
Federalist (tenth) (Madison), 32
Feinstein, Diane, 167
Fiorina, Morris, 48, 160, 197–198
foundational agreements, 73–79,
101, 105, 179
Franklin, Benjamin, 77
Franks, Tommy, 228
free votes, 175
friendship, 116–120, 123–124, 127

Gates, Robert, 137
George III, 39
Gingrich, Newt, 157, 244
Glorious Revolution, 5
Gonzales, Alberto, 220, 221–222,
224
Goodnow, Frank, 7
goods, of the body and the soul,
50–51
Gore, Bush v., 77, 238
government: trust in, 122, 185;
Reagan on, 131, 171, 215, 258;
citizen ambivalence toward,
257–258
government employees, restrictions
on partisanship, 226

loyalty: importance to democratic citizenship, 17–20; virtue of, 98; politics' need for, 111–112, 128–130; effect of, on negative capacity, 111; as patriotism, 114; essence of, 116; basis for, 127

MacArthur, Douglas, 230
Machiavelli, 252–254
Madison, James, 32–33, 35, 58, 88, 203, 205, 261
Madisonian constitutionalism, 32–35
majority, moral claim to legitimacy, 88
majority of the majority rule, 191–195
majority rule, 90, 93–94
Mann, Thomas, 11, 15, 252
Mansfield, Harvey, 144, 271n35
Marx, Karl, 39
Massachusetts Democratic primary (1992), 154
mavericks, 46–47
Mayhew, David, 2
McCain, John, 146
McCarthy, Joseph, 60
McConnell, Mitch, 252, 253
McGovern-Frasier Commission, 152
Medicare, 1, 130, 214, 257
memory, partisan, 98, 128–134, 139, 171, 254
Michels, Robert, 45
Michigan Republican primary (2012), 153–154
middle class, 30–31, 32

military officers as voters, 227–232
Milkus, Sidney M., 278n26
Mill, John Stuart, 99–105, 107, 109, 245
Minnesota, nonpartisan legislature, 183
monarchic rule, rejection of, 74, 105
moral duty, 115
morality, political, 38, 53, 129, 239
moral purists, 41–42, 43, 46–49, 89, 91
moral unity, threats to, 57–59
moral urgency, 47–48
Morse, Wayne, 46
muddling through method, 141–145
The Myth of the Independent Voter (Keith), 10

national unity, source of, 76
Nebraska, unicameral and nonpartisan state legislature, 183–190
necessity of parties and partisanship, 7–10, 183–184
negative capacity, 98–99, 106–107, 111, 247–248
New Deal: bipartisan cooperation and the, 13, 242; Supreme Court and the, 14; Reagan and the, 72, 131, 133, 171, 208, 258–259; Democratic identity and the, 171, 206–209, 212, 215; centrism and the, 195
New Deal era, 14, 183
Nixon, Richard, 131, 258

APSA report on, 7, 176, 243, 260; suspicion of, 23; function of, 144; Wilsonian reformist hope, 260–262; fate of, 260–264
party-in-campaigns, 174
party-in-the-electorate, 134, 174
party-in-the-legislature, 174
party loyalty: ambition and, 112–114; choice in affirming, 112, 127; connection to identity, 114–115; moral danger of, 116; enforcing, 155; patience component of, 254–255; memory component in, 254. *See also* loyalty
party loyalty, pathologies of: reason and judgment incapacitated, 115–119, 120–123, 126–127, 139; epistemic closure, 121–122; facticity obliterated, 123–127, 138–139; lack of community, 125–126
party organizations, importance of, 7–8
party spirit, ix–xii, 2–6, 12–13, 15–18, 20–22, 35, 54, 56, 58, 73, 82, 109, 129, 131, 167, 198, 200, 204, 223, 232, 253, 264
party votes, 247–248
patience, partisan, 98, 128, 130, 134–141, 143–145, 254–255
Patient Protection and Affordable Care Act. *See* Affordable Care Act
patriotism, party loyalty as, 114
patronage parties, 6–7
Patton, George, 227, 229
Pelosi, Nancy, 113, 167
Petraeus, David, 227, 229, 231
philosophy, political, 5, 24–29

Pitt, William, 39
Pledge of Allegiance, 60
political action, effective, 111
political imagination, modern, 52
politics: ancient ideal of, 34–36; goals of, 37; basis of, 73–74, 210–211; definition of success in, 129–130; requirements of, 129; business analogy, 187–188; coercive nature of, 201
politics, modern: traditional conception of vs., 24; beginnings, 35–36; characteristics of, 36–37; purpose of, 37–38, 186–188; antipartisanship of, 41; denial of partisanship, 43; basis of, 50–56; ancient vs., 53–54; indeterminant nature of, 97–98; holistic ideals of, 187; normal machinations of, 249, 252
post-partisan fantasy, 255–256
power seekers, 41–45, 48, 52
presidency: separation of powers and the, 201–202; power of, 203–204, 225–226; leadership role, 204–208; post-partisan branding, 208–211; ideal of nonpartisan administration, 224–226. *See also specific administrations*
presidency above party, 237
president: ambition and the, 204–205, 216; vision of the partisan, 204–205; basis of dignity, 223–226; duty of care, 231–232, 234–237
presidential election (2000), 2, 77, 88, 238

Supreme Court: presidential
  election (2000) decision, 2, 77,
  238; social/labor laws overturned, 14; partisanship,
  203–204, 237–239; Office of the
  Solicitor General role, 232;
  DOMA challenge, 234–237
A System of Logic (J. S. Mill), 100

tactical voting, 153–154
taxation and tax reform, 132–133,
  135–137, 171, 192
Tea Party, 48, 259
Texas voters, 146
A Theory of Justice (Rawls), 40, 81
Thompson, Dennis, 101
Thoreau, Henry David, 47–48
Tocqueville, Alexis de, 12–13, 38,
  44, 108
Toomey, Pat, 113
top-two primary, 151, 152,
  167–168
Tory party, 5
"Toward a More Responsible
  Two-Party System" (American
  Political Science Association
  Report of the Committee on
  Political Parties, 1950), 7, 176,
  243, 260
tradition, 102–103
Troubled Asset Relief Program, 1
Truman, Harry, 212, 214, 230
trust, in government leaders, 122,
  185
truths, self-evident, 104
Tsongas, Paul, 154
Tuvalu, 183

Uganda, 183
Ulrich, Marybeth, 231
"Unabomber" (Ted Kaczynski),
  49–50
unicameral and nonpartisan state
  legislature, Nebraska, 183–190
United States v. Windsor, 234–237
unity, national, 58–62
Urbinati, Nadia, 188, 272n42
USA PATRIOT Act, 219

value politics, 51
values, fundamental, 1–2, 179
Van Buren, Martin, 6–7, 108,
  206
Verba, Sidney, 62, 63
Vietnam War, 46, 171
violence: zealots and, 42, 49–51;
  ethical partisan's renunciation
  of, 55, 77–79, 98, 107; hyper-
  partisanship and, 72–73;
  partisanship and, 73–74
Virginia Plan, 205
virtues: of partisanship, 18–19, 48,
  53, 90–91, 98; political, 41–42,
  45, 50, 52–54; of good representatives, 179
voter fraud, 220–223
voter identification laws, 220
voters: as partisans vs. loyalists,
  43; encouraging partisanship in,
  44; as loyal partisans, 114; Texas
  primary, 146; civic education for,
  168–172. *See also* citizens
voter turnout: primaries, 147,
  156–159; voter identification laws
  and, 220